The Very Life of Life

The Very Life of Life

A second year of daily reflections

Tom Gordon

wild goose
publications

www.**ionabooks**.com

Copyright © 2018 Tom Gordon

First published 2018

Wild Goose Publications
21 Carlton Court, Glasgow G5 9JP, UK
www.ionabooks.com
Wild Goose Publications is the publishing division of the Iona Community.
Scottish Charity No. SC003794. Limited Company Reg. No. SC096243.

ISBN 978-1-84952-599-2
Cover photograph © Mary Gordon

Overseas distribution:
Australia: Willow Connection Pty Ltd, Unit 4A, 3-9 Kenneth Road,
Manly Vale, NSW 2093
New Zealand: Pleroma, Higginson Street, Otane 4170, Central Hawkes Bay
Canada: Novalis/Bayard Publishing & Distribution, 10 Lower Spadina Ave.,
Suite 400, Toronto, Ontario M5V 2Z2

Printed by Bell & Bain, Thornliebank, Glasgow

Dedication

To my friends in Chalmers Memorial Church, Port Seton,
who have given me more than they will ever know.

Preface

When *Look Well to This Day* was published in 2014, I had no intention of writing a second volume of daily reflections. That task had been completed and I could now move on to something else. But the feedback I got from people who told me they were using my book on a daily basis made me think again. What I had put into people's hands was obviously useful: as part of their daily devotions; as a thought to reflect on at the start or end of the day; as a resource for illustrative material for talks and sermons; to be used alongside Bible readings, or even, as one man told me, instead of reading the Bible. I know homes where *Look Well to This Day* sits on coffee tables and at bedsides, on kitchen tables and even on a toilet windowsill. One lady showed me her personal, well-thumbed copy, which she carries around in her cavernous handbag, to be dipped into from time to time as the mood takes her. So I have been encouraged to make available more accessible, bite-sized chunks of reflective material. The result is what you have in your hands. And, however you use it, or wherever you keep it, I hope it continues to be of use to you as you reflect on your own daily journey of life.

My most important testing ground for this has been among my friends in Chalmers Memorial Church in Port Seton where I live, and to whom this book is humbly and appreciatively dedicated. I have been a member of this congregation for sixteen years, and these wonderful people have done much to restore my faith in the Church and the worshipping and serving community. They have been unfailingly warm, supportive and encouraging. In their search for faith and truth, they offer each other openness and understanding. In the strengthening of their fellowship, they continue to be an exemplar of commitment and service. As they have pulled together in times of crisis and sorrow, challenge and rejoicing, they have been more than could be expected of a Church of Scotland congregation. I have laughed and cried with them. They are a very special group of people. It would be invidious to name names, but they know who they are, and I say thank you to them all.

My thanks, also, to the many groups who, in recent years, have invited me to read my stories and reflections when they meet together. We've had a lot of fun, and a few tears too. But it has been a privilege to read some of what I've written and share my thoughts with a wider audience.

I am grateful, too, for the encouragement I've experienced from other writers in the Scottish Arts Club Writers' Group, and for the permissions I've received from people and organisations which allow me to include their material in this book. Their graciousness and support does them great credit.

Once more, I pay tribute to Sandra Kramer and her colleagues at Wild Goose Publications, for their patience with me and tolerance of my foibles. They have been the epitome of professionalism and dedication.

I leave the most important thanks to the end, as I take the opportunity to say a huge thank you to my family. My children and their partners are a delight, and I love them all deeply. To my two grandsons – both of whom pop up in this book from time to time – I say that I hope I can still be 'acceptable' (find that story in the pages that follow …) or perhaps even a little better than that from time to time.

And to my wife, Mary, I say this … you are the most special person to me in the whole world. You have immense talent and ability, and I'm delighted that others can see what I have known for many, many years. What you give to me and do for me is immeasurable. I hope what I give you in return works half as well.

Cover design and title

My grateful thanks go to my wife, Mary Gordon, for the photograph for the cover of this book.

The book's title comes from the same Sanskrit poem which gave us *Look Well to This Day*, the full text of which is:

> *Look to this day, for it is life, the very life of life.*
> *In its brief course*
> *lie all the realities and truths of existence*
> *the joy of growth, the splendour of action,*
> *the glory of power.*
> *For yesterday is but a memory*
> *and tomorrow is only a vision.*
> *But today well lived makes every yesterday*
> *a memory of happiness*
> *and every tomorrow a vision of hope.*
> *Look well, therefore, to this day.*

January 1 – First

'... the more imperative the need
not to take the first step without considering the last.'
Karl von Clauswitz, On War

The train line from Fort William to Mallaig in the north-west of Scotland is arguably one of the most beautiful in the world. Nowadays the train is driven by a steam engine for some of its journeys, and the carriages are packed for a wonderful trip through glens and around lochs, and, of course, across the curved viaduct at Glenfinnan made famous in the *Harry Potter* movies.

In times past, there's been an observation car on the back of the train. The best views could be had by sitting in the observation car and looking backwards. Not for the aficionados of train travel being up-front with the driver, or sitting in a compartment with the scenery flashing by too quickly. But, instead, they were relaxing, looking back the way, seeing the scenery slowly fall into place and taking a more leisurely view of where they had come from.

On the first day of the year we start a new journey. There will be new things to see, new people with whom to travel, new stations along the way, new experiences to absorb. You can't always be the driver. You'll go where you go, and what will happen will happen. And, as with most of our journeys of life, things will often flash by too quickly. So why not sit at the back of the train for a while as it's moving off and ponder where you've come from. There's no better time to do that than at the start of a new year.

Don't take the next step without considering the last one.
It might help you enjoy the journey all the better.

January 2 – Resolutions

'It may almost be a question whether such wisdom
as many of us have in our mature years has not come from
the dying out of the power of temptation,
rather than as the results of thought and resolution.'

Anthony Trollope, The Small House at Allington

Whatever I know about human nature, I know this ... you will be
reading today's thought having failed to keep the new year resolutions
you made only 48 or 24 hours ago. It's tough to keep promises to
change this or that part of our lives. I hope you can keep some of the
resolutions you've made. But, more than that, I hope you cope with
your sense of failure when resolutions have been broken so quickly.

However, it's worth considering that Anthony Trollope may be
right. By thought and resolution – in other words, by our decision-
making and choices – we may not be able to change what needs
changing. We are not, and cannot be, in control of everything. Perhaps
the wisdom we have in our mature years comes from adjusting to the
changes that happen despite our best efforts – whether from the dying
of the power of temptation or anything else.

Lord Thomas Macaulay, the 19th-century politician, described the
progress of science since the time of Charles I:

> *It is a philosophy which never rests, which has never attained, which
> is never perfect. Its law is progress. A point which yesterday was invisible
> is its goal to-day and will be its starting-point to-morrow.*

I hope you achieve some of your goals today, and, if not, that you find
a starting point for some future progress.

January 3 – Guidance

'Be thou my guardian and my guide.'
Title of a hymn written by Isaac Williams in 1842

In 1993, three classes of five-year-olds were admitted to my local school – about 70 children. The school catchment area was almost exactly the same as the parish where I was minister, and I had baptised none of these children.

I enquired of some parents why they chose not to have their children baptised. The replies were always similar: 'I don't want to impose on them.' 'We live in a pluralist society, so why should I label them when they're small?' 'They can make up their own mind when they're older.'

But don't children need guidance – open, informed, inclusive and fair guidance – so that they *can* make the reasoned decisions parents seem to want? When we are good guardians, should we not also seek to be good guides?

The poet Coleridge once listened to a diatribe against religious instruction of the young. 'I am determined not to prejudice my children in any form of religion, but to allow them at maturity to choose for themselves,' his visitor intoned. Coleridge made no reply, but instead invited the visitor to see his garden. They stood beside a strip of lawn overgrown with weeds. 'This is no more than a weed patch,' the visitor exclaimed. 'Indeed,' Coleridge replied. 'That is because it has not yet come to the age of its discretion. The weeds have taken the opportunity to grow, and I thought it unfair of me to prejudice the soil towards roses or strawberries.'

Who are the guides we most value, and why?
And what guidance might we offer to others today?

January 4 – Back-story

'The wolf shall lie down with the lamb
and the leopard shall lie down with the kid;
and the calf and the young lion and the fatling together;
and a little child shall lead them.'
Bible, Isaiah 11:6

I didn't much like my grampa. He suffered from Parkinson's disease and shook uncontrollably. And he had a temper, was over-acquainted with pubs and reeked of pipe-smoke. He'd had a chequered life as a husband and father too, and stories abounded about drink, violence and wastefulness. No, I just didn't like my grampa.

I knew my grampa had been orphaned aged one – in 1892. But it was when I discovered his 'back-story' that I saw him in a different light. His father had died of TB just after he was born. His mother, an alcoholic, had set fire to their home through smoking in bed and died in the fire. My grampa and his three brothers went to an orphanage. He was transported to Canada to work on farms when he was 14, along with a hundred other orphanage boys – and many more before and after. He came back at 21 and married my granny when he was 24 – and the rest, as they say, is history.

Who is my grampa now? In my mind he's become a vulnerable, frightened, unhappy little boy. I still don't like the old man he became, but I have a deep fondness for the child he once was. The wolf I had known could now lie down with the lamb I'd discovered – and a little orphaned child could lead them to me.

'The child is the father of the man,' we are told.
How then can a grandfather be the father of the child I know and love?

January 5 – Justice

'Justice is the constant and perpetual wish
to render to everyone his due.'
Justinian, Institutes, Book 1

The book of Amos in the Old Testament has always fascinated me, and for two reasons. Amos was the first prophet in the Bible whose message was recorded at length. Though he originated from a town in Judah in the south, he preached to the people of the northern kingdom of Israel around the middle of the eighth century BC. It was a settled time for Israel, a time of prosperity, religious piety and peaceful security. All appeared to be well. But God gave Amos a challenging message. Prosperity was limited to the wealthy and it was built on injustice and the oppression of the poor. Religious observance was insincere and devoid of meaning. National security was more apparent than it was real.

With passion and courage, Amos reminded people of the ways of his God. He didn't hold back. With powerful metaphors – locusts, fire, plumb lines and baskets of fruit – and dynamic language, he told it as it was. He faced people with the fundamentals of a just and fair society.

And the second reason? Amos was a sheep farmer from Tekoa. A humble man from a less-than-notable town became one of the great prophets with a transforming message we would all do well to heed.

This verse from Amos 5:15 *[Today's English Version]* sums it up for me. Might it also become our watchword, wherever we come from and whatever we face?

Hate what is evil, love what is right,
and see that justice prevails.

January 6 – Work

'Set thy heart upon thy work, but never upon its reward.
Work not for reward, but never cease to do thy work.'
Bhagavad-Gita, Hindu scripture, 2nd century BC

Whether it is paid work or a voluntary activity ... the commitment of a homemaker or the toil of a carer ... in the public eye or always private ... our work matters. Of course we try to follow the Bhagavad-Gita's advice or that of St Ignatius Loyola when he suggested that we are 'to labour and not to seek reward'. Yet society mostly measures the value of work by the rewards it brings. But when the value of work is in the satisfaction of a job well done, where no material rewards ensue, how might we measure that? We can't, other than to know we did our bit and we did it well.

A traditional Celtic blessing offers us this insight. It's called a 'Milking Croon'.

Bless, O God, my little cow,
Bless, O God, my desire;
Bless thou my partnership
And the milking of my hands, O God.
Bless, O God, each teat,
Bless, O God, each finger;
Bless thou each drop
That goes into my pitcher, O God.

When our desire, our motivation to do any work, is blessed ... when our partnership – the worker and the workplace together – is blessed ... when every finger of our toil, and every drop of our productiveness, is blessed ... then we surely have the reward we need.

January 7 – Anger

'Ira furor brevis est.'
Anger is a short madness.
Horace, Epistles, Book 1

In the Bible story of Balaam and his ass (Numbers 22), Balaam beats his beast when it stops suddenly (it's seen an angel!) and crushes his master's foot against a wall. Imagine Balaam's consternation when the ass speaks back and remonstrates with him for his cruelty. And the angel has some words of admonition to offer too ...

An English duke and his two companions were climbing in the Alps. A blizzard blew up and their donkey refused to go further. A couple of guides came to the rescue and found that they were all within a step or two of a deep crevasse. The donkey had saved them, for without its awareness three climbers could have fallen to their deaths.

During the Depression a poor widow lived in an English cotton town with her three girls. They had no bread, so the widow prayed for relief. There was a knock at the door. It was a baker selling bread. 'I have no money,' the woman replied, and the baker tried to drive away in his cart. But his donkey refused to move. Knocking again, the baker asked the same question and got the same answer. But again the donkey refused to shift. So the baker whipped his beast. 'I don't understand it,' shouted the angry man. 'This has never happened before. So I'm going to give you what's left on my cart and be done with it.' And, with that, he unloaded the remains of his delivery into the woman's arms. And only then did the donkey move on ...

Aware Donkeys 3, Angry Humans 0

January 8 – Territory

'It's not in my power to decide
such a great dispute between you.'
Virgil, Eclogues No. 3

There's a funny song we sing in Scotland, much beloved of children's gatherings. It's called 'The Three Craws' (crows). If you know it, you can sing it with me. The first verse goes:

Three craws sat upon a wa',
Sat upon a wa', sat upon a wa',
Three craws sat upon a wa'
On a cold and frosty mornin'.

The rest of the song tells the story of what was troubling each of the craws in turn. These three craws, with all their troubles, were on the one wall. On a cold and frosty morning, the three craws were in it together.

The same can't be said for the three pigeons on the roof of my garage. As one settles, another comes along and chases him (or her, I can't tell …) away. Within seconds, another one comes and gives the current incumbent short shrift. And the first one comes back (or is it the second one, I can't tell …) and takes over. It's a fight over territory.

Three pigeons mirror what we see in the world's trouble-spots. Territorial ownership, borders, power, destruction, displaced refugees. Where would you rather be – with 'three craws' sharing their troubles, or three pigeons fighting over territory? I know which wall I'd rather be on.

One? Not so good. Two? Better. Fifty? A million?
We'll see that day come round. I think there may be a song in that …

January 9 – Flattery

'Even till I shrink with cold, I smile and say,
"This is no flattery."'
William Shakespeare, As You Like It

My grandsons have always been observant. Sometimes we have a 'noticing walk'. We once came across a tree festooned with a dozen or so pairs of trainers, tied together with their laces, hanging like fruit from different branches. 'Look, grampa, it's a trainers-tree,' I was informed.

One day I was aware that I was being observed closely by Cameron, my second grandson (then aged four), when I was sitting on the floor against the sofa. 'Grampa,' he announced with a serious look. 'Yes?' I replied. 'Grampa, you're fat!' 'Well,' I rejoined, surprised by a four-year-old's bluntness, but conscious that my sitting position did over-emphasise a distinct paunch, 'you might well be right.' 'Yes, grampa,' he concluded, 'you've just got a fat tummy.'

Satisfied with his 'noticing' ability, he wandered across the room to where my wife was sitting and recommenced his intent scrutiny. *'Oh, no,'* I thought, *'this'll be another devastating put-down.'* 'Granny,' he said after a while. *'Here it comes, the withering, destructive observation.'* But he was better than that. 'Granny,' he said seriously, 'you *used* to be fat, but you're not fat any more.' And my wife smiled broadly, with undoubted pleasure.

Shakespeare is right. 'This is no flattery' for me. But, whether he meant it or not, a four-year-old had begun to learn that flattery, properly directed, is well worth offering.

Tell the truth. A bit of flattery goes a long way.
So if there's nothing good to say, better to say nothing.

January 10 – Joined together

'When each separate parts works as it should,
the whole body grows and builds itself up through love.'
Bible, Ephesians 4:16

Samuel Hebich, the son of a German pastor, founded the Basel Mission in India in the 19th century. He had a remarkable ministry despite his poor English and eccentric manners. That's what makes this story all the more endearing. It's the 'Tale of a Tub' – or Hebich's tob!

You and I cannot make a tob. It requires a good carpenter to make a tob or it vill hold no water, because it is not made of von piece of wood, but of many, and they must be fitly shoined together.

Dere are four tings to make a good tob: it must have a cood bottom; each of de pieces must be fitly shoined to de bottom; each von must be fitly shoined to his fellow; each von shall be kept close by the bands outside.

Von piece may be narrow and de next piece wide, yet it shall be a cood tob; but if a leetle shtone or a bit of shtick vill come between de pieces, it vill not do at all; and if all de pieces but von touch, and are fitly shoined togeder, and dis von fall in or out of de circle, it is no tob at all.

Vat is de shmall shtick or shtone between de pieces of vood that falls out of de circle? It is de proud, unforgiving spirit dat efry von can feel is in de meeting and vich causes all heavenly peace to run out. Oh beloved, be fitly shoined together.

Fitly joined together ... I like that. If it keeps heavenly peace in, that's a good job done.

January 11 – Death

'O death, where is thy sting?
O grave, where is thy victory?'
Bible, 1 Corinthians 15:55

As a hospice chaplain and now in bereavement support work, I know all too well the devastation death brings. The 'sting' of death, and the experience of loss rather than victory, are often too hard to bear for those who mourn. So, like Paul, we ask big questions about death and the grave.

But the questions he airs are rhetorical, and he goes on to say that, for the Christian, there is no 'sting' in death because there is ultimate victory through faith in Christ. Paul is positive that, even in the face of our mortality, we have hope and purpose, and he wants people to believe that.

That's not the way it's seen by everyone, however. In one of our hospice bereavement support groups we had a woman who was passionate about her faith and was convinced that the only way anyone could cope with the death of a loved one was to believe in Jesus. Another member of the group spoke privately with me afterwards. 'If you put that woman in my group next time, I'm gonna punch her! She's too certain. It isn't real. She's not listening to my pain.'

We begin to deal with bereavement when we begin with the pain, not when we cover it up with faith or anything else. The pain of loss is the human reaction to death, and we must listen to that first.

*It is the greatest wisdom, in time of health and strength,
to prepare for sickness and death:
he that really doth so, his business of dying is half done.*
Richard Illidge (1636–1709)

January 12 – Poor in spirit

'Whoso stoppeth his ear at the poor
shall cry himself and not be heard.'

Hebrew proverb

There's a Latin proverb which reminds us, 'Not he who has little, but
he who wishes for more, is poor.'
On the same theme, Jesus said, 'Blessed are the poor in spirit.' I
offer two interpretations of that concept today.

From the Rule of St Benedict:

*More than anything else is this vice of property to be cut off root and
branch from the monastery. Let no one presume to give or receive anything without the leave of the abbot, or to retain anything as his own.
He should have nothing at all; neither a book, nor tablets, nor a pen
– nothing at all. For it is not allowed to the monks to have bodies or
wills in their own power.*

And from the Rule of St Francis:

*The brothers shall possess nothing, neither a house, nor a place, nor
anything. But as pilgrims and strangers in this world, serving God in
poverty and humility, they shall confidently seek alms, and not be
ashamed, for the Lord made himself poor in this world for us. This is
the highest degree of that sublime poverty, which has made you, my
dearly beloved brethren, heirs and kings of the Kingdom of Heaven;
which made you poor in goods but exalted in virtues.*

January 13 – Family

'And drops on gate bars hang in a row,
And rooks in families homeward go, and so do I.'
Thomas Hardy, Weathers

Polly knew her place in the family. In fact, she knew her place *all* the time, for mostly she sat cross-legged on the corner of the sofa in the lounge, minding her own business, and never causing a fuss. Her mother and father were there as well, of course, standing guard, always behind her, keeping a watching eye. They knew their places too.

Polly always wore bright-coloured clothes. It was a family thing: bright-red dungarees; a garish-yellow jacket; a purple bobble-hat; remarkably colourful socks, shoes *and* mittens. Her outfit was very similar to her mum and dad's – different colours, but the same over-the-top, bright ensemble. Polly was happy enough knowing her place, but she often wished for someone else, a brother or sister, or even a playmate. Life would be more fun. So she wanted *anyone* to be added to her family. *She* couldn't do that. And her mother and father didn't seem to be making any effort.

Just then, Miriam came into the lounge. Miriam was nice. She talked to Polly, and smiled at her, and always sat beside her on the sofa. Miriam unearthed her knitting from a cavernous bag, took out the brightest ball of green wool you've ever seen, turned to Polly and her parents, grinned widely and said, 'Well, folks, today's the day! I'm going to start knitting a little brother for you, Polly. Green legs and yellow dungarees, I think. That'll make the family complete, eh?' It was the *best* news that Polly had ever heard ...

Family matters – for rooks, and knitted dolls, and me!

January 14 – Stepping stones

'A man of sorrows, and acquainted with grief.'
Bible, Isaiah 53:3

In Chalmers Memorial Church in Port Seton where I live, we offer a bereavement support service to the local community. It's a six-week programme, where, together with a trained and experienced group from the congregation, people can explore aspects of their journey of loss. It helps them 'normalise' their experiences, find common ground, feel less isolated and gather confidence for the journey forward.

When we were setting up our support service, we talked through possible names. We came up with *Stepping Stones* because it concisely represented what we were intending to offer.

People use many phrases to describe the journey of loss. 'You'll get over it.' 'I'm getting there.' 'Coming to terms.' 'Time's a great healer.' We know why such platitudes are used, but we also know the effect they can have. Is a death something to be 'got over', or is it about learning to live with it? Where is the 'there' people are expected to get to when it's hard enough living in the 'now'? What are the 'terms' you'll come to – as if the death will no longer have an impact? And as for the 'time' bit ...

So we talk about 'stepping stones', small steps, sometimes wobbly ones; taking it slowly, even though you're afraid; having small successes when you thought you'd never make it at all. 'Stepping stones', with a guiding hand to help you when it's needed.

Take my hand and I'll support you across the stepping stones.
I know they're solid, because I've tried them out before you.

January 15 – The greatest

'Seek to be good, but aim not to be great.'
Lord George Lyttelton, Advice

I'm writing this not long after the death of the legendary heavyweight boxer Muhammad Ali. Among Ali's numerous one-liners and catch-phrases – such as 'Float like a butterfly, sting like a bee' – his most memorable and long-lasting is 'I am the greatest', first reported in the *Louisville Times* in 1962. The greatest *boxer* of all time? Arguably. But '*The* greatest'? Well ...

It's in our nature to aspire to greatness. But when that desire to be great carries with it the wish to be 'the greatest' over everyone else, do we not have a problem?

Matthew's Gospel (18:1-5) gives the account of Jesus' disciples asking, 'Who is the greatest?', perhaps even hoping it might be one of them.

At that time the disciples came to Jesus and asked, 'Who, then, is the greatest in the kingdom of heaven?' He called a little child to him, and placed the child among them. And he said: 'Truly I tell you, unless you change and become like little children, you will never enter the kingdom of heaven. Therefore, whoever takes the lowly position of this child is the greatest in the kingdom of heaven. And whoever welcomes one such child in my name welcomes me.'

That turns the greatness argument on its head, doesn't it? Who would ever have thought it?

I know some children who are great.
I know some great adults too –
and being childlike is part of their greatness.

January 16 – Gifts

'The gods themselves cannot recall their gifts.'

Alfred Lord Tennyson, Tithonus

The gods may not 're-call' their gifts in the sense that they want them returned. But they must surely be able to recall, to remember, their gifts and the importance of their giving.

I've received many gifts over the years. I recall a family having a 'whip round' – in front of me, too – as a 'thank you' gift for a funeral I'd conducted. I recall being given a gift of a beautiful autoharp because I'd admired a similar instrument when I was visiting a couple in their home. I even recall the gift of a frozen chicken, offered in gratitude for a wedding service! (I didn't risk cooking it, but I appreciated the sentiment nonetheless.) But perhaps the most moving gift I recall was from a little child.

As a school chaplain, I would often play my guitar and sing with the children. One day I shared the chorus of a Russian folk-song, along with a story about the importance of the love of family.

May there always be sunshine;
May there always be blue sky;
May there always be Mama;
May there always be me.

The next day I was approached by a seven-year-old. He presented me with a crayon drawing – a blue sky, a fat, yellow sun, and a woman and a child. 'That's me and my mama,' he said. 'My mama loves me.' And he was gone.

What a gift, to recognise what love means.

January 17 – Disaster

'If you can meet with triumph and disaster
And treat those two imposters just the same …'
Rudyard Kipling, If

The funeral director was responsible for a funeral at the crematorium. They were running late. By the time the cortège arrived, everyone was in a rush. Sensitivity prevailed as the family were ushered to their seats, the organ played, and the coffin was carried in. But the arranging of the flowers around the catafalque was hasty and disorganised.

Among the floral displays was one, in white and red carnations, which boldly proclaimed that the deceased was a BROTHER. Such was the rush, this floral tribute was the responsibility of only one attendant and not the usual two. It broke in half before he got it to the front. He hastily rearranged it and placed it alongside the other flowers. The service that followed was rescued by the clergyman completing *his* task, at least, with dignity and warmth.

After the mourners had gone, the clergyman was approached by the organist. 'You never said the deceased was German, vicar,' he announced.

'But he wasn't,' the clergyman replied. 'He was Scottish.'

'So, what's that, then?' the organist responded, pointing to the floral display, especially the broken-and-hastily-rearranged one, in red and white carnations, which boldly said – HER BROT.

In the midst of life there is death.
In the midst of sorrow we can still smile.
In the midst of seriousness we can learn to laugh again.

January 18 – Legends

'I'd rather believe all the fables in the legend ...
than that this universal frame is without a mind.'
Francis Bacon, Essays, 'Of Atheism'

Spoiler alert: This tale is somewhat gruesome ... Sawney Bean was a celebrated 17th-century murderer who ate his victims. (I warned you, didn't I?) Sawney Bean's ghost is said to haunt the family's cave beneath Bennane Head, north of Ballantrae in South Ayrshire, Scotland.

Bean's common-law wife, Black Agnes Douglas, had been driven out of Ballantrae as a witch, so the cave became the family home. For twenty-five years, so legend has it, they and their family survived by eating the bodies of waylaid travellers. King James VI of Scotland, hearing of these terrible events in his kingdom, sent a band of men with bloodhounds to flush them out. In the cave the hunters, to their horror, discovered human limbs hanging from the roof and an assortment of human flesh pickled in barrels. Bean, Agnes and their forty-six assorted family members were rounded up and taken to Edinburgh for execution.

Before he died, the story concludes, Bean put a curse on the cave. And from that day till this, strange incidents have been recorded in that area. Even in recent memory, the local police have logged reports of drivers on nearby roads having to brake sharply to avoid ghostly figures.

True? Well, who knows? But if I'm ever driving down Ballantrae way, I'll make sure I drive pretty quickly.

I've heard someone called 'a legend in his own lunchtime'.
Wouldn't we want our legendary status to last a bit longer?

January 19 – Promises

'Statesman, yet friend of Truth! of soul sincere,
In action faithful, and in honour clear;
Who broke no promise, served no private end,
Who gained no title, and who lost no friend.'
Alexander Pope, To Mr Addison

Here is a story from India. A man on a long voyage encountered a great storm. He prayed to his god, and vowed to sacrifice ten fat oxen if his life were spared. The storm passed and he arrived safely at his destination. Before he disembarked, however, he reconsidered his promise. 'Ten oxen? A bit rash. I'm sure the god will be satisfied with five.'

At home he decided he was still being over-generous. 'I'll sacrifice two oxen because I got home safely,' he promised. But he couldn't sleep and vowed the next day he would take one fat bullock and make a public sacrifice to his god in thanksgiving for his safe return. But, waking in the night, he changed his mind again and reckoned a goat would do. In the morning he shared his decision with his wife, but she objected, saying they needed the milk the goat was producing. 'All right,' said the man, 'I'll take a bag of peanuts to the temple – more pleasing than an animal sacrifice.'

So he prepared a basket of peanuts and was on his way to the temple when he realised he hadn't tasted peanuts for a long time. He took a few, but he liked them so much he had eaten them all in no time.

Keeping his promise? All that was left to pay his vow at the temple was a basket of husks.

A promise matters. Break it, and you might break
someone's heart – and possibly your own.

January 20 – Listening

'The reason why we have two ears and only one mouth
is that we may listen the more and talk the less.'
Zeno of Citium, as recorded by Diogenes Laertius
in 'Lives of the Philosophers'

A wise old abbot was instructing a novitiate in the ways of prayer.
'You must be still, my brother, and be aware of God. Speak less. Listen
more. Come! Walk with me a while.' He guided his companion into
the abbey gardens. They walked in silence – or at least the abbot did,
for his enthusiastic brother had much to say about many aspects of
the spiritual life. Suddenly the abbot stopped. 'Listen!' he exclaimed.

The young man looked around him. 'Listen to *what* Father? I hear
nothing out of the ordinary.'

'The cry of a lark, high above. But it has gone now.'

The two men walked on, the novitiate continuing his chattering
discourse on prayer. Again the abbot stopped abruptly. 'Listen!' he said
once more.

'Listen? But what is there to listen to?'

'It was the chirping of a sparrow, in the corner of the garden. But
it is silent again.'

By now they were on a paved path and the abbot secretly dropped
a small coin on the ground. The young monk stopped immediately.
'What was that?' he said. 'Was that not a tinkling sound? Did I hear a
coin fall, Father?'

The abbot smiled. 'You have much to learn, my brother. You may
hear, but you do not yet know how to listen to what matters.'

Listen! Still your chattering, empty noise.
Listen! Let the silence use its voice.

January 21 – Glory

'But glory doesn't mean
a nice knock-down argument for you.'
Lewis Carroll, Through the Looking Glass

There is no doubt about it, Alice in *Through the Looking Glass* was right. Glory *is* more than a knock-down argument. It shines above the ordinariness of life. It stands out as special. It is worthy of our gratitude and praise. 'Mine eyes have seen the glory of the coming of the Lord,' we sing; 'Solomon in all his glory,' we read; 'Land of hope and glory,' we hear. We speak of glorious victories, the glory of the morning, *Gloria in excelsis Deo*. Yes, there are no doubts about it, glory matters.

But what of the glory that's never seen, or lauded, or raised above the ordinary? What of the glory of humble and faithful service? What of the glory of a life-long commitment to loving someone? What of the glory of a personal goal achieved, a sin forgiven, a fault overcome? What of the glory of a job well done, to the best of our ability?

An anonymous poem reminds us where the roots of such glory might be.

Oh, you gotta get a glory in the work you do;
a hallelujah chorus in the heart of you.
Paint, or tell a story, sing or shovel coal,
But you gotta get a glory or the job lacks soul.

The next time I'm shovelling coal, maybe I'll find a hallelujah chorus in my heart as I'm doing so.

Some people say they have joy in their heart.
I do wish that their heart might talk to their face.

January 22 – Influence

'Canst thou bind the sweet influences ...'
Bible, Job 38:31

I've never been a great lover of camping. But one of my rare camping trips had more of an influence on the remainder of my life than I could ever have imagined.

It was in the late 1960s during a week's camping on the island of Iona. In those days – before regulations and necessary restrictions – you just turned up, pitched your tent and roughed it for a week. There was only one shop on the island, which opened on a few afternoons and had little beyond the bare essentials. So whatever you needed, you had to take it with you. I had my tent – check; sleeping-bag – check; camping-stove – check; food – check. Yes, I had it all – apart, I discovered, from my razor and sugar. No problem! I could go unshaven for a week and try coffee without sugar. Roughing it would have to be the way of things. And anyway, the little shop would be open on Tuesday afternoon ...

The shop was, indeed, open on the Tuesday. It had sugar. But after three days of unsweetened coffee ... Nah! I could give it a miss! But I wasn't comfortable with my weekend stubble. So, razors? None left! No delivery till the Friday. And that was it! No sugar in coffee or tea since then. And by the end of the week my stubble was ... well ... not too bad. I hated shaving anyway. I've had a beard ever since.

Small things, big influence, long time ... Clearly, I'm one of those who can't 'bind the sweet influences' like Job. There's more than one influence that's changed me for ever.

What influences have changed the direction of your life?
And ... what influence might you have on others?

January 23 – Sceptical

'I am too much of a sceptic
to deny the possibility of anything.'
TH Huxley in a letter to Herbert Spencer, 1886

Three game-hunters were always in competition with each other – the most birds bagged; who owned the best gun-dog; who was the most accurate shot. One day they were out on a lake on a duck-hunting expedition. One hunter provided the gun-dog which lay curled up in the bottom of the boat as they rowed out to the best spot from which they could bag the ducks to be flushed out from the shore.

'This dog is the best gun-dog any of you will ever have seen,' the man announced. 'This dog can do things no other dog can do. Just wait till she springs into action.'

Suddenly there was a disturbance on the bank and a flock of startled ducks rose into the air. One by one, the hunters bagged their trophies. The shooting spree over, the proud dog-owner snapped, 'Go girl! Go fetch!' The alert dog leapt over the side of the boat, walked on the water, picked up the first duck and sprinted back to the boat. One by one the fallen ducks were retrieved, each time the dog walking, trotting or running over the surface of the lake.

The hunters declared themselves satisfied with their day's work and headed for shore. 'Well,' the gun-dog's owner exclaimed, 'what do you think of that? Wasn't my dog amazing, just like I said?'

'Oh, not too bad,' one of his friends replied. 'But isn't it a great pity your poor dog can't swim?'

What a pity ... when competition destroys appreciation,
and scepticism wins out.

January 24 – Children

'... to be sensible of his natural rights ...'
Joseph Priestley, An Essay on the First Principles of Government

In chapter 9 of the Gospel of Mark, there is a powerful admonition to Jesus' hearers to care for the rights of children.

If anyone causes one of these little ones – those who believe in me – to stumble, it would be better for them if a large millstone were hung around their neck and they were thrown into the sea.

Yes, says Jesus, it's *that* important.

This is nowhere more clearly laid out than in the *UN Declaration of the Rights of the Child.* Accepted by resolution of the UN General Assembly in 1959, it's the basis of the *UN Convention on the Rights of the Child* adopted in 1989.

We might do well to ponder the natural rights of a child enshrined in this important Convention – the right to affection, love and understanding; adequate nutrition and medical care; free education; full opportunity for play and recreation; a name and nationality; special care if disabled; to be among the first to receive relief in times of disaster; to learn to be a useful member of society and to develop individual abilities; to be brought up in a spirit of peace and universal brotherhood; and to enjoy these rights, regardless of race, colour, sex, religion, or national or social origin.

Our children are our future. They are also our present.
That makes them a gift worth looking after.

January 25 – More children

'Out of the mouths of very babes and sucklings ...'
The Book of Common Prayer (1662)

My daughter Kathryn is a teacher with nursery and infant school children. As with most teachers, she could write a whole book by herself of the funny things children say in class.

Jason, a four-year-old, asks Mrs Harrison, his classroom assistant, to tie his shoes. Mrs Harrison, taking the opportunity to remind him of the need for politeness, enquires, 'And what is the magic word, Jason?' To which Jason excitedly replies, 'Abracadabra, Mrs Harrison.'

An American teacher of children aged six and seven had been sharing a lesson about the early settlers in America, including the Pilgrim Fathers from England. Towards the end of the lesson, she had one or two questions to satisfy herself that the important elements in the lesson had got through. 'And finally, children,' she asked, 'how did the Pilgrim Fathers come over to America all those years ago?' To which an over-enthusiastic child shouted out, 'On the cauliflower, Miss.'

I liked this conversation overheard by a class teacher.

Johnny: 'I've learned to spell my mum's name.'
Andrew: 'Oh yeah? And how do you spell it, then?'
Johnny: 'Easy-peasy. It's M – U – M.'
Andrew: 'Wow! That's amazing. That's exactly how I spell my mum's name too!'

More of that please, children, more and more ...

January 26 – Paradox

'Man is an embodied paradox,
a bundle of contradictions.'
Charles Caleb Colton, Lacon, vol. 1, no. 408

A paradox is 'a statement that is apparently self-contradictory or absurd but really contains a truth'. In *The Rainbow*, William Wordsworth uses the phrase, 'The child is father of the man.' A paradox? Here it is in context.

> *My heart leaps up when I behold*
> *A rainbow in the sky:*
> *So it was when my life began;*
> *So is it now I am a man;*
> *So be it when I shall grow old,*
> *Or let me die!*
> *The Child's the father of the Man;*
> *I wish my days to be*
> *Bound each to each by natural piety.*

Wordsworth shares with us his feeling of joy when he sees his rainbow, and tells us that this feeling was the same when he was a child as it is now he is a man. He hopes that he will still feel that way when he is old.

A paradox? The openness and wonder of the senses of a child have given birth to the man that he is. Why would he not yearn for that to continue into his old age?

To know joy, to live with wonder, to be open to childlike pleasures when you are old? No paradox for me ...

> *Keep the child that's in you close to your heart.*
> *You never know when you might need it.*

January 27 – Building

'He builded better than he knew;
The conscious stone to beauty grew.'
Ralph Waldo Emerson, 'Ode' inscribed to WH Cummings

The writer Eric Blair, better known as George Orwell, spent the last few years of his life on the island of Jura on the west coast of Scotland. Jura is a beautiful but remote place, and Blair lived at the far north of the island, in an isolated house called Barnhill – a 25-mile drive along a single-track road and a four-mile hike to get there. On Jura in 1949 Blair wrote *Nineteen Eighty-Four*, a remarkable novel which imagines the superstate 'Oceania' in a time of government surveillance, persecution of independent thinking known as 'thoughtcrime', and the tyranny of 'Big Brother'. As many have done before and since, George Orwell – as in his equally powerful book, *Animal Farm* – was asking questions about what kind of society we envisage and how to build a better world in which we can live safely together.

On the journey through Jura to Barnhill you pass Lagg Bay. Beside the bay there is a stone house built by a local man, who, to provide a home for his family, hewed every piece of stone for the building out of solid rock, and built the house by himself, piece by piece, stone by stone.

What he built has stood the test of time. He 'builded better than he knew'. For him, 'the conscious stone to beauty grew'. Now that we are well beyond 1984 and Orwell's critique of society's future, we ask ourselves 'Will our society be builded better' as a Jura man has shown us?

Building love and nurture into the stones
creates memories that will stand the test of time.

January 28 – Waiting

'Friends are those rare people
who ask how you are and then wait for the answer.'
Anonymous

On a recent visit to Iona, I came across a flock of geese in a field beside the parish church. The wild goose, we are told, was a Celtic representation of the Holy Spirit, and this meaningful symbol has become commonplace in the Iona Community, epitomising freedom, movement and hope. This community of geese happily pecked their way around the field until a crowd of people came along. The startled birds flew off – apart from one. And, as the geese came and went over the next half hour, it was always the same one that was left behind.

Was it a rebel, not easily startled, or just plain lazy? Then I realised that this goose had only one leg. It could hop about and feed like the others. And it could fly, I discovered later. But it couldn't keep up with its mates when they flew away. So, it stayed – a one-legged goose, alone in a field.

I don't know much about societal norms for geese. But I do know that community matters. When someone is abandoned because they are different, or can't keep up, or are damaged, community suffers.

And the fate of the one-legged wild goose? I didn't stay to find out. There were too many isolated people to get back to, who needed to know the nurture of friendship until they could fly again, or to find that the community stayed with them and cared for them – no matter what.

I wondered why somebody didn't do something.
Then I realised, I am somebody.
Anonymous

January 29 – Learning

'It's never too late to learn.'
17th-century proverb

A young man travelled from village to village selling hats. One warm afternoon he rested in the shade of a mango tree, placed his bag of hats beside him and fell fast asleep. When he woke a little while later, his bag was empty. All his hats had gone. Just then, he saw that the mango tree was full of monkeys, all wearing colourful hats. 'Come back here with my hats,' he yelled. But the monkeys just screamed back. He made faces at them, but the monkeys made faces back. He threw a stone at them, but the monkeys threw raw mangoes back. In frustration he took off his hat and slammed it on the ground. To his surprise, the monkeys threw their hats on the ground too. The man didn't waste a moment, but collected the hats, stuffed them in his bag and hurried on his way.

Fifty years later his grandson travelled the same way selling hats. He found a shady mango tree and rested a while. But when he woke, all his hats were gone. He saw some monkeys sitting in the tree wearing his hats. Then he remembered a story he'd heard from his grandfather. So he waved at the monkeys, and the monkeys waved back. He scratched his ear, and the monkeys scratched their ears. He stuck out his tongue, and the monkeys did the same. Finally, he threw his cap on the ground.

One of the monkeys jumped down from the tree, walked up to him, slapped him on the back and said, 'Do you think you're the only one who has a grandfather?'

> *There are lessons in life; there are lessons from history.*
> *Why we don't heed them is always a mystery.*

January 30 – Support

'May He support us all the day long ...'
John Henry Newman, 'Wisdom and Innocence'
in 'Sermons Bearing on Subjects of the Day'

John Henry Newman's words quoted above are also found in 'An Evening Prayer' in the 1928 *Book of Common Prayer*. Newman sought support from his God. But in a more basic and human sense, support from those around us is also important.

I'm not a cyclist, but I love *Le Tour de France*. The spectacle of the *peloton* and its entourage making its way around France and elsewhere for three weeks in July is always amazing. And I'm constantly impressed by *les domestiques* (literally 'servant riders'). Each team has its rider whom they hope will win The Tour (and secure *Le Maillot Jaune*, The Yellow Jersey) or win a stage, either for the best climber or in a sprint finish. *Les domestiques* are there to ride for the team, not for their own personal glory or success. If their best guy wins, they all benefit. If they do their job, the whole team is successful. Support is what *les domestiques* do.

Here's a prayer from St Ignatius Loyola – for all of us who find ourselves in the role of *les domestiques*.

Teach us, good Lord, to serve you as you deserve,
to give and not to count the cost,
to fight and not to heed the wounds,
to toil and not to seek for rest,
to labour and not to ask for any reward,
save that of knowing that we do your will.
Amen.

January 31 – The future

'To complain of the age we live in, to murmur at the present
possessors of power, to lament the past,
to conceive extravagant hopes for the future,
are the common dispositions of the greater part of mankind.'
Edmund Burke, Thoughts on the Cause of the Present Discontents

In Scotland there is a long tradition of claims to have Second Sight, the ability to foretell the future. The most famous 'seer' was Coinneach Odhar, the *Brahan Seer*, who is reputed to have foretold the site of the Battle of Culloden and the construction of the Caledonian Canal, while the 'black rain' he spoke of is believed to be the coming of the oil industry in Aberdeen.

Another, Thomas of Ercildoune, lived in the Scottish Borders. The story goes that he met the Fairy Queen in the Eildon Hills and she took him to Fairyland for three years. When he returned, he had the gift of prophecy and a skill with poetry. He became known as 'Thomas the Rhymer'. It's said he predicted the Union of the Crowns of 1603.

A minister friend, the late David Ogston, always greeted me with 'It's Thomas the Rhymer.' I'm delighted to be identified with such a remarkable figure from Scottish history. An ability with poetry or a claim to have second sight? The first, perhaps, for this Thomas, but, sadly, not the second. I'm happy to leave conceiving 'extravagant hopes for the future' to the dispositions of others.

But thanks, David. I was always the better for your company and positive greeting.

The past is history. The future is mystery.
Today is a gift. That's why it's called 'the present'.

February 1 – Food

'Give me neither poverty nor riches;
feed me with food convenient to me.'
Bible, Proverbs 30:8

A family of mice went on holiday to Blackpool. (Remember, this is only a story ...) The mice loved it, but found themselves tired out trudging around the sights. They happened to bump into Blackpool's Lord Mayor. (It's just a story ...)

'Are you enjoying yourselves, little mice?' the kindly mayor enquired.

'Oh yes, sir. But your city is so big, and there's so much to see, that we are very tired walking around,' was the reply.

'Don't you worry your little heads. I have the very things for you.' And the mayor arranged that every member of the mouse family should have a set of roller-skates. So the mice had an even *better* time whizzing around the city on their new mode of transport.

A country cat went on holiday to Blackpool. (It's just a story, remember ...) and bumped into the Lord Mayor on his travels.

'Are you enjoying yourself, Mr Cat?' the mayor enquired.

'Oh yes, sir,' was the reply. 'And I've particularly enjoyed the meals on wheels.'

I hope you enjoy your food today.
But, as you do, spare a thought for families
who have nothing to feed on,
not even meals on wheels,
who remain in poverty while we have riches a-plenty.

February 2 – The call of nature

'Natura dat unicuique quod sibi conveniens est.'
'Nature gives to each what is appropriate.'
A medieval classical proposition

In 1929 the British Aluminium Company completed a hydro construction programme, one part of which was to carry millions of litres
of water to their new aluminium smelter at Fort William. The main
source of water is from Loch Treig, along a 24km-long pipe, 4.5m in
diameter, driven through the hillside. The pipes descending from the
shoulder of Ben Nevis are the last section of the waterway, and the
drop of hundreds of metres gives the power for the factory turbines.
There are five pipes, a familiar sight on the hillside as travellers leave
Fort William *en route* to Inverness or Mallaig.

One of my summer jobs when I was a student was to clean the
inside of one of these pipes. Each pipe was cleaned every five years,
the inside scrubbed to wash away peat deposits, scoured to remove
old paint and then repainted. It was dangerous work, but it was satis-
fyingly well paid.

On my first day we were taken to the top of the pipes, given our
instructions and safety briefing and kitted out with protective gear.
Responding to the call of nature, I enquired of the charge-hand
where the toilets were. 'Come with me,' he beckoned and led me outside till we were standing on an outcrop of rock surveying the magnificent vista of mountains and lochs below us. Then, with an
extravagant swing of his arm over the hillside, he announced, 'If it's a
toilet you want, just help yourself. Anywhere out here will do. There's
plenty enough space for everyone. That's the call of nature for you.'

Nature calls to everyone. It doesn't belong to you alone.

February 3 – Bent

'For the rest of it, the last and greatest art
is to limit and isolate oneself.'
Johann Wolfgang von Goethe,
JP Eckermann, 'Conversations with Goethe in the last years of his life'

In the thirteenth chapter of Luke's Gospel there's this story:

> *One Sabbath Jesus was teaching in one of the synagogues, and a woman was there who had been crippled by a spirit for eighteen years. She was bent over and could not straighten up at all. When Jesus saw her, he called her forward and said to her, 'Woman, you are set free from your infirmity.' Then he put his hands on her, and immediately she straightened up and praised God.*

A big discussion ensued, the synagogue leaders complaining about Jesus 'working' on the Sabbath, and Jesus saying that compassion will not be bound by the law.

But this story isn't just about a 'healing miracle' or the Sabbath. It's about lifting people out of their limited view. Try bending over and touching your toes. Now stay there for a bit. What can you see? Your feet ... the dog walking by ... about a metre of carpet ... not much more. Now stand up again. What can you see now? People's faces ... blossom on the trees ... sunshine and clouds ... and much more besides.

If you have a limited view,
you won't have much of a perspective on things.
If your view is expanded,
the possibilities of life and love are endless.

February 4 – Prayer

'Why [does Yohanan say that one may pray all day long]?
Because prayer never loses its value.'
Jerusalem Talmud, Berakhot 4:4

Every week there is a service in Iona Abbey which includes prayers for healing. Requests for prayer are left in various places – in a box in the quiet corner of the Abbey; pinned to a wooden cross in the south aisle; on the altar in St Oran's chapel; in St Columba's shrine. There are prayers for situations and circumstances and for people experiencing difficulties, as well as for personal yearnings, and thanks for healing and celebration. There is also the opportunity for people to request help from the 'prayer circle' of the Iona Community which prays for people across the world on a regular basis.

During the service of healing in the Abbey, names from prayer requests are read out. But what means most to me is the taking of a basket with all the little pieces of paper containing the prayer requests from around the Abbey complex and placing it on the communion table. These prayers were offered when they were written, prayed again when people read them and are now prayed in the silence as they're laid on the table. The prayers go on and on, and aren't left to one person, or place, or moment in time.

Today, someone is praying my prayers, even when I can't.

As o'er each continent and island
The dawn leads on another day,
The voice of prayer is never silent,
Nor dies the strain of praise away.
John Ellerton

February 5 – Still life

'Life isn't finished for us yet! We're going to live!'
Anton Chekhov, The Three Sisters

One of my favourite paintings in our home is a still life by the Scottish artist Gillian Goodyear. We acquired it in 2002 when we were on holiday in the north of Scotland. My wife and I are suckers for local art galleries. And when we saw Gillian Goodyear's still life, it was irresistible. It consists of one large and two small bowls of fruit, with several apples on the table beside them. There's a pot of pansies in the background too. The whole picture is vibrant and attractive.

That's what I like about still life paintings. Though they capture a moment in time, they aren't still at all. They are shot through with life and colour and interest.

The 'still life' emblem of the Church of Scotland is the burning bush, and the motto which goes along with it, *Nec tamen consumebatur,* 'Nevertheless, it was not consumed', gives the key to the emblem's significance.

Moses was called by God out of the burning bush. The bush was burning, but it wasn't being consumed by the flames. The symbolism is powerful – the God of Moses and his people would not disappear in a puff of smoke and a cloud of ash; the Church, and the message from God which the Church is entrusted to share, will survive and remain vibrant. It's not a 'still life' emblem for Moses or the Church, but one that remains alive, full of life and colour and interest. It isn't still for a moment.

Here are life and love that are never still.
Here is life that isn't finished yet.
Here is love that may only just be beginning.

February 6 – Infant feet

'But what am I?
An infant crying in the night:
An infant crying for the light:
And with no language but a cry.'
Alfred Lord Tennyson, In Memoriam

The words quoted below are from a familiar baptismal hymn, written in the 19th century by Thomas Herber. The metaphors of 'the early feet' and 'upward drawn to God' speak of the Christian nurture enshrined in the sacrament.

By cool Siloam's shady rill,
how sweet the lily grows!
How sweet the breath beneath the hill
of Sharon's dewy rose!

Lo! such the child whose early feet
the paths of peace have trod,
whose secret heart with influence sweet
is upward drawn to God.

The 'early feet' of a child are unstable. It's not surprising, therefore, that families will remember when a baby took its first steps. It's a milestone and a real sign of progress. But does that mean that the nurture and support are over? Not at all, for a toddler also needs support, and so does a pre-school child, and a teenager, as well as the child in every adult. We never cease being on our 'early feet'.

Life is about learning and growing,
and always being nurtured so that we may go forward.

February 7 – Mortality

'Who then to frail mortality shall trust,
But limns the water, or but writes in dust.'

Francis Bacon, The World

In the hymn *By Cool Siloam's Shady Rill* there are two of Herber's stanzas not included in the baptismal version. They speak not of birth and childhood, but of maturity and death.

By cool Siloam's shady rill
the lily must decay,
the rose that blooms beneath the hill
must shortly fade away;

And soon, too soon, the wintry hour
of life's maturer age
will shake the soul with sorrow's power
and stormy passion's rage.

From life's beginning we need to face our mortality. Only then will our childhood faith grow and develop such that we are able to face the ultimate fragility of our mortal lives.

O thou, whose infant feet were found
within thy Father's shrine,
whose years, with changeless virtue crowned,
were all alike divine,

Dependent on thy bounteous breath
we seek thy grace alone,
through every stage of life, and death,
to keep us still thine own.

February 8 – Walls

'Dancing on the top of the wall.'

The title of a sermon by the author

One of my sermons I am most pleased with was called 'Dancing on the top of the wall'. I had been uplifted by the images from Germany of the fall of the Berlin Wall on 9th November 1989. Footage of people breaking down the wall with mallets, tearing chunks out of it with bare hands, and eventually singing and dancing as they climbed on the rubble, was immensely powerful. 'Dancing on the top of the wall' seemed to me to be a metaphor for freedom and unity, and an end to separation and disharmony.

Walls are around us all the time. They can be like the 'drystane dykes' familiar in Scotland, keeping animals from wandering; they can offer security, providing the shelter of a home; they can promise safety, like the Hadrian and Antonine walls of the Romans, keeping the marauding Scots at bay. In the Bible, Joshua's trumpeters caused the walls of Jericho to come down – a metaphor for the triumph of God and his people. Ezra organised the rebuilding of the walls of the Temple when the Jews had returned from exile – a metaphor for restoration and renewal. And walls can separate people, like the infamous Berlin Wall.

Look at your walls. Are they like those of Berlin or Jericho – needing to come down because of the divisions they cause? Or are they a symbol of safety, peace and stability, like 'drystane dykes' or the walls of Ezra's Temple?

Do your walls need to be strengthened,
or do you need to dance on the top of them when they fall?

February 9 – Taking things for granted

'Familiarity breeds contempt.'
Late 14th-century proverb

I didn't have a shower in my house when I was a boy. We had a bath, of course, though when I was very little I was washed standing up in the big Belfast sink in our kitchen. We had a rubber 'skooshy-thing' fitted onto the taps of the bath so that my mother and sister could wash their hair. But we didn't have a shower. My granny's house didn't have a shower either, so it was a bath there too.

I can't remember when or where I first had a shower, but I can certainly remember how it felt. It was *amazing*, the best thing *ever*. We have two showers in our house now, one downstairs (a cubicle one) and one upstairs (over the bath). We've certainly gone up in the world since I was young, haven't we?

Why am I telling you about my domestic arrangements? Because I like having a shower so much, I have never taken it for granted. I've become so familiar with many other modern conveniences that contempt has been breeding, I'm afraid – toaster, DVD player, remote control, electric blanket ... The list is endless. But I've never taken access to my shower facility for granted.

The next time you have a shower, give thought to the people who have no access to clean water, far less a warming, cleansing, instant hot shower. Then you might dispel contempt for something that has become over-familiar to you in your comfortable domestic arrangements.

Have you told someone today that you love them?
Wouldn't it be a shame if we took our love for granted?

February 10 – Progress

'Creating the illusion of progress.'
Petronius (attrib.), but probably anonymous

'What do you dislike most about housework?' I was asked.

'All of it,' I replied.

'Not good enough. What's the worst part – dusting, ironing, cooking, vacuuming ... the bit that you just *hate*?'

I pondered my aversion to dusting, my occasional forays into ironing, my loathing of using the vacuum on the stairs, and responded, 'Dislike the most? That's got to be emptying the dishwasher ...'

My parents would be turning in their graves. A mother brought up in a farm-labourer's house, going into service, working as a domestic when I was small; a father, one of eight children living in two rooms, losing his father when he was seven, orphaned when he was fourteen ... I can hear them, and they're not laughing.

'Dishwasher? *Emptying* the dishwasher?' my father is saying. 'When we were young, a dishwasher was whatever child happened to be on the rota for dishes. No luxuries for us, son. Dishwasher! You don't know you're living.' 'Dishwasher? *Emptying* the dishwasher?' my mother is saying. 'What do you expect to happen? The dishes to magically fly back into the cupboards? Or are you expecting the women to do it? Dishwasher! I'll give you dishwasher ...'

And they're right. To take our labour-saving devices for granted isn't good enough.

> *Don't let's make our home comforts*
> *no more than an illusion of progress.*
> *What progress is there in that?*

February 11 – Confusion

'He set my feet upon the rock and ordered my goings.'
Bible, Psalm 40:1

My Paisley granny was steeped in west of Scotland working-class culture. So from time to time she would lapse into the Broad Scots tongue. The words she used were expressive and vibrant, and yet they were strange to my Highlander ears.

One word I loved to hear her use was 'boorach'. When a kitchen was in a mess because the cook had been enthusiastic but disorganised – it was in a boorach. She'd look at my bedroom, with socks, underwear, football boots, games, toys, all over the floor, and say, 'Your room's a boorach, son.' Looking around my study as I'm writing this, she'd be saying that's a boorach too – organised chaos.

If anything is in a state of untidiness or confusion, boorach is an apt description. It's like a guddle, but worse! The word has its roots in the Gaelic word *búrach,* which described 'a digging', and went on to mean a rubbish mound. It's a lovely, expressive word, and brings my granny back to mind when I use it or hear it.

We all get into a boorach sometimes, not just physically, but mentally, emotionally and spiritually too. We might trust our belief system to offer us order, but our human untidiness of mind and spirit creates more confusion than we would like. And the solution? I think my granny would suggest that recognising your boorach is a good place to start, and then to set about a bit of tidying. Right, granny?

Let all things be done decently and in order: The Bible
Aye, right: The author

February 12 – Pilgrimage

'His first avowed intent to be a pilgrim'
John Bunyan, The Pilgrim's Progress

Every week on the island of Iona, the staff working on behalf of the Iona Community organise two pilgrimages. One is 'off-road', a trek to parts of the island which have historical and spiritual significance. It lasts about six hours, with stops at various points for worship, thought and silence, and with a picnic lunch on the *machair,* the common grazing land on the west of the island. The other is 'on-road' on more level ground, from the Abbey to the village and back, lasting a couple of hours, and stopping at various places for prayers and reflection. Strenuous or easy, long or short, in foul weather or fair, these pilgrimages mirror the pilgrimages of life and faith, purpose and direction with which we are all engaged.

There are two things that are significant for me on the Iona pilgrimages. The first is that you do it together with other pilgrims. You talk on the way, with people you know well and with strangers. Sometimes you have brief and intense conversations with people you will never meet again. These are not solo pilgrimages. There are companions on the journey.

The second is that the pilgrimages have stopping places – times for reflection and prayer, rest and lunch. We need to stop sometimes on life treks to gain strength and to clarify ideas for the rest of our journey. Or else the tramping onwards takes over, and the pilgrimage isn't a pilgrimage any more, but just another step-by-step hike.

Together we walk as we go on our way.
Together we talk when we've something to say.

February 13 – Faith

'O come, all ye faithful.'
Anonymous

The 18th-century philosopher David Hume wrote this in *An Enquiry Concerning Human Understanding:*

> *The Christian religion not only was at first attended by miracles, but even at this day cannot be believed by any reasonable person without one. Mere reason is insufficient to convince us of its veracity: and whoever is moved by faith to assent it, is conscious of a continued miracle in his own person, which subverts all his principles of understanding, and gives him a determination to believe what is most contrary to custom and experience.*

The writer of the Letter to the Hebrews in the Bible puts it this way *[Good News Bible]:*

> *To have faith is to be sure of the things we hope for, to be certain of the things we cannot see [11.1] … What a record all of these have won by their faith! [11:39]*

I wish I had the faith I see in many others. But I don't. But does that stop me still giving thanks for the 'miracle in my own person' that my faith creates? No it does not!

'Be a sinner, and sin strongly,' Martin Luther wrote in a letter to Melanchthon, 'but more strongly have faith …' That's the miracle that works for me!

Give me faith, Lord, enough for today.
Make me strong when sins get in the way.

February 14 – Love

'For verily love knows not "mine" or "thine";
With separate "I" and "thou" free love has done,
For one is both and both are one in love:
Rich love knows nought of "thine that is not mine";
Both have the strength and both the length thereof,
Both of us, of the love which makes us one.'

Christina Rossetti, I Loved You First

The hymn in praise of love in Paul's first letter to the church in Corinth is one of the most beautiful expressions of the depth of love that has ever been written. *[1 Corinthians 13:1-13]* The opening lines are quite wonderful:

> *I may be able to speak the languages of men and even of angels, but if I have no love, my speech is no more than a noisy gong or a clanging bell. [Good News Bible]*

W.L. Lorimer's Scots translation puts it this way:

> *Gin I speak wi tungs o men an' angel, but hae nae luve i my hairt, I am no nane better nor dunnerin bress or a ringing cymbal.*

I like 'dunnerin bress'. It's more expressive than the 'noisy gong' of the English version. When our 'dunnerin bress' approach leaves no space for thoughtfulness, tenderness, care, listening, compassion, and all the attitudes and attributes that love contains, then love is compromised.

'The love which makes us one'
is better than all your 'dunnerin bress', don't you think?

February 15 – Hope

'He that lives in hope danceth without music.'
George Herbert, Outlandish Proverbs

There was once an old donkey which accidentally fell into the farmer's well. When he discovered what had befallen the beast, the farmer at once faced a dilemma.

'My donkey is old,' he said, 'and the well is not my only source of water. Is my donkey worth rescuing? Is my well worth saving? Will I succeed? Is it worth the effort?'

He decided it was and called his friends together to help rescue the donkey. Together they began to shovel dirt into the well. The old donkey started to panic because he thought the farmer had decided he wasn't worth saving and was burying him instead. But then he realised what was happening. Every time a shovel of dirt landed on his back, he would shake it off and step up a little higher.

'Stay hopeful,' the farmer shouted.

But there was no need, for hope was always in the donkey's mind.

'Shake it off and step up,' he said to himself over and over again as every spadeful of dirt was thrown into the well. And so, after a while, as the dirt in the well rose higher and higher, the donkey was able to reach the top and step over and out to freedom again.

The farmer and his friends had done their job! But the donkey had always done his, for if he hadn't stayed hopeful and reminded himself to 'shake it off and step up' we might never have seen him again.

> *When the dust settles, I've got more dust to stand on.*
> *When hope settles, I've got more to rely on.*

February 16 – Language

'Our Father, who art in heaven ...'
Bible, Luke 11:1-4

The Church of the Pater Noster in Jerusalem stands on the traditional site where Jesus taught his disciples The Lord's Prayer. *Pater Noster,* the Latin for 'Our Father', gives its name to a church built over a cave by the Emperor Constantine in the 4th century. Through Crusader buildings, to a cloister modelled on the Campo Santo at Pisa, and reconstructions from 1915 onwards of the Byzantine church, the Church of the Pater Noster is still an incomplete project.

The Lord's Prayer is still important to the Christian tradition. Indeed, given that the plaques in the cloisters of the church bear the Lord's Prayer in 140 different languages and dialects – from Cree Indian, through ancient Greek, to Maori – it has clearly remained important and accessible to people of all languages and generations.

When I visited the Church of the Pater Noster I was delighted to find the Lord's Prayer displayed in the language of my granny's childhood – The Doric, or Broad Scots.

Oor Faither in Heiven,
hallowt be thy name;
Thy kingdom come,
Thy will be dune, on the yird as in heaven.
Gie us oor breid for this incomin' day;
forgie us the wrangs we hae wrocht,
as we hae forgien the wrangs we hae dree'd;
an' say-us-na sairlie, but sauf us frae the ill-ane,
an' Thine be the kingdom, the pooer an' the glory,
noo an' forivver. Amen.

February 17 – Trust

'Little Jack Horner sat in the corner,
Eating a Christmas pie;
He put in his thumb, and pulled out a plum,
And said "What a good boy am I!"'

Traditional nursery rhyme

The original Jack Horner, so tradition tells us, was a steward to Richard Whiting, the last of the abbots of Glastonbury.

In the 1530s, the time of the Dissolution of the Monasteries in the reign of King Henry VIII, it is said that the abbot, hoping to placate his king, sent Henry VIII an enormous Christmas pie – containing the deeds of twelve manors. The delivery of the pie to the king having been arranged, the trusted steward, Jack Horner, was charged with its safe delivery. However, the trust was misplaced, and Jack Horner managed to open the great pie and extract from it the Manor of Mells in Somerset – the 'plum' referred to in the rhyme.

Tradition doesn't tell us whether King Henry VIII was placated by the fact that he had the deeds of the eleven manors remaining in the pie, nor whether Jack Horner was found out or not. But 'a good boy'? I think not, for a dishonest act had been perpetrated, and a trust had been broken.

There's an old Italian proverb which runs, 'From those I trust, God guard me; from those I mistrust, I will guard myself.' It would be a sad state of affairs if we mistrusted even the people we trust, more than the people we don't.

Trust matters.
But I trust, Mr Horner, that you already know that.

February 18 – Communication

'A toast to the Queer Old Dean.'
Anonymous

I love reading stories to my grandsons. One evening, in a rush to finish a story, I got the beginnings of a couple of words wrong, and the 'soft and cuddly' bear somehow became the 'coft and suddly' bear. Much giggling ensued. From then on, making deliberate mistakes became a regular request, and 'Tister Mickle' (with apologies to Roger Hargeaves) and 'The Pransome Hince' (with apologies to Cinderella) are now commonplace.

I explained, of course, about spoonerisms, and how the Revd William Archibald Spooner, Warden of New College, Oxford in the early years of the 20th century, became legendary for juxtaposing the initial letters of words – to confusing and hilarious effect. And, of course, the Dear Old Queen might have been the better of a loyal toast than the Queer Old Dean!

Using language can be fun, deliberately or not. But it remains a serious business. Bad communication is often the cause of tensions, from individual relationships to the way nations cooperate – or don't.

Misheard communication often causes all sorts of problems. The order 'Send reinforcements, we're going to advance' can soon become 'Send three-and-fourpence, we're going to a dance' as it's hastily passed along the line.

Enough for now! I'm off for a tup of key.

Good communication matters.
When we say what we mean and mean what we say, everyone benefits.

February 19 – Laughter

'C'est une étrange enterprise
que celle de faire rire les honnêtes gens.'
'It's an odd job, making decent people laugh.'
Molière, Le Critique de l'École des Femmes

Laughter is important, even for decent people – like the folk in our churches who make such mistakes in their newsletters and noticeboards. And they're not even deliberate.

The peace and justice meeting scheduled for today has been cancelled due to a conflict.

Mrs Catherine Cuthbertson sang 'I will not pass this way again', giving obvious pleasure to the congregation.

Eight new choir robes are currently needed, due to the addition of several new members and to the deterioration of some older ones.

The retired men's group will meet at 6 pm. Steak, mashed potatoes, green beans, bread and dessert will be served for a nominal feel.

Come along to the fellowship gathering on Tuesday. You will hear an excellent speaker and heave a healthy lunch.

The church will host an evening of fine dining, superb entertainment, and gracious hostility.

Making people laugh isn't an odd job at all.
Thanks to some church people, it can be a lot of fun.

February 20 – Riches

'It is easier for a camel
to go through the eye of a needle
than for someone who is rich
to enter the kingdom of God.'
Bible, Matthew 19:24

I've always struggled with Jesus' assertion with which today's thought begins. On the one hand, it's such a strange metaphor. Why not suggest 'It's easier for a camel to enter a wardrobe', or 'It's easier for a dog to go down a mouse hole', and give us a metaphor we understand? On the other hand, is it really riches *per se* that's the barrier for us?

I was enlightened somewhat when I heard an alternative explanation. A friend suggested that 'the eye of a needle' to which Jesus was referring was really 'The Needle's Eye', or 'The Needle Gate', one of the many gates in Jerusalem's city wall. It was so narrow – 'needle-like' – that when a merchant arrived with a camel laden with too many fine things, the traveller had to dismount, unpack everything so that the camel could go through the narrow gate, then take all his goods and chattels through the gate piece by piece, load up the camel again, and only then be able to continue his journey into or out of the city. Too much baggage, and you can't get through the Needle's Eye.

In Luke 13:24, Jesus said, 'Do your best to go through the narrow gate; because many people will surely try to get in that way but will not be able.' The Needle's Eye can be for you, as narrow as it is.

Give thought to the kind of things you value,
or you may be stuck in the gate to a better life.

February 21 – Gentleness

'The gentle mind by gentle deeds is known.'

Edmund Spenser, The Faerie Queen

Saint Anselm was riding in the countryside with a group of young men when one of them saw a hare. The party of riders immediately gave chase with their horses and hounds. The frightened hare took refuge under the feet of Anselm's horse. Why, we are not told, as it seems a strange thing for a hare to do, but, nonetheless, it had the effect of bringing everyone up short. The whole party stopped in amazement.

Anselm steadied his startled horse and called on his companions to do the same, forbidding any of them to come near their prey. 'Be gentle with this creature, this child of God's creating,' he said. But the men were not for gentleness. They quickly dismounted and crowded around Anselm's horse and the startled hare. They were noisy with excitement.

One of them shouted, 'Now we have him cornered.' On hearing this, Anselm burst into tears. 'You laugh and cheer,' he said, 'but there is nothing to rejoice about for this unhappy creature. For it is indeed trapped, surrounded by its human enemies. And so it flees to us, those who would take its life, for sanctuary and safety and rescue and shelter.'

And, with that, Anselm walked on, with the hare still cowering under his horse, and all the while he forbade that the dogs should go near their quarry. When they were a good way apart from the rest, the hare, at liberty again, darted with all haste to freedom in the fields.

Let your compassion be gentle, and let your words of comfort rest lightly on the ears of those who need your care.

February 22 – Poverty

'Give me not to poverty lest I steal.'
Daniel Defoe, Review, vol. 8, no. 75, 1711

I'd signed up for the annual speech competition in Divinity College. Entrants had to offer a five-minute speech: 'A motivating talk as part of a church Stewardship Campaign.'

I was sitting in the college common room when one of my mates came in. 'Tom, you're on,' he gasped, 'after Jack. He's got the three o'clock slot. You're next. Ten past three.'

'On for what?' I asked.

'Speech prize, Seminar Room 6, now ...'

I looked at my watch. It said 3.05. I had nothing prepared. Choice ... Not turn up? Loss of face. Scribble something on the back of a fag packet? I didn't smoke. Wing it and make a fool of myself? Only option ...

So in Seminar Room 6 at ten past three I addressed a Pastoral Theology lecturer, the college speech therapist and a PhD student on the theme of Stewardship. I told them of a lad I worked with in a youth club. He'd stopped coming to the Tuesday club-night because his dad was wearing the shoes. They only had one pair between them, and Tuesday night was his dad's turn. I concluded with these words – 'If that's the kind of poverty that's on your own doorstep, in your own parish, around the church where you worship, doesn't it demand a better response in your giving?'

I won the speech competition's second prize. I got a cheque for £10. I spent it on beer. I know now I should have gone out and bought a young lad a new pair of shoes.

When we have more than we need, we are rich beyond imagining.
Beyond imagining the needs of the poor?

February 23 – Messy

'Another nice mess you've gotten me into.'
Oliver Hardy, in several Laurel and Hardy films

I mentioned earlier the way my West of Scotland granny would lapse
into Broad Scots to find a word to describe something which didn't
have an English equivalent. One such word was 'slaister'. A slaister is
a messy person, not in the sense of making a 'boorach' (see February
11), but in making a mess of themselves – spilling soup down their
front, slurping their tea, leaving stains on the tablecloth. Slaister can
also be used as a verb, to describe making a mess or working in a
sloppy way.

No one's quite sure where the word comes from. There's an equivalent in Orkney which is 'slester', and both words may have their roots
in Scandinavia. Who knows? But what I do know is that slaistering is
something we're all guilty of – when we rush at something without
proper care and attention ('more hurry, less speed'), or don't put our
all into something, leaving a botched job (the 'anything'll do' attitude).

'If a job's worth doing, it's worth doing well' is a good motto to
live by. Perhaps 'Take care and you won't meet a problem' would be
a bit simpler.

No one likes to be labelled a slaister. We live with enough messi-
ness that's created by other slaisterers without adding to the mess
ourselves.

'Watch ye dinnae spill that soup aff yer spoon, son.' Aye, right,
granny.

Thank God for dirty dishes, they have a tale to tell;
while others may go hungry, we're eating very well.
Anonymous

February 24 – Volunteers

'One volunteer is worth two pressed men.'
Proverb, 18th century

My friend, Ewan Aitken, is CEO of the Cyrenians. For nearly 50 years, Cyrenians has served those on the edge, working with the homeless and vulnerable to transform their lives. Although it's a secular organisation, the name 'Cyrenians' comes from the biblical story of Simon of Cyrene, the man who was pressed into service to carry Jesus' cross. So the work of the Cyrenians begins with an acceptance of people's own stories and the burdens they carry; it helps them believe that they can change their lives and walks with them in their own transformation. Their vision is an inclusive society in which all have the chance to live valued and fulfilled lives. They work to make that a reality through supporting people excluded from family, home, work or community.

As with every charitable enterprise, without volunteers Cyrenians would not have been able to walk with so many for so long over the years. I worked with an elderly widow recently in one of my bereavement support programmes. She's a volunteer driver with the Cyrenians. 'To be honest,' she told me, 'they might think I'm doing something for them, but they are doing *so* much for me. To see how my small contribution makes such a difference to people's lives is what gives me hope for my future. I didn't think I'd get anything good out of life after Bill died. But volunteering made me feel alive again.'

Compassion benefits the person who receives it and the one who gives it. Volunteering works for the volunteer and the person or organisation being supported. Everyone wins.

February 25 – Together

'And all that believed were together,
and had all things in common.'

Bible, Acts 2:44

I mentioned yesterday a widow who had derived great benefit from working as a volunteer with the Cyrenians. She got more out of it than she ever put in. Volunteering gave her hope for her journey of loss and finding purpose again.

It's interesting to read what the Cyrenians say about this for themselves. I'm sure they speak for all charities who look to volunteers to support their work.

We believe both Cyrenians and our volunteers should benefit from the experience of working together. Volunteering can help build your confidence. It's fun and you'll make friends. You can learn new skills and find out what type of work you enjoy; many of our volunteers like the freedom of physical work, while others take pleasure in working with people face to face. It's great for your CV: you'll gain valuable work experience and may get a qualification too. You'll make a big difference to other people and it feels great to use your talents to give something back. Most importantly, you'll see people's lives changing – including your own. You can volunteer full-time or simply support us whenever you have the time. You can offer your own skills and experience as a way of helping out, or you can take on new challenges, learning as you go. As a Cyrenians volunteer you will make a difference, and it will make a difference to you.

Everyone's a winner when we work together
and have aims, purpose and values in common.

February 26 – Patience

'Patience is power;
with time and patience the mulberry leaf becomes silk.'
Chinese proverb

When Henry Morton Stanley, the American explorer, went out to
Africa in 1871 and found David Livingstone, the missionary-explorer
from Scotland, he spent months in Livingstone's company. But, we
are told, Livingstone never spoke to Stanley about spiritual things.
Throughout these months Stanley constantly observed the old man.
He could not understand Livingstone's habits. Nor could he com-
prehend his patience. Try as he might, he never got to an understanding of Livingstone's empathy for the indigenous people with
whom he was working.

All he knew was this – for the sake of his Christian faith Livingstone lived out what he believed. He was patient, tireless, hard-
working, committed and self-effacing, giving of himself for his people
and his Lord. Stanley wrote: 'When I saw that unwearied patience,
that unflagging zeal, those enlightened sons of Africa, I became a
Christian at his side, though he never spoke to me about it.'

A Scottish schoolgirl was asked by her teacher, 'What is patience?'
She replied, 'If you wait a wee while, miss, I'll try to give you an
answer.' We learn more when we're patient, do more and – as Stanley
found – have a greater influence on others than we can ever imagine.
The mulberry bush of our Chinese proverb can't do anything to
change things for itself. But if we have time and wait with patience,
we will marvel at the fine silk it produces.

Patience is a virtue, in a woman or a man.
And if you fail to find it, be as patient as you can.

February 27 – More prayer

'Pray as though no work would help,
and work as though prayer would help.'

German proverb

A man went hunting. Suddenly he saw a big lion coming towards him. He waited with his gun till the lion got nearer to make absolutely sure he would not miss it. Then he pulled the trigger, and nothing happened! The gun had jammed! Terrified, the man sank to his knees in prayer. The lion came bounding up to him and, seeing the man on his knees, it too knelt on the ground in front of him.

'What are you doing?' asked the trembling man.

'I always say grace before meals,' the lion replied.

Well, that's as maybe, but a hunter and his prey had this in common – prayer mattered, for the one at a time of panic, and for the other at a time of preparation. That's what we do with prayer. It's left to particular circumstances, and doesn't always fit in to the rest of our lives.

Journeying on horseback one day, Saint Benedict met a peasant walking along the road. 'You've got an easy job,' said the peasant. 'Why don't I become a man of prayer? Then I too would be travelling on horseback.'

'You think praying is easy,' replied the Saint. 'If you can say one "Our Father" without any distraction, you can have this horse.'

The peasant began to pray. 'Our Father, who art in heaven, hallowed be thy name ...' He stopped, looked up and asked, 'Shall I get the saddle and bridle as well?'

*When you pray, rather let your heart be without words
than your words without heart.*

John Bunyan

February 28 – Courage

'Sing unto the Lord a new song;
sing praises lustily unto him with a good courage.'
Bible, Psalm 33:3

The Victoria Cross (the VC) is the highest UK military award for conspicuous bravery 'in the face of the enemy'. It is awarded to members of the British armed forces, sometimes posthumously. Instituted by Queen Victoria in 1856 to honour acts of valour during the Crimean War, it consists of a bronze Maltese Cross with a royal crown surmounted by a lion under which is a scroll bearing the words 'For Valour'. Tradition suggests that the metal from which the medals are struck derives from Russian cannon captured at the Siege of Sevastopol.

One of the first awards was to a boy-midshipman who, when a bomb from a Russian battery fell on the deck of his warship, picked it up with its fuse still burning, carried it to the side of the ship and dropped it into the sea.

We are all rightly moved with admiration for such acts of courage, and the VC is an important way of recognising bravery. But, at the same time, it's important to give thought – and our gratitude and admiration – to those who will receive no medal or public recognition, but who exhibit courage every day – coping with disability; caring for a loved one; working in dangerous places.

Let's admire courage when we see it and know it. Let's give thanks for all the inconspicuous 'For Valour' people we see every day.

For Valour. For Service.
For you? For me?

February 29 – Names

'A good name is rather to be chosen than great riches.'

Bible, Proverbs 22:1

My father was one of eight children, the youngest of whom was named Catherine after a family aunt. Well, that's the name on her birth certificate, at least. She was known as Katy – or Katie – in the family, following the normal pattern of shortening names to a more intimate 'diminutive' version. I knew her as 'Auntie Katy' when I was young. I discovered in later years, however, that she was known as Kate to my father and his older sister, and Kit to her husband, my uncle John. And in her church she was always called Mrs Dorward.

Mrs Dorward, Catherine, Katie, Kate, Katy, Kit, depending on who she was with and what their relationship was with her – and she answered to them all!

It's well documented that when her husband, Prince Albert, died Queen Victoria went into deep mourning. At one point she wrote in her grief, 'I have no one to call me Victoria now.'

Names matter. They are precious, intimate and relational. A formal name, a nickname or a diminutive, a name holds our uniqueness and the uniqueness of our relationship with the people that matter to us.

A new patient was admitted to our hospice. His name was above his bed: 'William Robertson'. I asked him what he would like to be called, thinking Bill, Willie, William or the like. He smiled and said, 'Thank you for asking. My best friends call me Mr Robertson.'

On an extra day that gives us a Leap Year,
don't leap over someone's name. It might just ruin their day.

March 1 – Penance

'Spirits overwrought were making night do penance ...'
William Wordsworth, The Prelude

St David's Day, the national day of Wales, has been celebrated since the 12th century. Today's celebrations usually involve lots of singing, followed by a *Te Bach,* tea with *bara brith* (Welsh fruited bread) and *teisen bach* (Welsh cake). In some areas the women put on the national costume, and leeks and daffodils are worn. But who is the patron saint who's at the heart of it all?

Legend has it that both David's parents were descended from Welsh royalty, the young David being trained as a priest before he went off to be a soldier in battle with the Saxons. In later life, he made a pilgrimage to Jerusalem where he was consecrated bishop, founded twelve monasteries, including Glastonbury, and travelled round Wales and the rest of Britain sharing the Christian message. But preacher, bishop and hero though he was, David never forgot his human imperfections. Sometimes, as a self-imposed penance, he would stand up to his neck in a lake of cold water reciting scripture!

Brrrrr! Not for me, I'm afraid. And yet, from St David and many others, we learn that penance matters. And, whatever form it takes, it begins with an honest recognition of our failings. The prayer of confession in the Iona Community's morning liturgy says this:

I confess to my brokenness, to the ways I wound my life,
the lives of others and the life of the world.

You don't have to stand up to your neck in freezing water as a penance for that, I'm sure.

March 2 – Contrite

'O God ... that despisest not
the sighing of a contrite heart ...'
The Book of Common Prayer, The Litany

I'm not a Roman Catholic but I do know a bit about penance. Penance is a sacrament of reconciliation that 're-establishes a right relationship with God'. The penitent person must have a contrite heart, perform verbal confession and be completely humble. It is part of the process that restores the person to God's grace. That's what St David was about in his self-imposed penance of standing up to his neck in freezing-cold water while reciting scripture. Good man!

My friend Davie wasn't a Roman Catholic either. He would never darken a church's door. He'd had a chequered life. His marriage had broken up. He was estranged from his children. He was a recovering alcoholic. He'd 'done time' for being violent to his mother. Davie was no saint. Yet, every Friday, rain, hail or shine, he walked two miles to see his elderly mother when she was dying. Every week he spent his last few pounds buying her 'something nice', so he had no bus fare. Walking there and back was his penance, he told me. It was the working out of his reconciliation with his mother. Davie was a penitent man.

Davie was with his mother in our hospice when she died. He was 'completely humble' and, to me at any rate, with his contrite heart, had been restored to God's grace. Davie never needed to stand in freezing-cold water. But God accepted his penance. I did too. Davie was a good man!

Being contrite is an empty gesture
if it doesn't fill you with a resolve to change.

March 3 – Watching

'From humming-bird to eagle,
the daily existence of every bird
is a remote and bewitching mystery.'
Thomas Wentworth Higginson, The Life of Birds

I was travelling by bus across the island of Mull early in the morning. Half-awake and half-asleep, I was conscious of the movement of people around me and the person sitting next to me invading my space. Shaking myself out of my reverie, I was aware that the bus had slowed to a crawl and that everyone, including the driver, was peering at the hillside. For there, not far above us, were two magnificent golden eagles. The driver pulled into the next lay-by, and for a few minutes we were transfixed by the beauty of the eagles soaring on the thermals. Cameras were unearthed. Binoculars were trained. There was much pointing and many appreciative comments.

As we drove on and my sleepiness returned, I wondered what happened to the timetable when the driver spent time watching golden eagles. She explained later that there were often golden eagles at that spot on the journey, so she knew where to look. And, of course, she didn't keep the event to herself but shared it with the rest of us.

Watching – and not worrying about timetables; waiting – and knowing your patience could be rewarded; and sharing – helping others to see what they wouldn't be aware of on their own. Watching, waiting and sharing – oh to be a bus driver across Mull …

''Tis now the very watching time.'
William Shakespeare, Hamlet

March 4 – Old age

'I'll tell you everything I can:
There's little to relate.
I saw an aged, aged man,
A-sitting on a gate.'
Lewis Carroll, Through the Looking-Glass

I don't know if this old man was sitting on a gate or just leaning on it and letting the day go by ... but an aged gardener was once asked how old he was. He smiled and replied with no more than a moment's thought, 'I am an octogeranium.'

Mrs Malaprop would be proud of him! What a lovely blunder and surely an improvement on the meaning of the word the old man meant to use. The octogenarian was also an octogeranium – an old man who was young at heart, a veteran with an open mind, an ancient who maintained a forward look. Perhaps it's not too much to say that here was an aged man with a youthful soul. Are we not the better for meeting people like this?

There's a story told of a man who was well into his eighties – another octogeranium. He was informed that a friend of his, aged a mere seventy-five, had affirmed that a man is at his best in his seventies. But the octogenarian knew better and would have none of this nonsense from a man he clearly considered to be an upstart. 'He will know better when he has grown up,' was his withering retort.

A 16th-century proverb reminds us,
'You're never too old to learn.'
Perhaps learning of the value of youthfulness in old age
is learning enough of itself.

March 5 – Silence

'For words divide and rend;
But silence is most notable to the end.'
Algernon Charles Swinburne, Atalanta in Calydon

In the East Lothian village of Athelstaneford there is a library in a red telephone kiosk. A redundant phone-box halfway through the village and a local library that had long-since closed stimulated the creativity of the villagers – and a library in the red telephone kiosk is the result.

It's all done on an 'honesty principle'. You sign a book out and return it when you're finished with it. And you might even add books to the library from your own personal stock.

But one more thing strikes me about Athelstaneford's little library – inside its tiny space there is no room for photocopiers and computer terminals, children's corners or play areas, community noticeboards or information desks, coffee-machines or comfy reading chairs. There is no room inside for anything other than books, and you – and silence.

Silence – once the primary rule of library usage years ago – is hard to find anywhere these days, even in libraries. Oh the pleasure of being in this little library, with no one to bother you, no interruptions or distractions, and browsing your chosen book – in absolute silence.

'Words divide and rend,' said Swinburne. We might disagree with words we read and debate words people use. So we need to remember that 'silence is most notable to the end', and that precious moments of silence in a noisy world can offer the healing, peace and insight we crave.

Why not sit in silence for a moment now
before you rush on to something else?

March 6 – Old and wise

'With the ancient is wisdom;
and in length of days understanding.'
Bible, Job 12:12

Beware of assuming that old age is something it isn't. From a poem I had published in *Common Ground* some years ago there are these two contrasting stanzas:

I'm old, so they tell me, I'm old.
In the pensioners' club I've enrolled.
I'm way past my prime,
For my bus-pass, it's time.
'Cause I'm old, no denyin' it, I'm old.

But ...

Yes, I'm old, and I know it! I'm old!
But that bell that you've just heard being tolled
Is not for my death.
I've not breathed my last breath!
Oh, I'm old, but not dead yet. Just old!

We can be too quick to label the elderly as 'past it'. But has the passing of the years not resulted in the accumulation of wisdom? And wouldn't we be the better for spending time drawing on that wisdom and learning from it?

For there's life in the old dog, some life.
No, I won't cause you trouble and strife.
But there's more I can do,
More to offer to you!
For there's life in me yet. Yes, my life!

March 7 – Being at one

'All things and I are one.'
Zhuangzi, Chuang Tzu Chapter 2

Chief Crazy Horse of the Native American Oglala Lakota Sioux is quoted as speaking the words below in the 1870s when he sat smoking the Sacred Pipe with Sitting Bull for the last time. Crazy Horse was killed four days later by US Army soldiers in a hand-to-hand scuffle as they attempted to imprison him. He and his people knew about 'suffering beyond suffering'.

Upon suffering beyond suffering
the Red Nation shall rise again
and it shall be a blessing for a sick world;
a world filled with broken promises,
selfishness and separations;
a world longing for light again.
I see a time of Seven Generations
when all the colours of mankind
will gather under the Sacred Tree of Life
and the whole Earth will become one circle again.
In that day, there will be those among the Lakota
who will carry knowledge and understanding of unity
among all living things
and the young white ones will come to those of my people
and ask for this wisdom.
I salute the light within your eyes
where the whole Universe dwells.
For when you are at that centre within you
and I am that place within me,
we shall be one.

March 8 – Balance

'Nature does not proceed by leaps.'

Latin proverb

In 1309 AD, an Aztec, an inhabitant of what is now Mexico City, was tried and found guilty of burning charcoal in the town and thus polluting the air. For this offence, he was sentenced to death by hanging. In the late 1970s, Mexico City had a carbon monoxide level greater than that of the greater New York metropolitan area, a sulphur dioxide level higher than that found in London and ten times the industrial contaminants of the industrialised Rhine valley. What a contrast with 1309!

We know things have improved and that much has been done in the past thirty years to raise the world's awareness of the damage caused by pollution. Yet we are even now facing the effects of global warming and, sometimes effectively and sometimes not, we are trying to deal with it.

The damage that increased industrialisation and population does to our fragile planet is more in the public domain now than ever before. But there seems to me to be an imbalance between an Aztec burning charcoal in 1300 and – 700 years later – millions of tons of pollutants being pumped into the atmosphere without an apparent 'by your leave'.

We may not be able to restore *that* balance, but we must surely give constant thought to maintaining the balance in nature, so that we can get the best out of our world and not destroy it in the process.

A balanced ecology; a balanced economy;
a balance in caring; a balance in sharing.

March 9 – Learning

'Learning is a treasure
that will follow its owner everywhere.'
Chinese proverb

I was talking with some tradesmen who were swapping stories about their apprentices. One journeyman was bemoaning the fact that half of the apprentices' time was spent in college, while in his day – 'when we were properly trained' – everything was learned 'on the job'.

'Everything learned', it appeared, included initiation traditions – tricks played on the unsuspecting youngsters. 'You send a young lad to the store,' one of the tradesmen recounted, 'to ask for a "long stand", and the store man, being in the know, would have the apprentice waiting for an age till the penny actually dropped.' There were nods all round. Another told us, 'You ask the new boy to request a tin of tartan paint or a left-handed screwdriver.' And yet another, 'The welder would ask his apprentice to bring over a metal bucket to catch the fiery sparks so they could be used later to heat up the yard.'

Another Chinese proverb suggests: 'A single conversation with a wise man is better than ten years' study of books.' I'm not sure the apprentices who are the butt of initiation tricks would agree with that. But, nonetheless, there is much to be learned if we draw on people's experience, the kind of wisdom from years of learning that isn't found in books. We learn important things if we are prepared to listen to those who have done all their learning long before we became an apprentice in life.

You can learn something every day.
You can teach something every day.

March 10 – Laughing

'The case will be dismissed with a laugh.
You will get off scot-free.'
Horace, Satires, Book 2 No. 1

I had my bike stolen. It wasn't the most traumatic experience of my life. I didn't use it much; it wasn't worth a lot; it was my fault for leaving my front door open and not chaining the bike. But it had been stolen, and I dutifully reported the theft to the local constabulary. The bobby was attentive, efficient, but not at all encouraging. 'I think you can say ta-ta to this one,' he announced. 'And you'll have a fat chance getting anything out of the insurance.' I knew that but what's done is done.

I was the butt of jokes for a while and the focus of some *terrible* puns.

'I hear you've been saddled with an insurance claim,' a so-called friend announced.

'I thought you were looking a bit tyred,' said another.

'Are you gearing up to buy another bike?'

'If you've got no evidence, you and the polis will have nothing to go on.'

So it went on, unsympathetic people trying to make light of my misfortune by cracking jokes and falling about laughing at their own attempts at humour. What would it have been like if it had been something *really* traumatic. Would anyone be laughing then?

Oh, I got the bike back, by the way. The police got an anonymous tip-off. They'd racked up another success!

Humour and sorrow. Loss and redemption.
Disaster and success. Wheels within wheels.

March 11 – Wit

'And wit's the noblest frailty of the mind.'
Thomas Shadwell, A True Widow

The 17th-century Scot George Buchanan, a counsellor to the King, could answer any question put to him, by fact or by humour. In the court of King James VI, he also acted publicly as the King's Fool.

At that time a poor Scotsman dined on eggs one day at a public house in London, but, not having money to pay, arranged credit till he should return. The man went on to acquire a vast fortune and after some years called at the tavern and enquired of the publican how much he owed for his dinner of eggs. The landlord, seeing how rich the man had become, gave him a bill of several pounds.

'The reason for the charge,' he said, 'is that that these eggs, had they been hatched, would have been chickens, and the chickens, laying more eggs, would have produced more chickens. With the eggs so multiplying, in time their value would come to what I have charged you.' The man, however, refused to pay and was charged with fraud. He got George Buchanan to represent him in court.

When he appeared at the trial, Buchanan was carrying a bowl of mushy peas. 'What is this?' the judge asked.

'I am going to sow them, my Lord,' George replied.

'Will they grow?' enquired the judge.

'Indeed, sir, when scrambled eggs grow chickens.'

The answer convinced the judge of the extravagance of the innkeeper's demand. The Scotsman's bill was reduced to two-pence ha'penny.

What's wit? Wit's what's what, when it's needed.

March 12 – Signals

'I really do not see the signal!'
Horatio, Lord Nelson, Robert Southey, 'Life of Nelson'

Admiral Lord Nelson could not see a signal at the Battle of Copenhagen. 'I have only one eye ... I have a right to be blind sometimes,' he said.

I have two eyes and I have no right to be blind at all, but, nonetheless, I was surprised when I *did* see a signal in a suburban garden in Edinburgh. It was a big, red railway signal, on top of a typical white support structure, high above the garden hedge. Not being a railway buff, I don't know what the signal was signalling – a train to stop, or slow down, or travel safely on the line? And what was a train doing running through a suburban Edinburgh garden in any event when there wasn't a railway line in sight?

No, it was just a signal for the sake of having a signal in your garden. It wasn't a signal that signalled much to me.

When Peter was at the beginning of his ministry, he had a dream of animals being lowered to the ground in a big cloth. [Acts 10:9-16] 'Take, and eat,' a voice said. 'No!' Peter replied. 'I can't eat anything that's unclean.' 'Do not consider anything unclean that God has made,' the voice said. It was a signal, not for its own sake, but because it pointed Peter in a new direction – towards inclusiveness, openness, equity, embracing the whole people of God.

We need *those* kinds of signal, ones that say a lot when other signals say nothing – signals of welcome, fairness, justice, sharing, to point us in the right direction.

'Read the signs,' we are told often enough.
'Make the right signals,' we should also tell ourselves.

March 13 – Walking

'Walking, and leaping, and praising God.'
Bible, Acts 3:6

Some years ago, I walked the West Highland Way with my good friend Farquhar McArthur. Sadly, Farquhar is no longer with us, so the memories of the six days we spent together are very precious to me.

There are many things I remember from that walk. The first is that my rucksack was too heavy. I'd simply taken along too much 'stuff'.

Second, my feet hurt. I had blisters on the first day. I had started the walk without proper preparation.

Third, Farquhar was terrific company. Humour, encouragement, silences, meals together, shared pleasures, all made the walk special. I treasure those days with my friend. Good companionship on the journey matters.

Fourth, despite the trials of the hike, there were still memorable, spectacular things to see. Notwithstanding the troubles of our living, it is still a beautiful world.

And finally, we made it to Fort William. We'd achieved small goals along the way – Conic Hill above Loch Lomond, the Black Mount at Rannoch Moor, the Devil's Staircase in Glencoe – and the completion of the whole thing. The satisfaction of achieving our goals is very special.

Will I walk the West Highland Way again? Probably, but next time I'll travel lighter, be better prepared, make sure I have just as good company, appreciate the scenery again, and jump up and down along Fort William High Street shouting, 'I've done it! I've done it! I've done it!'

In the love of friendship, my friend still walks with me.

March 14 – Truth

'And you shall know the truth,
and the truth shall set you free.'

Bible, John 8:32

A king had one daughter, a princess who was perfect in every way, apart from one major flaw – she could never tell the truth. No one had seen the likes of her in the whole of the kingdom. So the king made it known that if anyone could outdo her in telling lies and could make her tell the truth, he should have her for a wife – along with half the kingdom.

Many tried to respond to the king's promise, but nobody succeeded. Three brothers thought they would try their luck. Two brothers fared no better than the others, but the youngest was undaunted. He set out for the palace, but arranged to meet the princess outside the cowshed.

'Good morning,' he said.

'Good morning,' she replied. 'You haven't got as big a cow as we have. Look at the milk we have in these barrels.'

'Let me tell you,' said the young man. 'I climbed right up to the clouds the other day and there I found the North Wind resting. I felt stranded as I hovered there in the wide open, but a warming wind gently let me down. I landed in a viper's hole – the nest of your mother and your father, I think it was! And, you know, your mother gave your father such a blow that a handful of figs dropped from his hair!'

The princess shouted, 'My father never grew figs in his hair!'

The truth! And the young man had won!

Truth or lies, which way to go?
Lies destroy, as truth will show.

March 15 – Image

'Dans le fond des forêts votre image me suit.'
'Deep in the forest glade your image follows me.'
Jean Racine, Phèdre

Some years ago, when we had a lady who did some cleaning in our home, we always tidied the place before she arrived. Why? Because we didn't want to present ourselves as untidy or slovenly. I'm sure she wouldn't have minded. But we did.

I spoke with a man recently who was just about coping with domestic chores since his wife died. He was wearing a crisp, white shirt, a beautiful tie and a smart three-piece suit. 'You're looking terrific,' I remarked. He smiled, 'But only on the outside. The only parts of my shirt I've ironed are the collar and sleeves. No one else sees the rest. Why do you think I'm wearing a waistcoat?'

I once turned up at a funeral having left my clerical collar at home. It was one of the 'insert' collars and not a full 'dog collar'. So I cut a piece from an Order of Service I had in my briefcase, slotted it in my shirt, and no one noticed the difference. There were also times when the collar-insert had been cut from a Fairy Liquid bottle and nobody knew.

Presentation matters. In an age when so many false images are projected, how we present ourselves is still important. We might be hurting inside, but we pretend to be 'together'. We might require a cleaner, but we also need to look after our own home.

When the presentation and the reality match, people see more than the display of a flashy image for its own sake.

If we are made in God's image, does that mean that God often has to cope with not looking as good as expected?

March 16 – Heaven

'When earth breaks up and heaven expands,
how will the change strike me and you
in the house not made by hands?'
Robert Browning, By the Fireside

A teacher, exploring some religious teaching, said to his class, 'Now, children, hands up all those of you who would like to go to heaven?' All the children put up their hands, except one who kept his hands firmly resting on his desk.

'Michael, don't you want to go to heaven?' the teacher asked.

'No way, sir,' was the reply, 'not if *that* lot's going ...'

The teacher, it is reported, did not enquire further of the honest Michael as to his preferred destination ...

We talk and think about heaven as somewhere 'out there', after death, a paradise after the toils and hardships of this world are over. That's as maybe, and there is much in this religious concept of heaven to commend the idea to us. But I recall an elderly patient in the hospice remarking to me, 'There will be another life. I can think of nothing surer. But the more definite I am about that, the more I am directed to *this* life, to make the best of it I can. Heaven will take care of itself. I have to take care of the here and now.'

Whatever the future holds for us we must make the best of the here and now. Heaven may be Browning's place 'not made by hands', but this life surely is. We have to make the best we can of this life before the 'earth breaks up'.

If little Michael was to put his energy
into getting along better with 'that lot', he might find
a tiny bit of heaven in his own classroom.

March 17 – Envy

'Indeed, I am not envious, rather I am amazed!'
Virgil, Eclogues No. 1

Every year on St Patrick's Day, cities and people across the globe deck themselves out in forty shades of green. Wherever there is a connection to Ireland, people will celebrate their homeland. And all over Ireland, from rivers to pets, from milkshakes to candyfloss, everything turns green on St Patrick's Day. And, of course, wherever there are the Irish, there's bound to be a party, and when it comes to their patron saint, there's no stopping them. In Dublin there's a festival programme, 'Greening the City', which encourages buildings and businesses in Dublin and beyond to light their buildings green in support of the St Patrick's Festival.

There's an old Irish saying which tells us:

> *There are only two kinds of people in the world –*
> *the Irish and those who wish they were.*

People from other countries might dispute that. But there is no doubt about it: you can take the people out of Ireland, but you can't take Ireland out of the people.

Pride in your nation and its heritage; bonds across the seas and the ages of history; pleasure in the culture and traditions of your land … it's all there, in Ireland and its people. Ireland is called 'The Emerald Isle'. So, if you ever go across the sea to Ireland, you'll know why, because, very quickly, you'll be green with envy, and absolutely amazed.

> *'Thou shalt not covet.' Damn! Why didn't Moses do a deal*
> *to get the Commandments down from ten to nine?*

March 18 – Grey days

'All cats are grey in the dark.'
Mid-16th-century proverb

The poem *The Match,* by the late-19th-century English poet Algernon Charles Swinburne, contains a wonderful series of metaphors of things coming together to become one in a deep and loving relationship – sorrow and joy, April and May, pleasure and pain, life and death … and the rose and the leaf, the words and the tune as in the opening stanzas:

If love were what the rose is,
And I were like the leaf,
Our lives would grow together
In sad or singing weather,
Blown fields or flowerful closes
Green pleasure or grey grief;
If love were what the rose is,
And I were like the leaf.

If I were what the words are,
And love were like the tune,
With double sound and single
Delight our lips would mingle,
With kisses glad as birds are
That get sweet rain at noon;
If I were what the words are,
And love were like the tune.

Life isn't all celebration. There are grey days as well as the green. The Irish know that too. Our task is to fit the differences into a compassionate and accepting world.

March 19 – Obedience

'Nature cannot be ordered about, except by obeying her.'
Francis Bacon, Novum Organum

A teacher left her class one day and when she returned she found all the children sitting in perfect silence with their arms folded. She was amazed and stood open-mouthed, absorbing what she saw in front of her. She was astonished not only by the profound silence but also by the behaviour of her normally unruly – and far from silent – class.

'Well, children. This is amazing indeed,' she said. 'So can somebody explain why you are all sitting silently like this?'

Several hands went up. Choosing a little girl at the back the teacher asked, 'Yes, Sophie. What's the explanation? And, yes, it's OK for you to speak.'

'Please miss,' Sophie replied, 'you told us one day that if you ever left the classroom and came back and found all of us sitting perfectly silent, you would drop down dead.'

Perhaps it was the same teacher who said to little Billy, 'This is the fifth time this week I've had to punish you. What have you to say, Billy?'

To which Billy replied, 'I'm glad it's Friday, miss ...'

Obedience among children? It's hard to find, sometimes, children being what children are.

St Benedict said,
'The first degree of humility is obedience without delay.' Obedience to some
kind of higher principle, and the humility which results, would make the
world – and every school classroom with it – a much better place.'

March 20 – Freedom

'When Israel was in Egypt's land:
"Let my people go!"'
A spiritual

We have a Cocker Spaniel called Amber. At the time of writing this she's three years old and is as mad as the first day we got her as a puppy. People tell us she'll settle down. 'The first year's the worst', they said. We're past that. 'Eighteen months, and she'll be fine.' No! Two years? Twenty years? She'll still be as mad as she is now.

It's most clearly seen when we're out for a walk. No matter how long a leash she's on – a short one or an expandable one that's ten feet or so in length – she's *always* at the end of it, trying to sniff that little patch of grass or pavement that's *just* out of reach. It's her bid for freedom, and a reminder that, as domesticated as she is, she'd rather be off the leash, exploring the world.

Freedom matters. Some of us take it for granted. For others, a curtailment of liberty is temporary. But for many in our troubled world freedom is that patch of grass or pavement that's always out of reach.

John Dalberg-Acton, 1st Baron Acton, wrote this in *The History of Freedom in Antiquity* in 1877:

> *No obstacle has been so constant, or so difficult to overcome, as uncertainty and confusion touching the nature of true liberty. If hostile interests have wrought much injury, false ideas have wrought still more.*

*Let's work for freedom and against the hostile interests
and false ideas that curtail people's liberty.*

March 21 – Wisdom

'So teach us to number our days:
that we may apply our hearts unto wisdom.'
Bible, Psalm 90:12

A wise old owl sat on an oak;
The more he saw, the less he spoke;
The less he spoke, the more he heard;
So why aren't we like that wise old bird?

Why indeed! Perhaps if we thought more, listened more, pondered more and took more care, we would have enough experience for people to consider that we might be wise.

One of my church elders, following an acrimonious discussion in a church meeting, said meaningfully:

Some people are wise,
And some are otherwise.

Here was a man who recognised wisdom when he saw it and clearly knew when it was missing. As far as I know, he didn't write the piece below. I don't know who did. I wish it had been me!

Who knows not, and knows not that he knows not, is foolish;
shun him.
Who knows not, and knows that he knows not, is humble;
teach him.
Who knows, but knows not that he knows, is asleep;
wake him.
Who knows, and knows that he knows, is wise;
follow him.

March 22 – Rubbish

'Cast as rubbish to the void ...'
Alfred, Lord Tennyson, In Memoriam

Not long after a new system of rubbish collection was introduced in Edinburgh, the following joke did the rounds.

Council cleansing operative: 'Where's yer bin?'
Edinburgh resident: 'I've been to Japan?'
Council cleansing operative: 'Naw, missus. Where's yer wheelie bin?'
Edinburgh resident: 'I've really been to Japan.'

When we use the word 'rubbish' and apply the label to a person, we are telling them they are worth nothing and should be thrown away. Towards the end of what we call 'The Sermon on the Mount' in Matthew 5, Jesus says:

> *You are the salt of the earth; but if the salt has become tasteless, how can it be made salty again? It's no longer good for anything, except to be thrown out and trampled underfoot.*

I know what Jesus is getting at. But this pithy saying is, for me, quite misleading. If the salt of the earth is the people of the earth, of course some of us can be tasteless. But surely that doesn't mean we're rubbish, fit to be thrown away, 'trampled underfoot'. We *can* find our purpose again, regain our saltiness. We'll always have another chance.

Most rubbish can be recycled. All people can be redeemed.

March 23 – Recycling

'So all my best is dressing old words new,
Spending again what is already spent.'
William Shakespeare, Sonnet 76

Recycling is big business these days. The more that can be recycled, and the less sent to 'landfill', the better it is. Bottles, cans, paper, garden waste, even food, all collected from your front door; wood, metal, rubble, engine-oil, batteries, and much more besides welcomed at your local 'recycling centre'. It's good for the Council, it's good for the environment and it's good for me.

I've been recycling sermons for years, but not in this way. I'd always thought that with all the hard work that went into a sermon it *deserved* to be kept and given another airing. So, after a reasonable passage of time or, even better, in another church where people hadn't heard the sermon before, it could be trotted out again. It's what preachers call 'the sermon barrel'. Keep every sermon; pull it out of the barrel when you're hard pressed for new ideas; preach it like it's brand new. Different date at the top, a note of when and where it was preached, topical references updated, and Bob's your uncle, a new sermon emerges, repackaged, refreshed – and nobody knows! Recycling works!

But after many years I've taken to recycling my sermon straight into the paper-recycling box. My sermons have gone, the barrel is empty, the recycling is total. I realise now that a sermon should be 'in the moment', given away. It was never designed to be kept or to be recycled in any form.

Excuse me. I have a sermon to prepare – new, pristine, fresh.
Who needs recycling when you have this opportunity?

March 24 – Pet

'An animal's eyes have the power
to speak a great language.'
Martin Buber, *I and Thou*

Bob had been looking for a pet for a while. Anything would do if it was good company, showed the right amount of affection and didn't cause too much bother. But he definitely needed a pet. Bob's career was over and he'd taken early retirement. Too much travelling, too many strange places, too much stress. The lifestyle had been hard and the rewards poor. Occasional successes had come his way. But that was scant compensation for a life of drudgery and always being at someone else's beck and call.

Now he *was* getting his pet, something to have a home with, to make it worthwhile getting out of bed in the morning, and, if he was honest, to share some love with. And today was the day! His new pet would be just the ticket. He *knew* that, and he was very excited. His ears pricked up at the sound of footsteps in the corridor. He jumped out of bed, tense with anticipation. The footsteps came closer. The door opened and a lady in a green sweatshirt appeared.

'Hello, Bob,' she said. 'How are you today?' And without waiting for an answer, she turned to the young man who was accompanying her. He was tall, balding and grinning from ear to ear. Bob liked the look of him right away.

'This is Bob, Terry,' the lady said to her companion, 'your very own rescue greyhound. Bob, say hello to Terry.'

Bob had been looking for a pet for a while. And he reckoned that Terry would do just fine.

'You're just a pet!' Who, me?

March 25 – More patience

'If all want sense,
God takes a text, and preacheth patience.'
George Herbert, The Church Porch

There's an apocryphal story of a Glasgow policeman, recently come to the city from Stornoway, who was patrolling the streets in the days when there was still horse-drawn transport. He came across a rag and bone merchant whose horse had collapsed at the top of Sauchiehall Street and who was calling for assistance. The policeman, having surveyed the scene, proceeded to try to drag the motionless horse and cart along the street.

'What on earth are you doing?' the merchant complained.

'If you just help me here, we can pull the poor beast round the corner. For if we leave it here, I'll have to write "Sauchiehall Street" several times in my report. But if we can say it happened in Bath Street, it would be much easier.'

My friend David Mitchell is minister in a parish in West Cowal in Argyllshire and lives in the village of Tighnabruaich. He's lost count of the number of times the name and spelling of his village has caused consternation on the telephone. 'Can you spell that, sir?' Even when he spells it *very* slowly, he often has to do so again – several times!

We need to listen to each other carefully, and not just with difficult names. It's amazing how complications can be overcome if we learn to listen with patience.

Patience is a virtue; I've told you that before.
If you think you've lost it, you'll have to wait some more.
Be patient while you're waiting, ev'n though it seems a bore.

March 26 – Meanings

'I pray thee, understand a plain man in his plain meaning.'
William Shakespeare, The Merchant of Venice

I was watching a flock of gulls as they languidly rose and fell in the air, carried by the prevailing wind. With their wings outspread and barely flapping, the gulls were almost stationary in the sky, only moving up and down, left or right as the wind took them. 'Ah,' I thought to myself, recalling a Richard Attenborough nature programme I'd watched the evening before, 'I know about that. They've "caught a thermal", as the wind is pushed upwards by the onshore landscape. They'll be "riding a thermal" for ages, using a minimum of energy and deriving the maximum amount of pleasure. Thermals, eh? What a way to spend your day ...'

Not many days later the weather changed and we were subject to a north wind, whipping across the Forth. No gulls to be seen that day! Maybe they were indoors looking for *another* kind of thermal. I know I was, as I raked in my 'winter clothes' cupboard to unearth those close-to-the skin winter-warmers designed to keep out the worst of East Lothian winds. *These* were the thermals that mattered now! No warm updraught of thermals for me when winter thermals were needed.

One word, two meanings. One word, two images. One word, two concepts. Isn't that the beauty of language, that it can convey a richness and variety of meanings?

'Be careful little lips what you say'
the old song reminds us.
'Be careful little words what you mean'
might be an equally important piece of advice.

March 27 – Misunderstood

'The only people who remain misunderstood
are those who either do not know what they want
or are not worth understanding.'

Ivan Turgenev, Rudin

I'm going to be controversial and suggest that Judas, the disciple who betrayed Jesus, is misunderstood. This isn't a new idea, but my proposition is that Judas believed he could force Jesus to reveal his true colours by betraying him.

Judas was a revolutionary and believed that Jesus had come to establish a new kingdom – not a 'heavenly' one, but an 'earthly' one – that would see Roman oppression overthrown and the people set free. Judas believed Jesus was a leader playing a cagey game. But time was running out. Something needed to happen that would force Jesus' hand. Selling himself as a fifth-columnist for thirty pieces of silver was the end-point of Judas' plan. Backed into a corner, Jesus would begin the revolution. He had to! He wouldn't succumb to arrest and torture and execution.

But Judas misunderstood Jesus. The revolution Jesus had begun wasn't one that would lead to being the ruler of a free people. This was a kingdom of attitude, not of power. This was a revolution of the heart, not one of violence.

In his misunderstanding, Judas is also misunderstood. His name is synonymous now with betrayal. Perhaps he's been given a bad press. Judas' intentions were honourable.

Controversial? Perhaps. But it allows me to emphasise this – be careful, be very careful, of judgement.

Motives might be honourable but not work out well.
The misunderstood need to be understood too.

March 28 – Eyes

'Eyes have they, but see not.'
Bible, Psalm 115:5

'What does Auntie Elizabeth do?' Katie asked.

'She's an orthoptist,' her mum replied.

'What's an orkopitriss?' Katie continued.

'Oh,' her mum replied lamely, 'she ... looks after eyes.'

'But what does she *do*, Mummy?' continued the insistent Katie.

Her mum was floundering now.

'Well ... eh ... she's ... a physiotherapist for eyes.'

Katie was quiet – but not for long ... 'but what's a fizzo ... terapinist, mum?'

'Not terapinist ...' her mum responded, reckoning it was going to be a *very* long day ...

Some weeks later, Katie had to get her eyes checked. 'We're going to the opticians,' her mum told her.

'What's an oktisyan?' Katie asked.

'Someone who looks after eyes.'

'Like Auntie Elizabeth?'

'No, she's an orthoptist. I've told you that.'

'What's the difference?' Katie's mum reckoned it was another very long day.

Katie liked the optician lady. 'My Auntie Elizabeth is an orkopitriss. She looks after eyes too, but not like you.'

'And do you know what an orthoptist does?' the optician asked.

'Yes. She's a physical terrorist for eyes.'

Katie's mother reckoned a long day had just got considerably longer.

The eyes have it! The eyes know it!
The words tell it. The face shows us.

March 29 – Good intentions

'I've started, so I'll finish.'
Magnus Magnusson, Mastermind

When I was about seven or eight, I found an old alarm clock in my grandparent's house which 'didn't go'. To my mind, a broken clock was no use to anyone, and if I could fix it, everyone would be pleased. If I couldn't, it would still be broken and no one would mind. This was before the days of Technical Lego, but being a lover of Meccano, the equivalent in my childhood, I had a high opinion of my fitting-together abilities. I'd never seen the inside of a clock before, but with fascination, and great gusto, I set about my task.

Very soon I had an array of little pieces spread over the kitchen table – screws, springs, cogs, wheels, hands, winders ... And then ... I tried to put them together again. You can figure out what happened. I didn't know which screw went with which cog, or how a spring fitted to a wheel, or where the winder slotted into the ...

It was a disaster! And even when I had got the clock into *some* semblance of order, there were still several pieces left over. I'd *started* with good intentions, but I didn't know how to finish.

Did the family discover my attempts at clock-fixing? No, they didn't. I just stuffed the leftover bits into the clock and screwed on the back. The clock was carefully hidden in the back of a drawer, never to be seen again.

Good intentions are OK.
But it's not the beginning of an enterprise that matters,
it's bringing it to a conclusion –
for broken clocks, or anything else.

March 30 – Holiness

'Worship the Lord in the beauty of holiness.'
John Samuel Bewley Monsell, 1863 hymn

A little girl notices several greying hairs on her mother's head. 'Why do you have grey hairs, mummy?' she asks. Her mother replies, 'Every time you do something wrong and make me unhappy or worry, one of my hairs turns grey.' The little girl thinks for a while, then asks, 'So how come *all* of granny's hairs are white, and have been for ages?'

A minister friend told me how when he was putting up a trellis to support some sweet peas he was conscious of one of his neighbour's children watching him. The minister asked him if he was trying to pick up some tips on good gardening. But the child replied, 'When my dad was fixing something, he hit his finger with a hammer and said some sweary words. I wanted to see if you would do the same.'

How quick we are to pick the faults in someone or expect them to do something wrong. Would it not be better if we looked for the good in people and commented on that? The late Billy Graham reminded us that in the Bible the term 'holy' means 'set apart', and indicates a person who is bound to God, or even to a place where God is present. Holy is *not* something unattainable nor does it describe people who are self-righteous. So, it would be better to see and comment on signs of holiness and not on the grey hairs or sweary words we are all too familiar with. Perhaps then people will feel they are 'set apart' to achieve better things.

But, like the Holy One who called you,
be holy yourselves also in all your behaviour;
because it is written, 'You shall be holy for I am holy.'
1 Peter 1:15-16

March 31 – Riddles

'Created half to rise, and half to fall;
Great Lord of all things, yet a prey to all;
Sole judge of truth, in endless error hurled;
The glory, jest and riddle of the world.'

Alexander Pope, An Essay on Man

Here's a couple of riddles – in the Scots tongue. I'll give you the answers at the end. Ready?

There's a wee, wee hoose,
And it's fu' o' meat;
But neither door nor window
Will let ye in to eat.
(hoose = house   fu = full)

Come a riddle, come a riddle,
Come a rot-tot-tot;
A wee, wee man,
Wi' a red, red coat;
A staff in his haun',
An' a stane in his throat.
Come a riddle, come a riddle,
Come a rot-tot-tot.
(haun' = hand   stane = stone)

'The wee, wee hoose' is an egg, of course. And the red-coated 'wee man' is – a cherry! Aren't riddles fun?

If we are the 'glory, jest and riddle of the world',
which part of us is the glory, and which part the jest.
There's another riddle worth pondering.

April 1 – Fool

'I care not whether a man is good or evil;
all that I care is whether he is a wise man or a fool.
Go! Put off your holiness and put on intellect.'

William Blake, Jerusalem

A court jester once said something in front of a king that was so foolish that the king, handing him a staff, said, 'Take this, and keep it till you find a bigger fool than yourself.'

Some years later the king fell very ill and lay on his deathbed. His courtiers were called; his family were summoned and stood around his bed; all his servants were in attendance.

The king, addressing them, said, 'I am about to leave you. I am going on a very long journey, and I shall not return to this place. So I have called you all to say goodbye.'

Just then, the jester stepped forward, and said, 'Your Majesty, may I ask you a question? When you journeyed abroad visiting your people, staying with your nobles, or paying diplomatic visits to other courts, your heralds and servants always went before you, making preparations for you. May I ask what preparations Your Majesty has made for this long journey that he is about to take?'

'Alas!' replied the king, 'I have made no preparations whatsoever.'

'Then,' said the jester, 'take this staff with you, for at last I have found a bigger fool than myself.'

Will you fool someone on April 1ˢᵗ?
Or will you try to be wise rather than foolish?

April 2 – Silly

'Mix a little foolishness with your prudence;
It's good to be silly at the right moment.'
Horace, Odes, Book IV

Emily Jane didn't like her dad being silly. When he cracked jokes with her cousins in the car, they laughed. But when he cracked the same jokes and Emily Jane and her brother and sister were in the car, they just groaned. And Emily Jane would say, 'Dad! That's just plain silly!'

But the worst *ever* was when she had friends to visit.

'Dad?'

'Yes.'

'You gonna be in tonight?

'Yes. Why?'

'Megan's coming round.'

'So?'

'Well, you won't do anything silly, will you?'

'Do I ever?'

'Yes, all the time. But not tonight, *please ...*'

Emily Jane's mother was amused to find when she talked with Megan's mum at the school gate that Megan reckoned her husband was 'cool'.

'How so?' she asked.

'Oh,' said Megan's mum, 'Megan thinks Emily Jane's dad is hilarious. "Why can't our dad be like that?" she said.'

Emily Jane's mum wondered if she should pass on this good news to her daughter. But, she decided, that would be just plain silly!

If it's good to be silly at the right moment,
then the moment of silliness is a good gift to the world.

April 3 – Weddings

'The voice that breathed o'er Eden,
that earliest wedding-day,
the primal marriage blessing,
it hath not passed away.'
John Keble, Holy Matrimony

I've lost count of the number of times I've been encouraged to turn water into wine. On the other hand, I heard someone remark recently of a fellow minister – not the sunniest of souls – 'He's got the kind of face that'll turn water into vinegar.' One way or another, the miracle at Cana in Galilee, when Jesus turned water into wine, is still in our consciousness.

The miracle has a theological message – water to wine, ordinary to special, human to divine, disaster to success. But I think it's more 'earthy' that that. Jesus was a guest at a wedding and was enjoying himself. The traditional Presbyterian marriage service includes the phrase 'Jesus sanctified marriage by his attendance at the wedding at Cana in Galilee.' No he didn't! Marriage was *already* sanctified before Jesus came along. He went to a wedding to enjoy himself like the rest, because the blessing of a marriage still mattered.

On a recent pilgrimage to the Holy Land, my wife and I visited Cana and what is now called 'The Wedding Church'. Deep underneath is an archaeological excavation that has unearthed a 1st-century synagogue and a 4th-century cross-shaped Christian church. Tradition has it that these were built on the exact place where Jesus performed his first miracle.

My wife and I had our marriage blessed at Cana.
After more than forty years of marriage, blessing still mattered.
Who needs the wine?

April 4 – Enterprising

'And fools who came to scoff, remain'd to pray.'
Oliver Goldsmith, The Deserted Village

There was a little old white-painted church with a high steeple out in the countryside. It was badly in need of repainting. The pastor talked with his people, but everyone knew there wasn't enough money in the funds for such a big job.

So the enterprising pastor checked the small ads in the local newspaper and was delighted when he found a notice advertising a paint sale the very next day. The sale in town was excellent, and the pastor returned to the church with a gallon of white paint. With enthusiasm, he started the job.

He'd finished one side of the church and it was looking terrific, he reckoned. But when he began the second side, he realised he had already used half a gallon of the paint. He didn't want to go to town again, but, being an enterprising person, he found some paint thinner in the shed at the back of the church, thinned down the paint and continued the job. He was delighted that he could finish the remaining three sides with the remaining half-gallon of paint.

That night it rained, and it rained hard. The next morning when the pastor went down to the church to admire his work, he saw that the first side was still looking great but that the paint on the other three sides had been washed completely away. The pastor looked up into the sky and wailed a heartfelt prayer. 'What shall I do, Lord, what shall I do?'

And a voice came back from above saying, 'Repaint, and thin no more.'

Why is it that people who normally scoff at prayer
often turn to prayer when they're in trouble?

April 5 – Devotion

'Pray without ceasing. In everything give thanks.'
Bible, 1 Thessalonians 5:16

One of the most holy and prayerful people I've ever met was a lovely elderly lady by the name of Gracie Allen. Gracie has been dead for many years, but I still remember her with fondness, for I learned much from her about being still and prayerful amid a busy world, and finding a time of calmness for prayer when it was most needed.

The first time I visited Gracie, I found her sitting by a roaring fire in her living room. There was an all-pervading sense of tranquillity in her home, and, whatever benefit she got from my visit, I knew I was going to benefit from being there. She invited me pull up a chair close to her, and we talked quietly about the 'things of God'. No trivialities in *this* pastoral visit. From time to time, she would take my hand, especially when our discussion got to deeper moments.

I was considering drawing the visit to a close when she took my hand again. 'Now, Gracie, I must be going soon,' I said. And with that, still holding my hand tightly, she slipped off her chair and sank to her knees on the floor. She was gripping my hand with such force she dragged me onto the floor too. I thought she was having a stroke or a heart attack. I looked at her, but she smiled back. 'Shall you start the prayer, Mr Gordon,' she asked, 'or shall I?'

Praying with the minister clearly mattered to Gracie. And, if prayer was on your knees, the minister had to do that too. That's devotion for you, don't you think?

Devotion creates a holiness
that surrounds people wherever they go.

April 6 – Nicknames

'A nickname is the heaviest stone
a devil can throw at a man.'
Eliza Haywood, Sketches and Essays

Jim MacDonald was known as Toastie Mac in primary school, because he always had toast and jam for his 'play-piece'. Jim's dad was also Jim MacDonald and was known by his profession – Postie Mac. So Jim (Jr) MacDonald was nicknamed 'Toastie Mac'. And it had stuck.

Jim had always been a wizard with electronics. And with the growing developments in computers, the world was his circuit-board. Computers had become his life, and he was now head of IT in a large college of further education. The Toastie Mac nickname was dropped, much to his relief. He was happily now 'Mac the IT guy' in his working life.

Jim doted on his nephew. Little Dennis was fascinated by computers, and Jim was happy to pass on his knowledge to the next generation. 'Why are you called "Mac the IT guy", uncle Jim?' his nephew asked one day.

'Because the Mac comes from MacDonald, and I do IT stuff, so it's a nickname that's kind of stuck.'

His nephew was thinking, and continued, 'I have an apple for snack in school every day.'

'Oh?' Jim replied. 'Why are you telling me that?'

'Because if I have an apple every day and I work in IT like you do, do you think I might be called "Apple Mac"?'

Jim reckoned that would be a very good nickname indeed. As a matter of fact, he might just possibly choose it for himself.

What's your nickname?
One of mine is 'eight men'. Get it?

April 7 – Pilot

'We often want ... to change the helmsman –
to replace the pilot of the calm with the pilot of the storm.'
William Bagehot, The English Constitution

The central core of the plot of Gilbert & Sullivan's *Pirates of Penzance* is confusion between two words, 'pilot' and 'pirate'. The maid, Ruth, explains:

> *I was a stupid nursery maid,*
> *On breakers always steering,*
> *And I did not catch the word aright,*
> *Through being hard of hearing;*
> *Mistaking my instructions,*
> *Which within my brain did gyrate,*
> *I took and bound this promising boy*
> *Apprentice to a pirate.*
> *A sad mistake it was to make*
> *And doom him to a vile lot.*
> *I bound him to a pirate – you –*
> *Instead of to a pilot.*

When we have responsibility to care for someone, there can be confusion there too. The best of carers takes the role of pilot, a companion who comes on board to offer reassurance to guide the ship through tricky waters. The worst of carers comes as a pirate, capturing the whole ship and depriving us of the power to make decisions – a 'sad mistake' indeed.

> *A pilot is a guest who brings experience and wisdom.*
> *When that pilot is trusted to do their job well,*
> *even the greatest of ships can come safely to port.*

April 8 – Weeping

'For seven months alone he wept beneath a crag,
high up by the lonely waters.'
Virgil, Georgics No. 4

Listening to a performance of Rossini's *Stabat Mater* recently, I was struck by one of the lines in a soprano/mezzo duet. *Quis est homo qui non fleret Matrem Christi si videret in tanto supplico?* 'Who is the man who would not weep if he saw the Mother of Christ in such agony?'

'Who is the man who would not weep?' In stoical western society, in stiff-upper-lip Britain, in Presbyterian Scotland, that man will be me, or you, or someone we know. For displays of emotion do not come readily to men. And when they do, they are often accompanied by apologies, embarrassment and a sense of letting people down.

I remember such feelings when my mother died. I felt I had to stay strong and composed. I was a son, a husband, a father, a brother, a grandson, a minister – and a man! If I cracked up, how would the rest of the family cope? If this man wept, where was his strength for others?

When I was a hospice chaplain there were times when I struggled with my emotions – with patients and families, and privately – after a moving encounter. The then Medical Director, Dr David Oxenham, said this to me: 'Sometimes, pain and suffering just slip under our defences. We're human, and if we lose our humanity, we lose everything.'

Weeping is human. And that humanity – including the part that weeps – is something I don't ever want to lose.

Weep if you must.
It may be all you have to show you care.

April 9 – Distress

'Far as distress the soul can wound
'Tis pain in each degree;
Bliss goes but to a certain bound,
Beyond is agony.'

Frances Greville, A Prayer for Indifference

In the Bible in 2 Samuel there is the harrowing story of the death of King David's son, Absalom, who, in torturous times, is killed in battle.

Then the Cushite arrived and said, 'My lord the king, hear the good news! The LORD has vindicated you today by delivering you from the hand of all who rose up against you.' The king asked the Cushite, 'Is the young man Absalom safe?' The Cushite replied, 'May the enemies of my lord the king and all who rise up to harm you be like that young man.' And the king was much moved, and went up to the chamber over the gate, and wept: and as he wept, he said, 'O my son Absalom, my son, my son Absalom! Would to God I had died for you, O Absalom, my son, my son!'

Many composers have set these sorrowful words to music – from the Renaissance musicians Thomas Tomkins and Thomas Weelkes, through the evocative 'David's Lamentation' from the Shapenote singing tradition, to the heart-rending modern version by Eric Whitacre. I've cried along with David in all of these. Entering David's time of distress and agony, I've learned again what it's like to weep.

We are distressed because we love.
Doesn't our love deserve that depth of response?

April 10 – Misunderstanding

'The offspring of cold hearts
and muddy understandings.'
Edmund Burke, Reflections on the Revolution in France

A friend told me he'd been framed. He looked and sounded crestfallen. 'Come to the house tonight and I'll tell you about it.' That evening, he laid it on thick, dabbed his eyes with his handkerchief and told me he'd never been framed before. It was the most dramatic thing that had ever happened to him.

'But what did you get framed for?' I asked. 'And who did the framing?'

There was a long pause. 'It was my mother,' he whispered.

'Your *mother*? But how could you have been framed by your mother?'

'Oh no,' he replied, 'she didn't do the framing. She got someone else to do that.'

'Someone *else*? My God, man,' I spluttered. 'Who framed you?'

He raised his hand and pointed to the wall behind me. 'Martin Archibald, the photographer in the High Street … did it last week … birthday present from my mother … big framed photo of me and the wife …' And there he was, grinning at me from the framed photo on the wall. 'Ah, gotcha!' he announced. I *was* framed! And you fell for it …'

A muddy understanding indeed – if not from a *cold* heart but a funny one. But an unfortunate misunderstanding, nonetheless.

Make sure you say what you mean
and you mean what you say.

April 11 – Solitude

'I had three chairs in my house;
one for solitude, two for friendship, three for society.'
Henry David Thoreau, Walden, 'Visitors'

I remember reading a story to my children from a series of books called *Frog and Toad are Friends* by the children's author Arnold Lobel. I've discovered recently that these books have been translated into many languages; there's a PowerPoint presentation that offers the stories in picture form; and there's a study-guide which examines lessons to be learned. I should reread the stories and make them available to my grandchildren. For all I recall is one image – Frog and Toad sitting in silence on a lily pad, 'being alone together'. They'd made up after a row. There was nothing more to be said. So they sat in silence, 'alone together'.

Bereaved people I work with – especially those who have lost a life partner – talk of the overwhelming loneliness they feel when they are bereaved of the companionship which had been integral to their lives; putting the key in the lock and knowing you're entering an empty house; dark winter evenings with no one to talk with. They don't crave chatter, or noise, or even conversation. They just yearn for company, just silent companionship, to make them feel complete. And when it isn't there, the solitude can be awful.

Perhaps we shouldn't take for granted our times of silent companionship with people we love. 'Being along together' – as Frog and Toad remind us – has much to commend it.

You can be alone in a crowd and feel lonely.
You can be alone with one other person and feel loved.

April 12 – Epitaphs

'If ye carve my epitaph aright.'
Robert Browning, The Bishop Orders His Tomb

Epitaphs can be amusing, poignant or revealing – and occasionally all three at once ...

Epitaph for a Mr Box
Here lies one Box within another.
The one of wood was very good,
But we cannot say much for t'other.

Epitaph for the *(clearly, somewhat corpulent)* Dr Chard
Here lies the corpse of Chard,
Who filled the half of this church yard.

But among the epitaphs of famous people, the one written for himself by Benjamin Franklin has much to commend it:

The body of
Benjamin Franklin, printer,
(Like the cover of an old book,
Its contents torn out,
And stripped of its lettering and gilding)
Lies here, food for worms!
Yet the work itself shall not be lost,
For it will, as he believed, appear once more
In a new and more beautiful edition,
Corrected and amended by its author.

What might be your own epitaph?
Is it worth giving thought to, even now?

April 13 – Prodigal

'And keep you in the rear of your affection,
Out of the shot of danger and desire,
The chariest maid is prodigal enough
If she unmask her beauty to the moon.'

William Shakespeare, Hamlet

Charles Dickens was asked what he considered to be the best short story in the English language. He replied, without hesitation, 'The Prodigal Son'. The story told by Jesus is, arguably, one of the most important of his Parables [Luke 15:11-31]. It is powerful in its imagery, graphic in its plot and sparse but profound in its telling. The son who wastes his inheritance on 'riotous living'; the father who welcomes him home again; the older brother who is resentful; the celebration of forgiveness and redemption – powerful stuff.

I've always been fascinated by the word 'prodigal' itself. One dictionary defines prodigal thus:

Prodigal (adj) 1, spending money or using resources freely and recklessly; wastefully extravagant: synonyms: wasteful · extravagant · spendthrift · improvident. 2, having or giving something on a lavish scale: synonyms: generous · lavish · liberal · unstinting · unsparing .

We are all 'prodigal', including Shakespeare's 'chariest maid' giving away her beauty – even if it's only to the moon – without a thought. So perhaps we should give more thought to the prodigal part of our nature than we do.

More care and less recklessness might be a good thought
with which to begin our day.

April 14 – Hills

'Before the hills in order stood, or earth received her frame,
From everlasting Thou art God, to endless years the same.'
Isaac Watts, Our God

My father, a native-born Highlander, brought up in the shadow of
Ben Nevis, chose the words of Psalm 121 for his funeral. Here is the
first verse from the original 1912 Psalter:

I to the hills will lift my eyes;
O whence shall come my aid?
My help is from the Lord alone,
Who Heav'n and earth has made.

However, when I was young, this psalm (sung to the tune 'French' or
'Dundee') had this as the opening verse:

I to the hills will lift mine eyes,
from whence doth come mine aid.
My safety cometh from the Lord,
who heav'n and earth hath made.

Notice the difference? There is no question mark at the end of the
second line! I always thought I was singing to the hills for my help,
Ben Nevis and all. But no! The Psalm properly asks, 'Does my help
come from those hills?' and then answers, 'No! My help is above and
beyond even the grandeur and strength of the hills that surround me.'
My father knew that. There was no question mark in it for him.

Beyond the hills, the beauty of a wonderful world.
Within the hills, the hope of more beauty to come.

April 15 – Questions

'Them that asks no questions isn't told a lie.'
Rudyard Kipling, A Smuggler's Song

A four-year-old went with her dad to see a litter of kittens in a neighbour's house. When they got home, the little one excitedly told her mother all about it. 'And, do you know, mummy, there were two girl kittens and two boy kittens?'

'Oh,' said the mother, 'and how did you know that?'

'Daddy told me.'

Mum smiled, and, half turning to her husband, continued her conversation with her daughter. 'And how did daddy know?'

'He picked them up and looked underneath,' the child replied. 'I think it must have been printed on the bottom.'

A priest in a confirmation class: 'Does anyone know what we mean by "sins of omission"?'

Class member: 'Aren't those the sins we should have committed, but didn't?'

It was Palm Sunday, but because of a sore throat five-year-old Danny stayed home from church with his big sister. When the family returned, they were carrying palm fronds.

'What are they for?' Danny asked.

'People waved them and threw them on the ground when Jesus went by,' his father told him.

'Wouldn't you know it?' Danny fumed. 'The one Sunday I don't go and Jesus shows up.'

Questions! Questions! Always ask your questions.
For how are we going to learn anything new if we don't?

April 16 – Self

'Everyone's oot o' step but oor Jock.'
The author's Granny, A West of Scotland proverb

There once lived an owl called Old Wisdom. Old Wisdom, being a wise owl, kept a school. Everybody went to him for lessons, not just the boys and girls, but all the creatures of the fields and rivers and hillsides. When he wanted to know what progress they had made, he gave them a question to answer.

'Why does the moon shine in the sky?'

The dog said, 'It shines to dispel the darkness, so that I might see any thieves who would dare to steal from my master's house.'

The nightingale said, 'It shines so that I might sing all night in its mellow light to the lovely rose.'

The hare said, 'It shines in the night so that there may be enough dew in the morning for me to lap at the beginning of the day.'

The lilies said, 'It shines so that we may open our petals and enjoy the gentle touch of its caressing rays.'

The glow-worm said, 'It shines so that it might glow more brightly than I do, for it envies my light.'

The fox said, 'It shines so that I can see my way into the hen-coop.'

'Enough!' cried Old Wisdom. 'You have learned little. You know that the moon shines, for there is but one moon for us all to see. Yet, each of you decides it is there for you and you alone. Each of you looks for the moon to serve your own purpose.'

Even when I think I'm the centre of my world,
my world shows me that I have much yet to learn.

April 17 – More to learn

'And gladly wolde he lerne and gladly teche.'

Geoffrey Chaucer, Prologue, The Canterbury Tales

I once enquired of my elder grandson, Alexander, then aged five, what he was learning about the Easter story. He told me it was about Jesus and the stone being rolled. I asked him what happened. 'Oh, it's easy,' he replied. 'A great big stone rolled down the hill and killed Jesus.'

Still got a bit to learn, methinks ... And so have the children who gave these answers to other religious questions.

The Bible is full of interesting caricatures.

The first book of the Bible is Guinness.

Adam and Eve were created from an apple.

Cain once asked, 'Am I my brother's son?'

When Mary heard she was to be the mother of Jesus she sang the Magna Carta.

One of the opossums was Matthew. He was also a taximan.

Moses got the 10 commandments up Mount Cyanide.

Moses died before he ever reached Canada.

Christians can have only one spouse. It's called monotony.

Unleavened bread is bread made without any ingredients.

April 18 – Grey

'The worthy gentleman … while his desires were as warm,
and his hopes as eager as ours, has feelingly told us
what shadows we are, and what shadows we pursue.'
Edmund Burke, From a speech in Bristol declining the poll

The artist David Hockney was once asked about his early years in
Bradford and what influenced him from that environment. Looking
through a portfolio of his work from his late teens, he said, 'There are
no shadows. My memory of it is that it was universally grey.'

He told of a visit in his later years to Japan in the cherry blossom
season. There were crowds of people around, all inspired by the
beauty of the blossom. Coming back to his native Yorkshire and
driving through the dales, it struck him that there was no one there,
and yet with hawthorns and briars the whole place was alive with
colour. And every time he went through a valley, as the light changed,
it was different.

Something had changed in the artist's eye – he had gained maturity, interest, understanding. Where once he'd been aware only of grey,
now he saw beauty, life and colour. Awareness of the changing light
had transformed what he saw.

Sometimes we live in greyness, and life is drab and devoid of
colour. When the mists of sadness come down, or the clouds of despair
obscure hope, or a curtain of depression throws a shroud over us, all
we can see is grey. We live with no shadows. But the light has not
gone away. Even in valleys which are places of darkness for us, there
is light and colour waiting to be discovered.

Tom Paxton, when love came into his life, wrote,
'Even a grey day is a good day now.'

April 19 – Messages

'The moving finger writes; and, having writ, moves on.'
Edward Fitzgerald, The Rubáiyát of Omar Khayyám

Do you ever receive mysterious messages of guidance?
Daniel was in the service of King Nebuchadnezzar. One night
Belshazzar, Nebuchadnezzar's son, invited a thousand noblemen to a
great banquet, and they drank wine together from the gold and silver
cups and bowls which Nebuchadnezzar had plundered from the
Temple in Jerusalem. Out of nowhere, a great hand appeared and a
finger began writing on the plaster wall of the palace. Belshazzar was
so frightened that his knees began to shake. He shouted for his magi-
cians, wizards and astrologers, but none of them could interpret the
writing on the wall.

Then the queen mother remembered Daniel and his previous success in interpreting dreams. Daniel was summoned, and he explained
the writing on the wall. It wasn't a message the king wanted to hear,
because it contained a judgement on his reign, and Daniel was
chucked into a den of lions because of it. But it was a message,
nonetheless, that had come through loud and clear.

I've never got any message from a giant finger writing on my wall.
But I do get guidance from thoughts that should be mulled over,
words of advice to be pondered, a sense of what's right that emerges
from times of prayer, calmness and reflection, a realisation that comes
out of a haze. Is it always a clear message? No it isn't. I have to be my
own Daniel and do my own interpretation.

The message is there.
Do we have the patience to work it out?

April 20 – Offerings

> 'Offering too little and asking too much.'
>
> *George Canning,* Dispatch to the English ambassador at The Hague

Three ministers were discussing the 'liberality' expected from their congregations – how much was given in church offerings. There was much grumbling about people 'offering too little', but when the discussion moved on to how the offerings were used, the conversation took a different turn.

'What do you actually *do* with the offerings?' one of the ministers asked.

'Oh, that's very simple,' one of the others replied. 'After worship, I take the offering plate back into the church, draw a circle in chalk in front of the Communion Table, throw the money into the air, and what falls inside the circle goes to the Church, and what falls outside I keep for myself.'

'Goodness,' said the second, 'that's quite remarkable. I do something similar. After worship, I take the offering plate back into the church, draw a circle in chalk in front of the Communion Table, throw the money up into the air, and what falls *outside* the circle goes to the Church, and what falls inside I keep for myself.'

'That's amazing!' said the third. 'I do almost the same. After worship, I take the offering plate back into the church, draw a circle in chalk in front of the Communion Table, throw the money up into the air, and what the Lord wants he keeps, and what he doesn't he throws back for me!'

What have you been given today that you can offer back to others?
And what have you kept today that you think belongs only to you?

April 21 – Hospitality

'Whoe'er has travelled life's dull round,
Where'er his stages may have been,
May sigh to think he still has found
The warmest welcome at the inn.'
William Shenstone, Written at the Inn at Henley

Hospitality – the 'welcome at the inn' – comes in many forms. I was visiting a couple in my parish who were, by all measurements, down on their luck. The lady was poorly and was lying on the settee with a blanket over her, with her husband fussing around. Two neighbours were there giving support. After a brief clarification on how things were, the devoted husband enquired, 'D'ye want a cuppa?' I always tried to avoid taking tea when I was visiting. But touched by 'the warmest welcome' and this expression of hospitality, I found myself saying, 'Yes, please.'

He bustled into the kitchen and came back a few minutes later with the lid of a biscuit tin as a tray holding four mugs (of dubious provenance) and a pot-noodle container. I took it that, of the five of us, someone wasn't having a cuppa, and that the pot-noodle container was the sugar bowl or the milk-jug. I was wrong. It was the extra cup for the guest. And who was that? Me! I looked around for an aspidistra that needed watering. There wasn't one. So I placed my 'tea cup' on the floor and carried on with our conversation. The 'cup' was still there when I left.

A warm welcome and good hospitality? Undoubtedly – despite my never having touched a pot-noodle since!

Hospitality only works if it's given in love
and accepted with graciousness.

April 22 – Surprise

'Never was heard such a terrible curse!
But what gave rise
To no little surprise,
Nobody seemed one penny the worse!'
RH Barham, The Ingoldsby Legends

In forty-five years of ministry, I've only been interrupted once during a sermon. It was, for me, 'no little surprise'. It was in 1976 when a new peace movement had begun in Northern Ireland. Mairéad Corrigan, Betty Williams and Ciaran McKeown had had enough, including tragedies in their own families. They began gathering signatures for a peace petition and took to the streets. The first peace march had 200 people. The next brought 10,000 Protestant and Catholic women together. Eventually they led 35,000 people onto the Belfast streets petitioning for peace.

The theme of my sermon was encouraging the congregation to be committed to Jesus' call to peace and reconciliation. With passion I said, 'And we should commend these women and their peace movement to our prayers ...'

Just then, one of my elders shouted, 'It's not enough!' To say I was surprised would be putting it mildly. But he continued, 'Prayer isn't enough. We must *do* something in solidarity with these women. Let's send a telegram of support. I'll be at the back to take contributions for the cost.'

The lesson of that day has never left me. Just as for the women of the Peace Movement, prayer wasn't enough. 'Let's do something ...' was their vital motivation.

The motivation to action took me by surprise.
But might it be our motivation too?

April 23 – Truth or fiction

'A petty fortress, and a dubious hand.'
Samuel Johnson, The Vanity of Human Wishes

According to legend, St George was a soldier and officer in the Guard of the Roman emperor Diocletian, who ordered his death for refusing to recant his Christian faith. As a Christian martyr, George later became one of the most venerated saints in Christianity. Pope Gelasius said that he was one of the saints 'whose names are rightly reverenced among us, but whose actions are known only to God'.

As patron saint of England, St George is identified with English ideals of honour, bravery and gallantry. Actually, he wasn't English at all. Indeed, everything we think we know about St George is surrounded by myth. It's believed he was born to Christian parents in an area which is now in Turkey, in the 3rd century AD. As a young man, he lived in Palestine, became a Roman soldier, but protested against Rome's persecution of Christians. He was imprisoned, tortured and beheaded at Lydda in Palestine.

St George is also patron saint of Aragon, Catalonia, Georgia, Lithuania, Palestine, Portugal, Germany and Greece; and of Moscow, Istanbul, Genoa and Venice (second to Saint Mark). He's also patron saint of soldiers, archers, cavalry and chivalry, farmers and field workers, riders and saddlers, and he helps those suffering from leprosy, plague and syphilis.

Truth or myth, you can't help admire someone who took a stance against persecution and died for his faith. That's enough sainthood for me.

St George and the dragon? Truth or fiction?
Maybe we should find a dragon to ask …

April 24 – Dragons

'Here be dragons.'
Marking on medieval maps

George had slain his dragon. Not that the dragon had been conquered completely, but George knew how to tackle it. Simply put, George could face his dragon – and win!

This George's dragon was 'the demon drink'. George was a man I knew well – at least, I *thought* I did. I'd visited his home, played with his children and shared church work with him. I liked him a lot. But the George I *thought* I knew wasn't the man who'd been fighting a dragon.

I met him at the local shopping centre two days into a new year. He was in a terrible state, unkempt, shaking, unshaven. 'I need help,' he said, and went on to tell me the story of a Hogmanay party at his mother's house. He was drunk, and an argument started between him and his mother. George lost his temper. He picked up an empty Vodka bottle, raised it above his head and was ready to bring it down on his mother's face. 'But my arm froze,' he said. 'It was as if something was stopping me. Eventually, I put the bottle down and left the party. I haven't been home for two days. I've been walking the streets, sleeping rough. But I haven't had a drink. And now I know I need help.'

George became involved with Alcoholics Anonymous. AA was his lifesaver – along with a forgiving mother, a church community and the growth of George's own self-esteem. But for two days and nights, wandering the streets and sleeping rough, George had begun to tackle his dragon.

We've all got dragons, not mythical, but real.
And they have to be named, faced and slain.

April 25 – Numbers

'There is safety in numbers.'
Late 17th-century proverb

6-7-0-7-1-2-9 was my university matriculation number from 1967. It's stayed with me ever since. Fifty years later I can trot it out as if I'd learned it yesterday.

Numbers are like that. Perhaps you'll remember phone numbers of houses you've lived in, pin numbers for credit cards or identification numbers for work or a chosen society. I know people who can recite their National Insurance Number (I can't! I still have to look it up ...) or their 12-digit bank-card number, or the numbers of every car they've owned. My father could reel off his service number from his time in the RAF during the war.

Numbers are important. They're familiar, offering reassurance, stability and security. So, in that sense, as the 17th-century proverb affirms, 'there *is* safety in numbers'.

But the more obvious sense of the proverb is that we feel safer when we are included in a number of people. The fourth book of the Old Testament is the Book of Numbers. It tells the story of the Israelites during their forty desert years, before they reach the land God had promised. The most prominent feature of the book is the census Moses took at Mount Sinai before their epic adventure began, and again a generation later. There was for them, as a people of God, safety in numbers. Together, belonging, sharing, bonded, in community, they could face their journey and reach their goal.

Who are you numbered with?
How important is that number to you?
And does someone feel safe numbered with you?

April 26 – Eternity

'For oh! Eternity's too short
To utter all thy praise.'
Joseph Addison, The Spectator, August 1712

What eight gramophone records would you take to a desert island as your Desert Island Discs? You're Roy Plumley's castaway, and you're being interviewed by Kirsty Young on Radio 4. What would your eight musical tracks be? It's an interesting exercise. Try it someday. And do the same with movies, or books, or even people … It'll tell you a lot about yourself. I'll start things off by giving you mine.

At least one would be an aria from an opera by George Frederick Handel. Perhaps 'Verdi Prati' from *Alcina,* or 'Ombra Mai Fu' from *Serses.* To be honest, there are too many to choose from. All eight could be Handel arias.

You'll gather from this that Handel is one of my favourite composers, and opera is among my most loved genres of music. Add to this the fact that my wife sings Handel arias, and you'll see where I am. We have a rose bush in our front garden called 'Handel'. My wife bought it to remind her of Handel's music. The rose bush doesn't sing, but every time she passes it she'll smell a rose, or hold a delicate bloom in her hand, and say a quiet 'thank you' to Handel.

Handel's music is timeless. It comes from eternity and will last for eternity. When my wife and I have passed from time into our eternity, a rose will still bloom, Handel's music will still inspire and castaways will continue to dream.

When time dips into eternity,
timelessness is in every moment of beauty and love.

April 27 – Observed

'Let observation with extensive view,
Survey mankind, from China to Peru.'
Samuel Johnson, The Vanity of Human Wishes

I was once in the home of a couple discussing the baptism of their child. I knew the father was a policeman, but I didn't know what he did or where he was based. In conversation, he revealed he was in the Special Branch, mostly in undercover surveillance. And then he surprised me …

'I was wondering what you were doing at No. 17 Canal Street, on Monday, Tuesday and Thursday of last week, each time around 10 in the morning?'

'How did you know that?' I asked.

'I was on a stake-out across the road,' he replied. 'We were keeping an eye on the comings and goings at No. 15. And I clocked you. I said to my colleague, "My minister's early on the go today." And there you were again the next day and a couple of days later. "Seeing a fancy woman," my colleague said. "Scrounging a bacon roll off some over-generous soul, more like," I told him.' He smiled widely. 'I've got some good photographs. You've got a nice profile …'

I'd been visiting an elderly lady who was dying, came back to see the family after she'd died, and returned a couple of days later to arrange the funeral. But it's always left me with a funny feeling. We can't go anywhere without being observed. And if we're *actually* scrounging bacon rolls, can we guarantee that someone isn't observing us – even if we don't want them to?

If I'm visiting in China or Peru,
might someone take a photograph of my nice profile?

April 28 – More food

'Food comes first, then morals.'

Bertolt Brecht, The Threepenny Opera

As a regular user of Facebook, I enjoy the interaction with people that social media platforms provide. Sharing news and photographs; being alerted to campaigns and events; reading interesting articles I might have missed; journeying with someone through good times or bad; learning from the passions of interesting people. It's all there, and, to be honest, I think it's one of the wonders of the 21st century.

But what is it, I ask you, with Facebookers and food? I'm delighted to hear that someone's had a family gathering for a birthday or an anniversary, but I do *not* need a photograph of their roast-chicken dinner; I'm very pleased that a friend is enjoying their holiday in an exotic clime, but I do *not* need a photograph of their fourth piña colada; I am over the moon that someone can force down a dessert after a substantial meal, but I do *not* need a photograph of their strawberry sundae; I am green with envy that someone has time to relax with a glass of good wine, but I do *not* need a photograph of the wine-bottle label and the large glass of red. Aaarrgghhhh ...

I suppose it's because food is such an important part of our lives that we give it so much attention. Good food is enjoyable. Special meals are worth remembering. I'll grant you that. But might I advise over-enthusiastic Facebookers to confine their food to their memories – and their stomachs – and leave social media alone?

I'm off now to have a cheese sandwich.
No one is going to get a photograph of that.

April 29 – Peace

'Peace on earth and mercy mild,
God and sinners reconciled.'

Charles Wesley, Hymns and Sacred Poems

The book of Isaiah in the Bible contains this passage: [Isaiah 65:17-25, *Today's English Version*]

The LORD *says, 'I am making a new earth and new heavens. The events of the past will be completely forgotten. Be glad and rejoice forever in what I create. The new Jerusalem I make will be full of joy, and her people will be happy … There will be no weeping there, no calling for help. Babies will no longer die in infancy, and all people will live out their life-span. Those who live to be a hundred will be considered young … People will build houses and get to live in them – they will not be used by someone else. They will plant vineyards and enjoy the wine – it will not be drunk by others. Like trees, my people will live long lives … The work they do will be successful, and their children will not meet with disaster. I will bless them and their descendants for all time to come … Wolves and lambs will eat together; lions will eat straw, as cattle do, and snakes will no longer be dangerous.'*

When we struggle to make sense of civil wars, conflicts across national divides, random acts of terrorism and the world's refugee crisis, is Isaiah's vision of a peaceful world just a pipe dream? Surely not! It's what we were put here to create for ourselves and the generations who follow us.

*Today we pray for peace, and for those who, like Isaiah,
still believe in a New Creation.*

April 30 – Shepherd

'The God of love my Shepherd is,
And he that doth me feed:
While He is mine, and I am His,
What can I want or need?'
George Herbert, The 23rd Psalm (1603)

Francis Rous (1579-1659) was a Puritan and one-time MP for Truro.
He was part of the 'Short' and 'Long' Parliaments, and was a member
of Oliver Cromwell's 'Council of State' as well as being Provost of
Eton. But this politician and parliamentarian was also author of many
theological works, including translations of the Psalms. One such
work is the familiar 'Twenty-Third Psalm'. Rous's version was first
published by William Barton, Vicar of Mayfield in Staffordshire, and
was revised for inclusion in the Scottish Psalter in 1650. It is traditionally sung to the tune, 'Crimond' – of which more tomorrow.

The Lord's my Shepherd, I'll not want;
He makes me down to lie
In pastures green; he leadeth me
The quiet waters by.

While we are familiar with a shepherd and his dogs driving a flock
of sheep from behind, the shepherds the Psalmist knew would walk
in front and the sheep would follow. A shepherd is a trusted leader,
and the sheep do well to follow.

Who is our shepherd?
And, if we're in front, who are our flock?

May 1 – Familiar

'Yea, even mine own familiar friend, whom I trusted.'
Bible, Psalm 41:9

Some songs and tunes are like old friends. You don't hear them for ages, but they are instantly familiar and take you back to earlier memories, often with warmth and pleasure. Hymn tunes do that for me. I come across a well-known melody in worship, and I'm embraced by its familiarity, security and depth. I've found an old friend once more.

'Crimond' is the tune most closely associated with the metrical version of Psalm 23 by Francis Rous. It was written in the mid-19th century by Jessie Seymour Irvine, the daughter of a Church of Scotland minister who served at Dunottar, Peterhead, and Crimond in Aberdeenshire. There was a long tradition in Scotland of talented amateur composers. Singing in Presbyterian worship was largely confined to the use of the psalms and paraphrases of biblical passages, so new tunes were almost exclusively associated with the psalms rather than being dedicated hymn tunes composed for newly written words – as was increasingly the case in Victorian England.

Jessie Irvine wrote 'Crimond' in her teens as an exercise for an organ class she was attending. It was originally credited to David Grant, but it was discovered later that Grant had only arranged the tune and not composed it, and it was rightly credited to Jessie Irvine in the revision of the *Scottish Psalter* in 1929. I know little more about Jessie Irvine. But I thank God that she has given me 'Crimond' as an old, familiar friend.

On my desert island, Crimond will be a companion
I'll always enjoy having around.

May 2 – Contentment

'He that has a little tiny wit,
With hey, ho, the wind and the rain,
Must make content with his fortunes fit,
Though the rain it raineth every day.'

William Shakespeare, King Lear

Cineas is trying to dissuade Pyrrhus from undertaking war against the Romans. 'Sir,' he says 'when you have conquered them what will you do next?'

'Sicily is near and easy to overcome,' replies Pyrrhus.

'And what if you have conquered Sicily?'

'Then we shall move onwards to Africa and capture Carthage.'

'And then?'

'Then we will fall upon Greece and Macedon and recover what we have lost there.'

'Well, when all are conquered, what fruit do you expect from your victories?' Cineas enquires.

'Ah, then, when all is subdued, we shall sit down and enjoy ourselves,' Pyrrhus responds.

'Sir!' cries Cineas. 'May we not do that now? Have you not already a kingdom of your own? He that cannot enjoy himself with one kingdom cannot with a whole world.'

Do we have Shakespeare's 'tiny wit' enough to learn from this? Of course we learn to live with the wind and the rain. But if it *is* likely to rain every day – and this is Scotland, after all – might we not be the better taking advice from Cineas and focusing more on contentment than we do?

*Jesus said, 'What good is it for someone
to gain the whole world, yet forfeit their own soul?'*

May 3 – Juggling

'As lookers-on feel most delight,
That least perceive a juggler's sleight;
And still the less they understand,
The more th' admire his sleight of hand.'
Samuel Butler, Hudibras Pt. 2

Anyone who must spend their day, or week, or all their life dealing with lots of things at once will know what it means to be a juggler. Onlookers may indeed have admiration for the performance. And if you're engaged in the 'juggler's sleight', you will know well enough how taxing it can be.

So, it's school holiday time … My wife and I do childcare on a Tuesday afternoon normally, but, during the extended summer break, we have responsibility for the boys *all* day on a Tuesday – from 8am till 6pm. Now, don't get me wrong, it's a genuine pleasure. So it was entirely my fault that one day recently I had far too much to think about. I was back to being a juggler – timings, meals, emails, phone calls, travelling, games, TV, walking the dog, shopping, seeing to the boys … Need I go on?

I'm not looking for sympathy. That was only one day for me. I know there are people who must be jugglers all the time. But here's one onlooker who knows how hard it is to be a juggler and is, there-fore, *full* of admiration for *all* jugglers. I will pray you don't drop any-thing. I will cheer loudly when you've done well. I will appreciate your ability when you manage to do it all again tomorrow. Jugglers everywhere, I salute you.

My friend gave me a set of juggling balls
and an instruction book for my birthday.
I wonder what she was trying to tell me?

May 4 – Couriers

'Vaunt-couriers to oak-cleaving thunderbolts
Singe my white head.'
William Shakespeare, King Lear

My local weekly newspaper is *The East Lothian Courier.* It's full of news from the East Lothian towns and villages; stories of local folk; special events; campaigns and political concerns; photographs of children on their first day at school, Gala Days and prettiest pets; and 'Court Reports', insights into the misdemeanours of East Lothian's finest. It's a fascinating read, keeping East Lothian's citizens up to date with news of their area and concerns that cover the whole county. I expect, in its day, *The Courier* has delivered the occasional oak-cleaving thunderbolt, though whether white heads have been singed in the process is open to debate. But, one way or another, *The Courier* is worth reading.

The Courier is a familiar name for many newspapers. There's *The Halifax Courier* and *The Kent and Sussex Courier* in England, for example, and *The Dundee Courier* in Scotland. But the term 'courier' isn't confined to newspapers. It's a commonplace description of a company that transports packages and documents. Or it could be the person who does the delivery, such as a motorcycle dispatch rider. In times of conflict, a courier is a person who carries messages in secret. And, of course, a courier can be a tour-guide, employed to assist a group of travellers.

We're all couriers when we have news to share, a message to pass on or guidance to offer. The question is, what kind of news or message or guidance do we deliver?

Will you be 'The Courier' that's worth reading?

May 5 – Honesty

'A few honest men are better than numbers.'

Oliver Cromwell, Letter to William Spring (1643)

William Muir, the owner of Willie's Mill in Tarbolton in Ayrshire, was a good friend of the poet Robert Burns and his family. He took in Jean Armour when she discovered that, for the second time, Burns had made her pregnant. Burns, as we know, was inclined to 'play the field'. After visiting Jean at the home of William Muir, he wrote to Clarinda (the pseudonym adopted by Agnes McLehose, an educated woman whom Burns met in Edinburgh in 1787, and who became another of his lovers) and called Jean 'a farthing taper beside the cloudless glory of the meridian sun'.

In his *Second Commonplace Book*, Burns wrote an epitaph on William Muir who died in 1793:

> *An honest man here lies at rest,*
> *As e'er God with his Image blest:*
> *A friend of man, the friend of truth,*
> *The friend of age and guide of youth;*
> *Few hearts like his with virtue warm'd,*
> *Few heads with knowledge so informed:*
> *If there's another world, he lives in bliss;*
> *If there is none, he made the best of this.*

A man who appears to have had such disregard for the feelings of women writes with frank admiration for William Muir. Burns clearly valued honesty in his friend. So where was his honesty with everyone else?

Value honesty where you find it – especially in yourself.

May 6 – More questions

'Puzzling questions are not beyond all conjecture.'
Sir Thomas Browne, Hydriotaphia

As they say in debating circles, 'questions are always in order'. In all aspects of life, questions matter. If we don't ask 'puzzling questions', how are we going to learn and develop?

You'll all be familiar with *Goldilocks and the Three Bears.* Goldilocks wanders into the house of the three bears. She tastes their porridge, finding one bowl too hot, one bowl too cold and one bowl just right. She tries their chairs, and one is too big, one too small and one just right. Then she tries out the bears' beds, finding one too hard, one too soft and one just right. She falls asleep in baby bear's bed, and when the bears return, they find that someone has been eating their porridge, sitting in their chairs and sleeping in their beds. They discover Goldilocks, and she runs away.

Questions about the story? How many bears? What did Goldilocks do? But what about the questions behind the obvious? Why did the bears leave their recently cooked porridge? And what would happen if Goldilocks was put on trial for breaking and entering?

There's a methodology of interpretation of biblical texts and philosophical writings called hermeneutics. It's derived from the Greek word that means to translate or interpret and goes back to the writings of Aristotle. In other words, even the Bible, which many determine should *never* be open to question, becomes all the richer if we apply a hermeneutic to it, if we're prepared to question, think, translate, interpret and get behind the obvious. Questions are *always* in order – thank God!

There's more to truth than just the facts.

May 7 – Careful

'If you can't be good, be careful.'
20th-century proverb

I did a bit of drama in school. It was nothing serious – farces mostly – but it kept the sixth form out of trouble, and made for a reasonably good performance before school broke up for the summer. Our director was David Chalmers, head of English in Lochaber High School. He was clear, calm and helpful – all you need in a director. And he gave us some useful acting tips too, like, 'Always act, even when you're not speaking.' 'Never speak "up stage" or the audience won't understand you.' 'Don't "crash the laughter" or else no one will hear your next line.' One of the most useful was, 'If you're going to sit down, don't look round for the chair. Instead, feel for the chair with the backs of your legs. That way the "sitting down" will happen seamlessly.' It works! Watch the professionals! It's great when they get it right.

It's also a disaster when you get it wrong. A minister friend was preaching in a new church. He had to enter the pulpit through a curtain at the rear and, as there was no seat in the pulpit, a bench 'on a hinge' would be put in place behind him. He'd obviously got good directions in his school drama class, for he didn't turn around to check where the seat was, but 'felt for it' with the backs of his legs. But no one had told him it was a very narrow seat, and that it was smoothly polished. So when he sat down, he slipped right off the back and disappeared in a flurry of cassock and legs through the curtain behind him and down the pulpit steps.

We might get the instructions right,
but if we're not careful, who knows what might go wrong?

May 8 – Loafing

'I have always looked on cricket as organised loafing.'
Anonymous

I visited two elderly sisters – one widowed, the other a spinster – in
a sheltered-housing complex around 12.15pm. When one of the sisters answered the door, there was a distinct frostiness in the air. An
Edinburgh stiffness and the fact that I was visiting for the first time, I
surmised. I was ushered into the front room. The TV was on. The
second sister declined to get up and shake the hand I offered.

'Do you like cricket?' she barked without looking at me. I was
somewhat taken aback.

I love cricket, even though I'd recently been teased by an American friend who couldn't figure it out at all, and would bombard me
with questions: 'What kind of game can be played for five days and
still end in a draw?' 'What on earth do "silly-mid-on" and "short leg"
actually mean?' Philistines might mock, but I still loved my cricket.

But I had obviously taken too long to respond. 'Well, do you like
cricket or not, minister?' she repeated.

'Yes, I do, actually. Very much,' I replied.

'Great!' was the response. 'There's three-quarters of an hour to go
till lunch in the Ashes match. Just sit down and enjoy it with us. This
is as much part of the Kingdom of God, you know, as all your Bible
stuff.'

I didn't argue. I had many happy hours of organised loafing in that
home over the years as part of the Kingdom of God – especially when
there was a Test Match on the TV!

Loafing can look like idleness.
But it's hard work when it's put to good use.

May 9 – Landmarks

'Remove not the ancient landmark,
which thy fathers have set.'
Bible, Proverbs 22:28

When Cockenzie Power Station was decommissioned in 2015, its two tall chimneys had to be demolished. It was a red-letter day for the local community, and the fall of the chimneys was nothing short of spectacular. But the demolition was more than an amazing one-off event. For when the chimneys came down, East Lothian lost a long-standing landmark. No longer could the chimneys be seen from the East Coast rail-line or the A1 as an indicator that the journey to Edinburgh was almost complete. No more could I say to my grandsons when we were high up on an Edinburgh hill, 'Your granny and grampa live close to there.'

Landmarks matter. When the Children of Israel had reached their Promised Land and Joshua, their leader, was close to death, he called everyone together at Shechem. And there, after reviewing their history, their journeying and their faith, he called on them to renew their commitment to their God. When that had been done, Joshua commanded that a great stone be raised up at Shechem, a memorial to a momentous occasion. And Joshua said, 'This stone is a witness against you.' Look, folks! Remember this important landmark. Let it remind you of this day, point you to the future and be a lasting sign of the commitment you've made.

Landmarks matter. Look around at yours and remember where you've come from.

Where are your landmarks?
Is there any danger that they will be knocked down?

May 10 – Indviduality

'Individuals pass like shadows;
but the commonwealth is fixed and stable.'
Edmund Burke, Speech in the House of Commons, 1780

I wonder what you make of personalised number plates. You know the kind of thing I mean – DES 51 E (Could it be that a 'Desmond' drives this car?); BIG 30 (A recent birthday, perhaps?); JUL 14 T (I suppose that's Juliet, but I'm not quite sure ...) The one I like best is COM 1 C (which has been doing the rounds of various well-known comedians for many years). I'm still looking out for A1 REV.

One website advertising personalised number plates (and some of them are available for *thousands* of pounds) suggests you might like to purchase one because it shows your creative side, helps you stand out from the crowd and is 100% unique. I suppose that's the point. In a world where there is so much conformity and similar patterns of behaviour, dress and even attitude, we crave recognition for our individuality. A personalised number plate is one way of emphasising our uniqueness.

But there must be other ways too. Not everyone can have, far less afford, a personalised number plate. So let's celebrate uniqueness where we find it. Let's use the right name for people we meet, for example.

Let's value that wee bit of eccentricity that makes someone stand out from the crowd. Let's learn from people who don't conform, and give thanks for variety and colour and life.

Isn't it our individuality
that makes our world an interesting place?

May 11 – Beginnings

'Mighty things from small beginnings grow.'
John Dryden, Annus Mirabilis

I've always been envious of people who can pinpoint a major development in their life to one moment in time. 'I knew I was going to be an astrophysicist from the very moment I heard Patrick Moore on *The Sky at Night* talk about ...' 'I can trace my career as a photographer back to when I saw David Bailey's photographs of ...' 'I was destined to be a politician from the day that ...'

I've never been like that. Developments in my own life have been more of a series of promptings than a one-off turning point. Ministry? It kind of grew on me. Writing? Well, it was always there.

That's why I was intrigued when I heard about the composer Edward Elgar writing his music for *The Apostles*. There was one event which sparked Elgar's creativity for this project. It occurred when he was a student at Littlehampton School in Worcester. His teacher, Francis Reeve, told his students that the Apostles were young men and very poor. 'Perhaps before the descent of the Holy Ghost,' Reeve said, 'they were no cleverer than some of you here.' So began for Elgar the idea of writing a religious work that would focus on ordinary men who were called to be the beginnings of Christianity. The concept remained with him into his adult life, and the wonder of *The Apostles* was the eventual result.

A definable moment, or a series of promptings; a specific event, or a growing awareness. I'm not sure it matters, if we're grateful for the beginnings that have led us to where we are. Those influences never leave us.

May 12 – Women

'Woman, much missed, how you call to me, call to me.'
Thomas Hardy, The Voice

Today I pay tribute to three much-missed women who 'call to me, call to me'. The first is my father's mother, Mary Cameron. She died when my father was fourteen, but her commitment to her children calls loudly to me of the beauty and strength of motherhood. Left by the death of her husband to bring up eight children, she gave herself unstintingly to her family's welfare. She took in washing, cleaned shop windows, looked after a lodger. She drove herself to an early grave. But the legacy she left, in my father and his siblings, is a tribute to a remarkable woman.

The second is my mother's mother, Maggie Gillick, who lived till she was ninety-five. She was married for over fifty years to a difficult man, whose own mother had died in tragic circumstances, leaving him a one-year-old orphan. He was violent and a heavy drinker. But through patience, feistiness and a strong faith, my granny brought up her daughter, lived a life of selfless compassion, and left many examples of innate goodness to her grandchildren.

The third is my mother, Jeanie McWhirr, a shining beacon of faith, compassion and service. As a young parent after the War, when money was tight and life was tough, she nurtured my sister and me, and kept our dad on the right lines too. She died young, aged fifty-eight. I'd love to have got to know her better in my later years. But her character is still with me, and her call to me remains very, very strong.

Commitment to family, selfless compassion, nurture and faith.
Which women call loudly to you?

May 13 – Refugees

'Jesus was a refugee.'
Pope Francis, General Audience Address, 2014

During one of his general audiences in 2014, Pope Francis made a poignant appeal on behalf of the world's refugees. Jesus, too, he said, knew times of hardship and danger.

We believe that Jesus was a refugee and had to flee to save his life, with Saint Joseph and Mary, he had to leave for Egypt. He was a refugee.

It's not surprising, therefore, that Jesus followed the injunction to show compassion that was fundamental to his Jewish upbringing. When the crowds asked him, 'Then what shall we do?' he answered:

The man who has two tunics is to share with him who has none; and he who has food is to do likewise.

In the Cathédrale St-Gatien in Tours in France there is a remarkable painting, *St Martin sharing his coat*. This key incident in the life of Martin of Tours depicts the aristocratic and military Martin leaning from his white steed to offer compassion to a wayside beggar, dividing his red cloak with his sword and giving one half of it to the poverty-stricken man. This life-changing moment in Martin's life is a metaphor for Jesus' command to show compassion to the displaced, stateless, broken people on the waysides of our life's journeys.

Might we do the same? And, if so, how?

May 14 – String

'I give you the end of a golden string.'
William Blake, Jerusalem

I was looking to add to my resources to help children cope with bereavement and get an insight into some of the aspects of grief and loss they might be experiencing. My daughter, who is a nursery and primary school teacher, pointed me to a book she uses in her teaching called *The Invisible String* by Patrice Karst and illustrated beautifully by Geoff Stevenson. It's a simple story designed to remind children – and adults – that they are never truly alone.

The mother in the story explains that people who love each other are always connected by a very special String made of love. Though it's invisible, you can feel it deep in your heart and know that you are always joined to someone you love. Even when someone dies, there is an invisible string that can still be tugged, as heart remains connected to heart. The power of love still connects us.

Juliette Drouet was a French actress who gave up her career after becoming mistress of the philosopher Victor Hugo. She was his secretary and travelling companion; she accompanied him in his exile in the Channel Islands and wrote many hundreds of letters to him during their love affair. In 1835, she wrote this:

There can be no happiness greater than that I enjoyed this afternoon with you, clasped in your arms, your voice mingling with mine, your eyes in mine, your heart upon my heart, our very souls welded together.

An 'invisible string' ... 'souls welded together' ...
Thank God for all that binds us to those we love the most.

May 15 – Awareness

'There is scarcely a single man sufficiently aware
to know all the evil he does.'
Duc de la Rochefoucauld, Maximes No. 269

The younger of my two grandsons was diagnosed with coeliac disease
when he was two years old. Very quickly, Cameron coined a new
word: 'gloonfree', and checking that something was *gloonfree* became
common in a little boy's vocabulary. When I collected him from
nursery, we always had a snack when we got back to the house.

'What would you like?' I would ask.

'What is there?' he would enquire.

There's a gluten-free cupboard in the kitchen full of interesting
things. I would rhyme off chocolate-chip cookies, brownies, bread-
sticks, bourbons, custard creams ...

'Can I have a brownie?' he would shout.

'Yes,' I'd respond. 'I'll bring it through.'

'Is it *gloonfree*?'

'Yes.'

'Are you sure?'

'Yes.'

'Can I see the box?' Box duly shown ... 'OK. It's *gloonfree*, grampa.
You were right. Can I have apple juice with that?'

Being conscious of his coeliac disease has made a little boy aware
that gluten-free is vitally important. Awareness matters – and not just
in a *gloonfree* world.

Can I develop an equal passion for injusticefree
and intolerancefree *and* prejudicefree *and* violencefree
to make our world a better place?

May 16 – Precision

'Some craven scruple of thinking too precisely ...'
William Shakespeare, Hamlet

I am constantly fascinated by quirky shop signs. I came across a shop which boldly announced that it was a *Precision Hairdresser*. Could it be that this shop's in competition with other hairdressing establishments of a less than satisfactory quality – *Slap-dash Hairdresser* perhaps, or maybe *Guesswork Hair Salon*, or even *The Couldn't Care Less Barber*?

There's a fish and chip shop which trades under the name of *The Cod Father*, a watch and clock repair shop called *Time On Your Hands* and a fishmonger's by the name of *Just the Plaice for You*.

Signs in shop windows make me smile too. What does the sign in the doorway of a baby-clothes retailer *actually* mean when it announces *We can deliver*? And I'm attracted by the message outside a second-hand bookshop which invites me to *Come and rustle in our reads*.

But when shop signs get it *wrong*, then my amusement turns to irritation – a fruit shop which advertises *Gala apple's – £2 per kiloe*, or the hair-stylist's which advertises *Mens haircut's half price on Monday's*.

And our *Precision Hairdresser*? Signs need to be clear, informative and correct. Yes, they might be quirky, and they may be designed to amuse. But they also need to do what they're there to do, and communicate in the right way.

You and I might be quirky, and we might make people smile,
but when the signs we show and the communication that goes with them
are way off beam, then no one benefits.

May 17 – Human rights

'All human beings are born free
and equal in dignity and rights.'
Universal Declaration of Human Rights, Article 1, 1948

Yad Vashem, Israel's main Holocaust remembrance and education centre, is situated on the green slopes of *Har HaZikaron* (The Mount of Remembrance) in Jerusalem. This commemoration project began in 1953 so that the Holocaust and its victims would be remembered by future generations.

I visited *Yad Vashem* during a two-week pilgrimage to the Holy Land in 2013. The gathering place outside the museum was crowded – tour parties such as ours, crocodiles of chattering youngsters, groups of Israeli soldiers and random tourists. But when all these people were inside, the atmosphere was different. It was subdued, solemn, respectful, dignified, sombre. And rightly so, for it is not possible to engage with the events of the Holocaust at any level and not be affected by it. We need to feel the pain.

I came back for a second pilgrimage two years later. Seeing illegal Israeli settlements encroaching on Palestinian land, and talking with Palestinians about their lives of fear and oppression, had an equally powerful effect on me. I was left with the conviction that when one nation, culture, religion or ideology oppresses another – in Hitler's Germany or in Israel/Palestine in the 21st century – nobody wins.

We *should* be subdued and sombre at *Yad Vashem.* But should we not be equally subdued and sombre in Bethlehem when we see the walls around the city, and the Shepherds' Fields being desecrated by illegal Israeli building?

*In Human Rights we need to determine what's right
for the whole of humanity.*

May 18 – Fear

'Whom then shall I fear?'
Bible, Psalm 27:1

Long ago, all the animals and human beings lived beneath the surface of the world in peace and harmony with the great god Kaang. Kaang began to plan the world above. He created a great tree, with branches that spread over the whole country, and then he created all the wonders within it. When he was satisfied, he dug a hole deep down to where the humans and animals were living. He took a man by the hand and led him to the world above. Then a woman wandered through the hole and the couple explored their new world. Soon the other people and all the animals were streaming out of the hole, excited by their new beginning. And Kaang said, 'You are to live together in peace and harmony. But under no circumstances must you make fire and bring evil to this beautiful world.'

All went well. But when the sun sank beneath the horizon, it became dark and cold and the humans couldn't see. 'What's happening? Will the sun ever return?' Fear spread amongst them. The animals too began to be afraid as they saw the people change. Then someone shouted, 'We must start a fire, then we will have light and warmth and we can survive.' So the fire was lit and the humans gathered around. They could see each other in its light and could feel its warmth. But the animals ran away, terrified of the fire.

Then the people remembered their promise to Kaang. By breaking it they had broken the understanding between humans and animals for ever. Fear was here to stay.

Is fear permanent? Can we make sure it isn't?

May 19 – Ageing

'In Manhood's more advancéd years,
We look on youth, and e'en its tears,
All fondly beaming on our gaze,
Seem bright thro' intervening days.'

Robert Howe Gould, Poetic Musings, Addressed to a Lady

All I ever knew about Sir Walter Raleigh was that he was a 16th/17th-century explorer who popularised tobacco in England having brought it back from the 'new world', and he put his cloak down over a muddy puddle so that Queen Elizabeth didn't get her feet wet. But it turns out that Walter Raleigh was a bit of a poet as well.

Raleigh could have been Gould's man looking back from his advanced years and seeing his youth – even through tears – as bright as it had ever been. Indeed, Raleigh *was* looking back to past years close to the end of his life and found himself reflecting on the ageing process. He died when he was sixty-four, old by the standards of his day. His reflections could well be ours, though we might live longer than he or his Elizabethan contemporaries were expected to. His poem was written the night before his death and was found in his Bible in the gate-house at Westminster after he died. It's entitled 'Even Such is Time'.

Even such is time, which takes in trust
Our youth, our joys and all we have,
And pays us but with age and dust;
Who, in the dark and silent grave,
When we have wandered all our ways,
Shuts up the story of our days,
And from which earth and grave are dust,
The Lord shall raise me up, I trust.

May 20 – Giving

'To give and not to count the cost.'
St Ignatius Loyola, Prayer for Generosity

A poor beggar was put up every night in a free *choultry* – a lodging house – sleeping on a mat on the floor and covered with old rags. Every day he sat by the wayside and passers-by would throw grains of rice or copper coins into his begging-bowl. On most days, the beggar had enough rice for a meal, money to buy sticks for a fire and a few vegetables for a curry which he ate by the *choultry.*

One day he heard that the Maharaja would come by on his chariot. 'Surely the Maharaja will give nothing less than a golden coin,' the beggar thought. The clattering of hooves signalled the Maharaja's arrival. Stepping into the road, the beggar stopped the chariot and begged the ruler for alms. But instead of giving anything, the Maharaja extended his hands and asked the beggar to give *him* something. Disappointed at a wealthy ruler begging from a poor man, the beggar counted out five grains of rice and placed them angrily in the Maharaja's hands.

With a sore heart, the beggar went back to his *choultry* to count the remaining grains of rice for his meal. As he did so, a small glittering object attracted his attention. It was a grain of gold. Soon he found another, and another, till he held five gold grains in his hand. Five grains of rice had been rewarded with five grains of gold. 'What a fool I was,' the beggar exclaimed. 'If I'd known this was the deal, I would have given away every grain of rice I had.'

Give freely,
for your freedom to give is a gift to be well used.

May 21 – Subversion

'Who would put up with the Gracchi
complaining about subversion?'
Juvenal, Satires No. 2

Father Roland Walls, who died in 2011 aged 92, was an Anglican priest for more than 40 years and chaplain at Rosslyn Chapel before converting to Roman Catholicism. In his conversations with the writer Ron Ferguson in *Mole Under the Fence,* Roland Walls shows himself to be a deeply spiritual man, impish in his sense of humour – and a subversive theologian!

I knew Roland Walls as a lecturer in Edinburgh's Faculty of Divinity in the early 1970s. In one class, when he was being typically subversive, provocative and challenging, he was soundly criticised by some students for not being 'orthodox' in his interpretation of Scripture. 'You are departing from the Truth,' he was told by one. 'You are dismissing received doctrine,' complained another. 'Where is your adherence to dogma?' questioned a third.

After listening calmly for a while, Roland Walls laid down his lecture notes and said, 'Ladies and gentlemen, today I have a suggestion.' The whole class listened attentively. 'I suggest we get a very large dustbin, and take *all* the books of dogma, and stuff them in the bin. And then, ladies and gentlemen, we shall take the dustbin lid and put it on top of the bin. And *then* ... we shall all sit on top of the lid, *just in case the books of dogma try to escape again.* I wish you every blessing. This class is now over.'

We need subversive thinkers
to challenge the purity and certainties of our beliefs.

May 22 – Time

'With thee conversing I forget all time.'

John Milton, Paradise Lost

We could time everything at home by our cocker spaniel's internal clock – pretty well to the minute. *Agitato* first thing in the morning, time for a walk and breakfast. Bouncing around at lunchtime, a walk again. Seeing someone move towards the kitchen, time for tea. Moping around during the evening, time for a wee walk. Nine o'clock (how does she know that?) time for an evening snack. What's the time? Ask Amber. She'll know.

There's a poem by Rabindranath Tagore about time which I've always liked, because it takes the measurement of time away from 'what's happening next?' – whether in relation to your dog or yourself – and places it in a wider context. It's called 'Endless Time'. Maybe it's that kind of understanding of time we – and our Amber – need to strive for.

Time is endless in thy hands, my lord.
There is none to count thy minutes.
Days and nights pass and ages bloom and fade like flowers.
Thou knowest how to wait.
Thy centuries follow each other perfecting a small wild flower.
We have no time to lose,
and having no time we must scramble for a chance.
We are too poor to be late.
And thus it is that time goes by
while I give it to every querulous man who claims it,
and thine altar is empty of all offerings to the last.
At the end of the day I hasten in fear lest thy gate be shut;
but I find that yet there is time.

May 23 – Parents

'A lad of life, an imp of fame,
Of parents good, of fist most valiant.'
William Shakespeare, Henry V

My mother died when she was 58, and my father aged 82. When he died, I wasn't ready to be an orphan. In my 50s, I had to grow up very quickly. Here's my tribute to my parents.

When I was young, you nurtured me,
fed me and clothed me, help me and loved me,
and let me learn and grow and find my way.
When I questioned and challenged,
you listened, corrected me and guided me,
rebuked me and affirmed me,
and helped me know and understand and love what I am.
When I left you, you watched me,
you let me go, believing in me and my going.
When I missed you, I cried at my leaving you,
at my frailty in coping without your security and warmth,
and I missed you more than I can say.
Now, when I remember you,
in your nurture and purpose for me,
and your healing and sustaining of me,
in your strength and commitment to me,
there is no leaving now, no separating,
no going, no returning,
only being in you and with you for all my days.

I hope I'm not 'an imp of fame', and I can't claim to be 'of fist most valiant'. But I thank God that I am 'of parents good', and for that I will be eternally grateful.

May 24 – Tears

'Thrice he assay'd, and thrice, in spite of scorn,
Tears, such as angels weep, burst forth.'
John Milton, Paradise Lost

I cried when I heard this story shared by a hospice chaplain at a study-day. The topic was empathy in end-of-life care, and we were exploring the boundaries between professionalism and our own humanity, touching on the emotion which caring for dying people creates in us.

There had been a particularly difficult death in the hospice, the chaplain told us. The patient had been a young woman, aged nineteen, one of twins. The last few days of her life had touched everyone deeply. When the young woman died, there were the 'last offices' to be done. The two nurses charged with this responsibility were struggling so they asked the chaplain to go with them. As the nurses went about their business, they were in tears. And the chaplain, understandably, was in tears too.

When the procedures were completed, one of the nurses asked if the chaplain would offer a blessing. 'Perhaps an anointing,' the other suggested. The chaplain had no prayer book and no sacramental oil. 'So I used what I had to hand,' she said. 'We were all crying. I took a tear from the cheek of one of the nurses and made the sign of the cross with it on the young woman's forehead. I did the same with a tear from the cheek of the second nurse. Then I wiped the tears from my own face and anointed the patient once more. She was anointed with our tears. It was all we had to offer.'

'It was all we had to offer' might be true.
But it was the offering of all that is human in our care.

May 25 – Laughing too

'And unextinguish'd laughter shakes the skies.'
Homer, The Iliad

If I ever get to be on *Desert Island Discs,* I would have to ask if I could be provided with a wind-up gramophone. One of my eight pieces of music would be a 78rpm record from 1922 of the wonderful Charles Jolly (the pseudonym of Charles Penrose) singing *The Laughing Policeman.* If you haven't heard it, search for it on YouTube. It's hilarious, and it always makes me laugh!

In the movie *The Dead Poets' Society,* Robin Williams' character says to one of his students, 'I'm not laughing at you; I'm laughing near you.' Well, I'm more than happy if people are laughing near me, because it will almost certainly make me laugh as well.

I was on a packed bus the other day. It was wet outside. No one was smiling. A woman came on with a baby. It was hard to squeeze her in and there were mumps and grumps of impatience from other passengers. She stood facing forward, the baby in her arms looking backwards over her shoulder. And the baby started to giggle. Within moments, everyone was smiling. The woman closest to the baby was pulling faces. The baby giggled louder. The man beside me started to chuckle. When the bus arrived at my stop, I was reluctant to get off. I was smiling for the rest of the day.

Laughter is infectious. It can make our day better – just what we need to cheer us up.

If there's a laughing policeman and a giggling baby
out there, what about me?

May 26 – Differences

'Why art thou then cast down my soul?
What should discourage thee?'
Scottish Psalter, Psalm 43 v 5

William Hazlitt, perhaps the greatest English literary critic after Samuel Johnson, wrote *Lectures on the English Comic Writers* in 1819. In 'On Wit and Humour' he wrote:

Man is the only animal that laughs and weeps; for he is the only animal that is struck with the difference between what things are, and what they ought to be.

I've shared thoughts over the past two days of the most common of human emotions – tears and laughter. In all of life, we inhabit the space between the two. Sometimes we laugh, sometimes we cry. We swing from one emotion to the other. We know the difference between what Hazlitt describes as 'what things are, and what they ought to be'.

Bereaved people tell me they are surprised how low they can feel, the 'cast down' feeling of the Psalmist. They are fearful that this will be permanent, that they will never laugh again. So they have to be helped to find this truth – that being low is but one dimension of the human condition. Laughter may be rare at the start. If it comes, it may not last long. But it will return, because we know the difference 'between what things are, and what they ought to be'.

*The art of life is to know how to enjoy a little
and to endure much.*
Hazlitt, 'Common Places', *The Literary Examiner,* 1823

May 27 – Impressions

'... this weaving and unweaving of false impressions ...'
George Eliot, Letter to Mrs Peter Taylor

I can remember my first day at school. Actually, I can't remember *much* of my first day at school, apart from two things. They may be real memories, or they may be simple impressions that have formed themselves into memories over the years.

The first is that my teacher, Miss Logan, was *very* old. My mother would have been in her early thirties when I went to school, and I learned later that Miss Logan, the teacher for the PI intake in 1954, would have been about 50. But, compared to my mother, my teacher was very old indeed. And she had grey hair. So she *must* have been ancient.

The second is that the classroom was *massive*. Compared to the small space of our house or even the medium size of the church we worshipped in, this classroom was huge. I remember the ceiling being *miles* above me. It was the biggest classroom ever.

I know now that Miss Logan wasn't ancient at all, and the classroom was no bigger than a normal-sized school-room. But through the eyes of a small boy, and in comparison to what I knew, Miss Logan was *very* old and the classroom was very, *very* big.

Be careful what judgements you make and what comparisons you use. Some things might look older or better or bigger ... and aren't at all. Some things can fall terribly short of your expectations, and don't deserve to.

Make sure you temper your impressions with reality.
Impressions may not always be reliable.

May 28 – Creation

'God looked at everything he had made,
and he was very pleased.'
Bible, Genesis 1:31

There are many myths suggesting how the world began. Here's one from China which I offer without comment.

In the beginning there was Chaos, and in the darkness an enormous black egg grew. Inside this egg was the sleeping giant Pan Gu. For eighteen thousand years Pan Gu slept and grew. Finally, he awoke and yawned, stretched his enormous limbs and broke the egg in two. The top half was lighter and flew up to become the heavens and the heavier bottom half sank down to become the earth. But Pan Gu was concerned that the two parts might come together again so that Chaos was remade. So he stood between them, his head holding up the heavens and his feet on the earth. And there he stood, growing bigger and bigger, pushing the sky and earth further apart for another eighteen thousand years.

Once he was sure that they would never come together again, Pan Gu, exhausted by his efforts, lay down and died. His last breaths became the wind and clouds, and his voice the rumbling thunder. One eye became the sun, the other the moon. His body and limbs became the mountains, his blood made the rivers and seas. The hairs on Pan Gu's head turned into millions of twinkling stars. His skin and other hair became plants and trees. His sweat flowed like the rain and dew, nourishing everything, while his teeth and bones turned into precious stones and minerals.

Finally, from the numerous small creatures that had lived on his body, came humankind, spreading out over the earth into every corner of the creation that was Pan Gu.

May 29 – Fringe

'Beyond the Fringe'
Title of a 1960s' comedy stage revue

Beyond the Fringe was a British comedy stage revue written and performed by Peter Cook, Dudley Moore, Alan Bennett, and Jonathan Miller. It played in London's West End and then in America. Hugely successful, it is widely regarded as having given birth to satirical comedy in Britain in the 1960s.

'The Fringe' of the title refers to the Edinburgh Festival Fringe – *The Fringe* – the remarkable cornucopia of events which make up the world's largest arts festival – over 50,000 performances of several thousand shows in hundreds of venues, wrapped around the Edinburgh International Festival, which takes place in Scotland's capital every August.

There's a story in Matthew's Gospel which tells of a woman with a blood disorder, who was so passionate to be close to Jesus that she caught hold of the hem of his cloak as he went by. Matthew tells us she was healed. But this isn't the part of the story that gets to me. Here is a woman who never got 'beyond the fringe' – beyond the hem of Jesus' cloak. She did not break into his inner circle, and was not even accepted in her own society. The fringe was as far as she got.

How many people do we know who are on the fringe of things – in family life, in circles of friends, in clubs, in societies, in school, even in church? Perhaps they're not easy to like. Perhaps they lack self-esteem. Perhaps they are you. People need to be helped to get beyond the fringes of things, to find acceptance, welcome, friendship and healing.

The Fringe is terrific.
Maybe 'beyond the fringe' is even better.

May 30 – Together again

'Rich or poor, we will keep together
and be happy in one another.'
Louisa May Alcott, Little Women

There's a slightly ghoulish Scottish ballad from the 17th century called
The Twa Corbies. It opens this way:

As I was walking all alane,
I heard twa corbies making a mane;
The tane unto the t'other say,
'Where sall we gang and dine to-day?'
'In behint yon auld fail dyke,
I wot there lies a new slain knight;
And naebody kens that he lies there,
but his hawk, his hound, and lady fair.

For the benefit of the non-Scots: *twa* = two; *corbies* = crows; *mane* =
a howl or lament; *tane* = one; *behint* = behind; *fail dyke* = a wall of
turf; *wot* = know; *kens* = knows.

A poor knight, fallen in battle or set upon by enemies, lies rotting
behind a wall, providing a feast of carrion for hungry ravens. Perhaps
a common occurrence in those days, but ghoulish nonetheless. But
there are *two* corbies at work here, in a secret conspiracy, plotting
together.

Planning and sharing a project can, of course, be a good thing. But
when a plan has a devious purpose, then it becomes what the Courts
call 'joint enterprise', where everyone involved is deemed guilty of
wrongdoing.

If you seek to do good, do it together.
If you seek to be together, make sure you do good.

May 31 – Giants

'Lo! Where the Giant on the mountain stands.'
Lord Byron, Childe Harold's Pilgrimage

Visiting the Giant's Causeway on the Antrim coast in Northern Ireland, I heard the story of how it came into being. Finn MacCool was an Irish giant, and his most fearsome enemies were the Scottish giants. Finn was so determined to get at them that he built a causeway from Ireland across the sea to Scotland, using six-sided cobblestones so they would fit neatly together like a honeycomb. It was an excellent and beautiful crossing.

One day Finn MacCool shouted a challenge to the Scottish giant Benandonner to cross the causeway and fight him. But as soon as he saw the Scot getting closer, he realised Benandonner was much bigger than he had imagined. Finn ran home, and, as he heard the stamping feet of Benandonner behind him, he had to stuff five pounds of moss into each ear to muffle the frightening noise. It all ends with a great fight. Finn chases Benandonner out of Ireland. Passing Portadown, Finn scoops a huge clod of earth out of the ground to fling at the retreating Scot. The hole fills up with water and becomes the biggest lough in Ireland – Lough Neagh. The clod lands in the Irish Sea – and becomes the Isle of Man. And both giants tear up the Giant's Causeway, leaving the ragged ends at the two shores.

A local man told us, 'If you go to Scotland, to the island of Staffa, you'll see the other end of the Causeway. You'll not see Finn Mac-Cool, or at least, not till you've had a pint or two of the Guinness.'

If you ever go across the sea to Ireland …

June 1 – Challenge

'No reward is offered, for they are gone forever.'
Horace Mann, Lost, Two Golden Hours

'Where did the money go?' I asked a friend who'd told me a story about a colleague who'd blown several thousand pounds over a stag weekend. 'It disappeared like snow off a dyke in summer,' he said. I knew exactly what he meant.

The last vestiges of snow will disappear very quickly during a spring thaw – from trees, fences, roofs, walls or dykes. But if there were to be snow on a dyke in *summer* it would last no time at all. It would disappear quickly and totally – like the drinks kitty on a stag weekend.

My dog's food disappears like snow off a dyke in summer! One moment, it's there, in a bowl, beside a hungry dog. The next moment, it's gone! Like snow off a dyke …

When Jesus was arrested in the Garden of Gethsemane and taken for trial before Pilate and the Sanhedrin, he had friends with him, disciples, dedicated, committed followers, called to be faithful. And when they were needed? They disappeared like snow off a dyke in summer. Gone – quickly, silently, fearfully, gone!

There's a well-known saying, as common in politics as it is in industry or commerce, that suggests: 'When the going gets tough, the tough get going.' In tough situations, the toughest rise to the challenge, and become bolder. But the disciples? They got going, right enough, but hightailing it away from the tough situation as fast and as far as they could go. Like snow off a dyke …

Getting going to face a challenge,
or getting going to run away?
Which way to go?

June 2 – Accidents

'Accidents will occur in the best-regulated families.'
Charles Dickens, David Copperfield

Jenny Atherton was an elderly widow. She was frail but feisty, and despite repeated suggestions that she would be safer and happier in a smaller, more 'user-friendly' house, she insisted on soldiering on in a rambling flat that had been her family home for over fifty years. Jenny's frailty, and the obstacle course that was her home meant that she was an 'accident waiting to happen'. I was distressed, therefore, but not at all surprised, when I heard that she'd had a fall, broken her hip, and was in a hospital orthopaedic ward.

When I went to see her, I found her to be as feisty as usual, frustrated that she couldn't get home right away, and not at all contrite for ignoring people's advice about moving to a safer house. It wasn't the time or place for me to put in my tuppence-worth. But I was interested to know how her accident had come about.

'Well,' she said, 'I was watching the snooker on the TV – that nice young man, Steve Davis, and that wild one, Alex Higgins – and they'd come to the end of a session. And I thought, "Time for a cuppa!" I got up from the chair, and my legs got tangled in the zimmer legs, and the zimmer legs got tangled with the table leg, and I didn't know which leg to move first, so I fell over!'

Jenny recovered from her fall, and, of course, went back to her own home. There was no way she was going to be snookered by the *smallest* of accidents, was there?

> *Oh, be careful little feet where you go.*
> *Accidents can happen, even so …*

June 3 – Light

'Thou, whose eternal Word,
Chaos and darkness heard,
And took their flight,
Hear us we humbly pray,
And, where the Gospel day
Sheds not its glorious ray,
Let there be light.'
John Marriot, hymn written in 1813

Most of us will know the 'Four Candles' sketch by the Two Ronnies. Written by Ronnie Barker under the pseudonym of Gerald Wiley, it was first broadcast on the BBC in September 1976. I could watch it over and over again. It is *so* funny!

But candles have also brought me tears. Ministering in a traditional Presbyterian church, while some of my modernity was appreciated, there were times when my innovations were not. It was an Easter service. My theme was 'Jesus, the light of the world'. We sang John Marriot's great hymn, 'Thou, whose almighty Word'. When we were singing 'Let there be light', I lit two large candles on the Communion Table. Some people were furious. 'Are we going Catholic?' 'Are candles in vogue?' 'Too much frivolity!' I was angry and upset. A little light in me had been snuffed out. The candles never appeared on the Communion Table again.

A week later I was visiting a family who'd had their electricity disconnected. They were lighting their home with candles and only had two stuttering lights. I gave them the church's rejected Easter candles. They burned for as long as they were needed in a home struggling with poverty.

A little flicker of light had begun to challenge the darkness.

June 4 – Farewells

'Ae fond kiss, and then we sever;
Ae fareweel, and then forever.'
Robert Burns, Ae Fond Kiss

One of my eight Desert Island Discs is a song from 1944 about Scottish soldiers leaving Sicily – *The 51st Highland Division's Farewell to Sicily.* It was written by Hamish Henderson while he was Intelligence Officer for the Highland Division. Henderson had been viewing the smoke curling from Mount Etna's crater in the distance behind the pipes and drums of 153 Brigade, when the band launched into the tune *Farewell to the Creeks.* The rhythm of the tune and the poignancy of the moment gave Henderson his words.

Fare weel, ye banks o Sicily,
Fare ye weel ye valley and shaw
There's nae hame can smoor the wiles o ye,
Puir bliddy swaddies are wearie.

He goes on to write movingly of the piper who's homesick and won't regret leaving Sicily, and the drummer who's sorry to be leaving Lola, his Italian girlfriend. The tune was composed by Pipe Major James 'Pipie' Robertson of Boyne, Banffshire, in 1915 when he was a PoW in Germany.

Farewells are part of life. Some are easy, and some are very hard. But if life is a journey, inevitably some people and places will have to be left behind.

Leave behind what needs to be left,
and carry in your hearts the things that matter.
Say your farewells and then move boldly on.

June 5 – Marriage

'O let us be married! Too long have we tarried:
But what shall we do for a ring?'
Edward Lear, The Owl and the Pussycat

My wife fell and broke a finger in her left hand. Apart from the fact that she is left-handed *and* that the break and the bruising were painful and took a long time to settle, she had to have her engagement, wedding and eternity rings cut off in A&E. It was the first time in forty-three years of marriage that she didn't have rings on her wedding finger. When we went to the jewellers to arrange for the rings to be repaired, the helpful staff member suggested she wait another four weeks or so till the swelling had completely gone, the indentations from wearing the rings for so long had dissipated, and the wedding finger had 'settled down'.

'Another four weeks without your wedding ring, I'm afraid,' he said.

'Four weeks pretending you're not married,' I joked.

'But our marriage was never defined by wearing a ring anyway,' my wife replied – putting us both in our place. And, as she remarked to me later, 'It's given us another chance to find meaning that a mere ring could never express.'

The 19th-century poet George Crabbe wrote this:

The ring, so worn as you behold, so thin,
So pale, is yet of gold:
The passion such it was to prove –
Worn with life's care, love yet was love.

Give thanks for the people who love you.
Give thanks that 'love is yet love' for you.

June 6 – Unique

'All my love is towards individuals.'
Jonathan Swift, letter to Pope, September 1725

My wife took her new spaniel to obedience classes. Obedience? Did the training make any difference? Not that that anyone noticed. But, nonetheless, she and her mad spaniel came back with a lovely rosette. Best dog in the class? Most improved animal? Special attribute?

'Why the rosette?' I enquired.

'Oh,' my wife replied, 'I think she got that just for being a dog.'

Just for being a dog ... No success, no achievement, no accolade, no degree, no qualification, just a rosette for being what a dog has to be – a dog!

Samuel Johnson, in his book *The Rambler,* written in 1750, offers us this reflection on the human condition:

Almost every man wastes part of his life in attempts to display qualities which he does not possess, and to gain applause which he cannot keep.

If we give our time and energy to our attempts to be what we are not, and if we seek affirmation for a 'pretend' person and not the person we really are, to what extent do we waste the quality of our life?

I wasn't born to be what I am not. I was given life so that I can find who I am and be the best that I can be. That's a difficult enough job without squandering time and energy trying to be something or someone else.

To be what you have to be,
to love as you were called to love,
is way above winning any rosette.

June 7 – Number one

'Tous pour un, un pour tous.'

'All for one, one for all.'

Alexander Dumas, The Three Musketeers

When I was a student at Edinburgh University, I played for the University shinty team. I was awarded a Blue in 1970, and I look back to my time in the shinty club with great affection. Shinty is akin to Irish hurling. The pitch is big, the game is fast and dangerous, the skill is technical and the enjoyment immense. Try field hockey without rules, and you've just about got it!

I played in goal, and so I was always listed as Number One. Phil McKenzie at full back was Number Two, all the way through the team to Dave Howarth, who, as full forward, was Number Twelve. We won the Scottish University Championship – 'The Littlejohn Vase'. The celebrations in the bus on the way home were understandably raucous. We always began with the team chant, which started,

We've got Tommy Gordon, Number One,
We're the best team in the land.

Phil McKenzie, Number Two, was the next to be lauded in song. But the team got bored singing the song for twelve verses and it was quickly abandoned, with other lewder offerings taking over. Poor Dave Howarth at Number Twelve never got a mention.

I can still hear the team singing my name.
'Tommy Gordon, Number One'
has helped me through the worst of days.

June 8 – An open door

'Open, ye everlasting gates, they sung.
Open, ye heavens, your living doors.'
John Milton, Paradise Lost

The late Charles Kennedy and I went to the same school, Lochaber High School in Fort William. Charlie died tragically young and is much missed in the Lochaber area and by many other people. Not long after he had been elected to the House of Commons and was the youngest MP, he appeared on *Question Time.* I was doing some work for the religious department of Scottish Television then, and, by coincidence, I was on STV at the same time as Charlie was on BBC. The following week this was commented on in the local Fort William paper. 'Remarkable,' the piece read, 'that two "sons of the Fort" should be on national TV at the same time.' I wrote to Charlie, enclosing the newspaper cutting. He was good enough to reply, suggesting, graciously, that people were more likely to benefit from a minister of religion than they were from any politician!

Charlie appeared on a BBC documentary recently about the workings of the House of Commons. Standing in the central lobby, he pointed out that there were four doors, above which were depictions of the patron saints of the four nations of the Union. 'St George,' he said, 'is above the entrance to the House of Lords; St David above the entrance to the House of Commons; St Patrick above the exit.' And with a twinkle in his eye he concluded, 'And St Andrew, the patron Saint of Scotland, is above the door to hospitality'.

An open door – not just for 'sons of the Fort',
but for anyone looking for hospitality.

June 9 – Choice

'Bankrupt of life, yet prodigal of ease.'
John Dryden, Absalom and Achitophel

Rembrandt's painting *The Prodigal Son* in the Hermitage Museum in
St Petersburg and my subsequent reading of Henri Nouwen's *The
Return of the Prodigal* have had a profound effect on me. Here's my
tribute to both.

Underneath the clouds I wandered;
Underneath the skies I squandered
Life – I had no clear direction,
Spurned all guidance and correction,
All because of the choice I made.

Down the slippery slope I travelled,
While my youthful life unravelled;
Self-esteem and value shattered;
Confidence and purpose battered,
All because of the choice I made.

Down the path to hope returning,
Failure in my heart still burning.
Will my father there be waiting?
Will he see me hesitating,
All because of the choice I made?

Underneath your hands you bless me;
Underneath your gaze assess me.
Here I kneel, my sin confessing.
Make me worthy of your blessing,
All because of the choice I made.

June 10 – Talk

'Man is caught by his tongue, as an ox is by its horns.'
Russian proverb

The 18th-century writer and satirist Jonathan Swift is reputed to have said, 'There are few wild beasts more to be dreaded than a talking man having nothing to say.' It's a statement that contains a great deal of truth. 'Empty barrels make the most noise,' I heard often when I was in school. Just because you talk a lot, it doesn't follow that you have much to say that's of any use.

I've always liked brevity and succinctness. An old minister once gave me sound advice about public speaking – and sermons – 'Stand up; speak up; and shut up.' Wise advice indeed ...

In ancient Sparta the citizens were stoical and noted for their economy of speech. Legend has it that when Philip of Macedon was storming the gates of Sparta, he sent a message to the besieged king saying, 'If we capture your city we will burn it to the ground.' The one-word answer was: 'If.'

In 1842, at the age of 60, Sir Charles James Napier was appointed Major General in the British Army in India. Many provincial rulers remained opposed to the British, so Napier's orders were to put down the rebels. He went beyond his mandate, however, and conquered the whole of the Province of Sindh. His campaign completed, Napier is reputed to have dispatched to his superiors the short, notable message, *Peccavi,* the Latin for *'I have sinned'* – the essence of cleverness and brevity.

Talk less, and 'if' you have to talk,
make it brief and to the point.

June 11 – Closed

'We never closed.'
Advertising slogan, The Windmill Theatre, London

During a recent period of gas mains repairs in Edinburgh there were frequent roadworks. Temporary traffic lights proliferated. Delays were common. But the most irritating part was the regular 'road closures'. When it wasn't possible for traffic to be guided past roadworks in a single lane, the road was simply closed off. There were diversions, of course, but unless you were aware of these early enough, you could come to a 'road closed' sign with no clue where to go. Giving yourself more time to navigate your way through city streets disrupted by roadworks is one thing. Having to find a completely new way of getting from A to B is quite another.

It would be great if all our roads were marked 'We never close' – similar to the Windmill Theatre during the war. Then all our journeys would be predictable. And in our journeys of life it would be great if we never saw 'road closed' signs. That way we would always be sure of our direction of travel and future plans. But, as with driving, life just isn't like that. It will throw up closed routes no matter what. It's how we adapt to road closures that matters.

I'm told that when people have a stroke, some of the receptor pathways in the brain become closed off. Rehabilitation, over time, allows new connections to be made and new receptor pathways to be opened up, so that speech, movement, memory, and the like, can return. When we meet road closures, we have no choice but to find new pathways, or else life, in all its fullness, just stops.

Stop if you have to. Change if you must. But keep going!

June 12 – Signs

'"What's the good of Mercator's North Poles and Equators,
Tropics, Zones, and Meridian lines?"
So the Bellman would cry: and the crew would reply,
"They are merely conventional signs!"'
Lewis Carroll, The Hunting of the Snark

Driving past the home-straight of Musselburgh Racecourse ...

Him: What's that sign for?
Me: Which sign?
Him: The one that says 3F.
Me: That's three furlongs.
Him: What's a furlong?
Me: It's a distance measurement.
Him: How long a distance?
Me: You get eight of them to a mile?
Him: So how long's that?
Me: A mile?
Him: No, a furlong thingy.
Me: Two hundred and twenty yards.
Him: How long's a yard?
Me: Three feet, or thirty-six inches.
Him: How long's that in centimetres?
Me: A yard's just under a metre, about 0.9.
Him: So why don't they use metres on the sign, then?
Me: There's not enough space to get all the numbers on.
Him: That one says 4F.
Me: Well, if there are two hundred and twenty yards in a
       furlong, and a yard's about nine tenths of a meter, roughly
       how many metres would four furlongs be?
Him: Too many to paint on a sign.

June 13 – Models

'You should turn the pages of your Greek model
night and day.'
Horace, Ars Poetica

Like many fishing communities, my village of Port Seton still has numerous homes which display model fishing boats in their windows. It's the fishing tradition. Families that nowadays have no engagement with fishing are still proud of the fishing heritage of parents, grandparents and generations further back in time. A model fishing boat in the front window of your home tells the world where your heart lies.

There are models of fishing boats in the local churches too. Prayers of thanksgiving for the harvest of the sea are more focused when there are model boats in front of you.

These boats are scale models of the real thing. I was passionate about Airfix model-making when I was younger – planes and ships, soldiers and kings, cars and motorbikes. Model railway enthusiasts are no different. Scale models of engines and tenders, carriages and trucks, tracks and stations are the delight of many. Sometimes, a model is made *before* the real thing is constructed. A shopping precinct or office-complex can be presented in model form so that we can see what the real thing will be like.

If we are models of something bigger, what do we model ourselves on – a person, a principle, an ethical standard, a religious code? We can't always *be* the big thing or person, but we can *model* what is right and good so that others can see what we have based our lives on.

What are we modelled on,
and how good a representation might we become?

June 14 – Prejudice

'When prejudice commands, reason is silent.'

Helvétius, De l'Homme

There's a story told of an eminent bishop who was sailing from England to the USA on one of the great transatlantic liners. The bishop, travelling as simply as possible, had arranged to share a cabin, though he didn't know who his companion would be. The two men, having been separately shown to their cabin, met briefly, deposited their luggage, and went about their business. The first thing the bishop did was to locate the purser's office.

After introducing himself and giving his cabin number, he enquired whether it might be possible for him to deposit his gold watch and other valuables in the liner's safe.

'Ordinarily,' the bishop explained, 'I would not avail myself of this privilege.' He dropped his voice to a conspiratorial whisper. 'But, you see, I have just been to my cabin where I met the man who is to occupy the second berth. And, judging by his appearance, I fear he may not be a trustworthy person, and so I am apprehensive that I might lose my valuable possessions to this stranger.'

'Thank you,' the purser replied, 'I shall be happy to lock your valuables in our safe. It's a service we're pleased to offer. And it's interesting that the other man in your cabin has been to see me just a few minutes ago and he left his valuables with us for the self-same reason.'

I wonder if that's why the philosopher Heraclitus once wrote, 'Dogs bark at everyone they do not know.'

Maybe it's time to stop and examine our prejudices.
Stop barking at – or about – the people you don't know.

June 15 – Acceptable

'Always acceptable in thy sight, O Lord.'
Bible, Psalm 19:14

It was a childcare day for my two grandsons during the school holidays. The morning was spent with grandson number one (aged 8) trying to teach me the technicalities of the Xbox and the intricacies of *Minecraft*. He was patient, tolerant and not a little amused by my stumbling efforts. After the umpteenth time that I muttered, 'I'm rubbish at this,' he turned to me and announced, 'Yes, grampa. You *are* rubbish. You're even worse than my wee brother.'

I was relieved, therefore, to escape from all of this as we went to collect grandson number two (aged 5) from nursery. I was strapping him into his car seat, when his older brother launched into a detailed explanation about how useless I had been on the Xbox, just at the point when I was struggling to get the seatbelt fastened around the car seat. In exasperation, I announced, 'Yes guys, I'm rubbish at everything, absolutely everything ... apart from being a grampa. Do you think I might be OK at that?'

To which the little one replied, 'Yes, actually, as a grampa you're quite acceptable.'

No sarcasm. Straight face. Factual and to the point. 'Quite acceptable', and from a five-year-old, at that ...

But it made my day! I'm happy with 'quite acceptable' when other things are going wrong. Acceptable is good, I've decided. And if my grandson reckons I'm acceptable as a grandfather, that beats being rubbish at the Xbox any day!

Acceptable?
I'll accept that in the spirit in which it's offered.

June 16 – Birdsong

'Each little flower that opens,
Each little bird that sings,
He made their glowing colours,
He made their tiny wings.'
Cecil Frances Alexander, All Things Bright and Beautiful

When Cecil Frances Alexander wrote the well-known hymn *All things bright and beautiful,* I wish she'd made reference to bird*song* alongside glowing colours and delicate physiology.

Some years ago I had a hearing problem. Repeatedly asking my wife to speak up, turning the TV volume up too high and complaining that people were mumbling had been signs of the deterioration in my hearing. Thanks to the wonders of the NHS, I was diagnosed with a loss of the 'upper register' of sounds and ended up with hearing aids.

When I wore them for the first time, I went for a drive and then for a walk with our dog. Two things stick in my mind from that day. The first was that I could hear the indicator in the car clicking *incredibly* loudly. And the second was that when I was walking the dog in the woods I could hear the birds singing. Maybe I'd just stopped noticing them. Or maybe I'd not been able to hear them at all. But I was noticing them again, and hearing them as if for the first time.

The 16th-century poet Edmund Spenser wrote this in *Epithalamion:*

*Hark how the cheerefull birds do chaunt their lays
and carroll of love's praise.*

Yes! I get that ...
now that I can hear the birds singing again.

June 17 – Nonsense

'His nonsense suits their nonsense.'
Charles II, said of the Bishop of Clonfert

Edward Lear, a 19th-century English artist, illustrator, musician, author
and poet, is known now mostly for his literary nonsense in poetry
and prose. But did Lear think he was ridiculous himself? His poem
How pleasant to know Mr Lear, makes us believe he did.

> *How pleasant to know Mr Lear!*
> *Who has written such volumes of stuff!*
> *Some think him ill-tempered and queer,*
> *But a few think him pleasant enough.*
>
> *His mind is concrete and fastidious,*
> *His nose is remarkably big;*
> *His visage is more or less hideous,*
> *His beard it resembles a wig.*
>
> *He has ears, and two eyes, and ten fingers,*
> *Leastways if you reckon two thumbs;*
> *Long ago he was one of the singers,*
> *But now he is one of the dumbs.*
>
> *He reads, but he cannot speak, Spanish,*
> *He cannot abide ginger beer:*
> *Ere the days of his pilgrimage vanish,*
> *How pleasant to know Mr Lear!*

Nonsense? Perhaps. But ridiculous? Not at all. In fact, I think Mr Lear
is a *very* pleasant man indeed!

June 18 – Sincerity

'There is no greater joy
than to examine oneself and be sincere.'
Meng-tzu, The Book of Mencius

The word for 'sincerity' in the original Greek of the New Testament
means 'judged in the sunlight'. The English word is derived from *sine
cera* which literally means 'without wax'.

When art flourished in ancient Greece, it was common practice
to repair any statue, pottery vase or wall-tile which had been damaged
by accident or carelessness with almost-invisible wax.

Many wealthy merchants or persons of high rank would employ
a sculptor to chisel their bust in marble. However, if the marble was
flawed or the sculptor careless, or if the chisel just slipped, it was easy
enough for the lobe of an ear or the end of a nose to be chipped
off. Rather than go to all the trouble of starting again – and taking
longer to finish the commission – the sculptor would seek to mend
the features with wax so that the flaw couldn't be detected – unless
by very close scrutiny. He would then palm it off to his customer as
a perfect carving.

But if the client was a knowledgeable person, he would examine
the bust carefully in the sunlight before he parted with his money. If
the statue was 'sincere' – without wax – the sculptor would be paid
for his fine work. But if the sculptor was devious, and the customer
less than careful, an ear or the nose of his bust might drop off in the
sunlight or the warmth of his home.

*If someone is not sincere,
they can't bear scrutiny in the sunlight.*

June 19 – Puzzles

'Multiplication is vexation,
Division is as bad.
The Rule of Three doth puzzle me,
And Practice drives me mad.'

Anonymous, 16th century

I have no idea what 'The Rule of Three' is. However, I *am* a fan of puzzles and the most avid lover of cryptic crosswords.

My fascination with cryptic crosswords and the beauty of language can be traced back to English classes in Lochaber High School under the tutelage of the head of English, David Chalmers. I adore words, and when they're presented in the puzzle of a cryptic crossword, I'm in seventh heaven. On holiday, I can happily work at a crossword all day, picking it up, putting it down, feeling the flush of success when I've solved a tricky clue, coping with frustration when I've been stuck with six across for ages.

My favourite crossword clue? Here's one.

A B C D E F G ... P Q R S T U V W X Y Z   *(5)*

A puzzle doesn't lend itself to an easy solution – or else it wouldn't be a puzzle, would it? There is a solution, but it requires patience, thoughtfulness and coping with frustration until it comes out right.

And the answer to the clue above? It's WATER – the missing letters H to O ... H_2O ... water, right? OK, I know! A puzzle looks simple when you know the solution, doesn't it?

I wish you well with today's puzzles, cryptic or otherwise.
There will be a solution for you somewhere.

June 20 – Free will

'We assure freedom to the free.'
Abraham Lincoln, Annual Address to Congress, 1862

Buridan's Ass is an illustration of a philosophical paradox in the conception of free will, named after the 14th-century French philosopher Jean Buridan. It's an attempt to satirise Buridan's philosophy of 'moral determinism' and it usually describes a hypothetical situation where an ass that is equally hungry and thirsty is placed precisely midway between a bale of hay and a pail of water. The paradox assumes the ass will always go to whichever is closer, but since the bale of hay is no closer than the pail of water, the ass is unable to make up its mind. So it will die of both hunger and thirst since it cannot make any rational decision to choose one over the other.

Would we have the same problem as Buridan's Ass? I don't think so. For we are not 'stuck' in the same way. We can apply our 'free will' to such a dilemma and make an appropriate decision. 'Ah, a bale of hay *and* a pail of water. Just the ticket! I think I'll just wander over to the hay and have a good lunch; then I'll toddle over to the pail and have a drink to wash it down; then I might have an afternoon snack, and another drink; and then I can have my final drink before I demolish what's left of the hay for my supper. Sorted!'

Free will is important. We have choices. We can work it out, apply all sorts of criteria to our decision-making, and come up with a solution that works.

Make the right choices. There's hay and water aplenty,
if only you get your decisions right.

June 21 – More names

'With a name like yours, you might be any shape, almost.'
Lewis Carroll, Through the Looking Glass

You don't have to spend long in Starbucks before you get to know everyone's name.

'Skinny latté for Caroline?'

'That's a flat white for Shaki!'

'Cappuccino and a regular Americano for Allan?'

You get it? You see, when you order your coffee at one end of the counter – and pay for it – they ask you your name, write it on a cup, pass it along the counter to the member-of-staff-who-actually-makes-the-coffee, and, when it is ready at the *other* end of the counter, they shout out your name so that you get what you ordered and not someone else's drink. Good, eh? Well, yes … but …

'Espresso for … I can't read this. Is it Shammi, no, Sammy … Sammy?'

'Hot chocolate for … someone beginning with M …'

'Frappuccino for … give me a minute … *your writing's terrible, Sonya. What on earth does that say?* Frappuccino for Godfrey?'

Names are precious. Yes, I understand that Starbucks' staff have a job to do. But names are *so* precious, I'm not sure they should be broadcast all over a coffee shop – especially when they're wrong!

Careful, Starbucks! Careful, all of us … We know how much we value people using *our* name with sensitivity, so let's make sure we respect other people's too.

What's in a name?
A precious life. A unique personality. A special individual.

June 22 – Temptation

'Lead us not into temptation.'
Bible, Matthew 5:9

A shopkeeper, seeing a street urchin hanging about outside his shop where there was a tempting display of various fruits, went out to remonstrate with him.

'What are you trying to do, young man?' the shopkeeper asked. 'Are you trying to steal my apples?'

'No, sir,' the lad replied. 'I'm trying not to.'

When King Edward I was collecting treasure for his great campaign against the Scots in the late 13th century, he deposited it in the crypt of Westminster Abbey, thinking there would be no safer place for it. But while the king was away in the north – from 1298 onwards – temptation set in. Some of the monks planted hemp in the cloisters and graveyard, knowing its quick-growing foliage would conceal what was going on, while others began purloining some of the treasure, selling vases, pots and gold artefacts in the City, leaving only the king's crown alone.

One monk, however, couldn't refrain from boasting how rich he'd become, and the theft was discovered – equivalent in today's terms to several million pounds. The Abbot and the monks were imprisoned in the Tower. The king got most of his treasure back. But not before he decided not to trust the monks of Westminster Abbey any longer and to store his treasure in the Tower of London instead.

When we succumb to temptation, there are long-lasting effects, especially on integrity, trust and standards.

The monks knew about temptation.
It would have been better for everyone concerned
if they'd tried not to give in.

June 23 – The natural order

'All things are artificial, for nature is the art of God.'

Sir Thomas Browne, Religio Medici

In one of the gorier parts of the Old Testament, when God's people are settling in their new land, Joshua and the Israelites have been slaughtering or enslaving people from every city and region they come across. In opposition, kings of five Amorite cities form a coalition to stop Joshua. But God tells Joshua not to worry. The Amorites would not prevail. Joshua attacks, while God confuses the Amorites and they run away. God 1, the Amorites 0.

But God is just getting started. He throws down giant hailstones from heaven and kills more Amorite soldiers than the Israelite army. God 2, the Amorites 0.

And then God makes the sun stop moving for 24 hours so that Joshua has plenty of daylight to finish killing off the Amorites. So victory is secured. God 3, the Amorites 0.

God stopped the sun for a whole day? It was this verse, among others, that got Galileo in trouble. If God stopped the sun from moving, then the sun must move around the earth – not the other way around as Galileo hypothesised. Like Galileo, I have a problem with the interpretation that God is in *all* of this. The winners will write history in their own way. But belief is one thing, going against the natural order is quite another. So let belief in God's involvement be explained in ways that reflect reality, and not in ways that make *everything* unbelievable.

Join us again next week for the return leg –
five kings killed and hung on trees …
No, I think I'll miss out on that one, thank you, God.

June 24 – More devotion

'Whatever I am offered in devotion with a pure heart ...
I accept with joy.'
Hindu teaching, from the Bhagavad Gita

Back in 1104 there was an Augustinian priory in the village of Little Dunmow, in Essex. The Lord of the Manor, Reginald Fitzwalter, and his wife dressed themselves as humble folk and begged blessing of the Prior a year and a day after their marriage. The Prior, impressed by their devotion, gave them a blessing along with a flitch of bacon. When Fitzwalter revealed his identity, he gave his land to the Priory on the condition that a flitch should be awarded to any couple who could claim they were similarly devoted.

So began the 'Dunmow Flitch Trials', which, by the 14th century, had achieved far-reaching notoriety, the winners of the Flitch being recorded from 1445. Over the years the custom lapsed. But since the end of WWII the Trials have been held regularly every leap year – not just because of historic precedent, but to give the organisers time to recover their strength to prepare for the next event!

The judging of the devotion of a couple around the 'Dunmow Flitch' is now simply a chance to have fun. But devotion *is* still a serious business. What measurements would we use to judge devotion in any of our relationships?

In Paul's letter to the Philippians (4:8) he says, 'Whatever is true, whatever is noble, whatever is right, whatever is pure, whatever is lovely, whatever is admirable, if anything is excellent or praiseworthy, think on such things.'

A good way to get the Dunmow Flitch, don't you think?

June 25 – Clues

'What's in a name? That which we call a rose
By any other name would smell as sweet.'
William Shakespeare, Romeo and Juliet

In the Tollcross area of Edinburgh there are lots of interesting establishments with fascinating names. Try these, for example: 'Killer'; 'Everest'; 'The Cuckoo's Nest'; 'Hotter Than Hell'. They're the names of a bar/club, a tattoo parlour, an Indian restaurant and a curry house. Which name goes with which establishment? (You'll find the answer later.)

Names often give a clue to what's important in a person or place. Think of what happens in the Forces: Chalky would be someone called White; Taffy would be Evans (or any Welsh name); Ronnie would be Barker; Flash would be Gordon; Buck for Rogers; Perry for Mason; Debbie for Reynolds; not forgetting Dicky Bird, Ding Dong Bell and Smudger Smith (though this one's origins are lost on me).

But some are just obscure. There's a soldier called Thrombo – short for Thrombosis – because the RSM labelled him 'a slow-moving clot'. And there are others that are too rude to include here.

Don't assume you know what someone or somewhere actually is just by their name or label. And don't assume that you know enough about someone or somewhere to think that a nickname gives you all the clues you need.

It's answer time: the bar/club is The Cuckoo's Nest; the tattoo parlour is Hotter Than Hell; the Indian restaurant is Everest; and the curry house is Killer. How did you do?

Clues? Maybe not …

June 26 – Tattoos

'If the doors of perception were infinite ...'
William Blake, The Marriage of Heaven and Hell

He looked scary. I was glad he was in front of me in the queue. That meant he would be well out of my way by the time I was finding a table. It was the tattoos – garish, lewd, too graphic by far. Both arms, neck, hands – and almost everywhere else too, I surmised. And the earrings – seven on one ear and four on the other, and a big black circle in one lobe that I could see right through ... And the big chunk of metal through his eyebrow ... And the nose clip ... And the bandana ... Just too scary for me. A biker, a Hell's thingy, I reckoned, given the look of him – and the leather jacket slung over his shoulder. Scary man; suspicious-looking man.

He paid for his two coffees and pastries and headed off. Good! Well out of my way ...

He was sitting at a table by the window, so I headed to a table as far away as I could. But I couldn't help noticing he wasn't alone. Sitting opposite him was an elderly woman with a tripod-stick beside her. 'D'you want me to cut up your pastry for you, gran?' I heard him say as I went by. 'No, son, I'll manage,' the old lady replied. 'But thanks for asking. You're such a good-hearted soul.'

'Such a good-hearted soul ...' And I was scared again, but this time by *my* tattoos, all those signs that could communicate my prejudices to anyone who happened to be behind me in the cafeteria queue.

Oh, be careful little eyes what you see.
And ask yourself, 'Is it something in me,
A prejudice from which I should be free?'

June 27 – Lift

'Oh, lift me as a wave, a leaf, a cloud.'
Percy Bysshe Shelley, Ode to the West Wind

I'm enjoying running again after many years of little or no physical exercise. I ran a lot when I was younger and fitter, and I have two marathon medals from the Glasgow and Edinburgh marathons in the early 1980s to prove it.

I had some quite odd experiences when I was in training for my marathons – falling over dogs, being sworn at by cyclists, bumping into pushchairs. But by far the funniest happened on one of my 'long runs' through the centre of Edinburgh. To head home, I had to turn off Princes Street and head up 'the Mound'. The Mound, which joins Princes Street to the Old Town's High Street, is one of the steepest hills in Edinburgh. It was murder getting up. And when I reached the top I was in a state of collapse. Fortunately, the traffic lights were in my favour and as I waited for 'the green man', I was glad of the brief respite. I jogged on the spot 'to keep my motor running' and a hearse pulled up at the lights beside me. It was one of the local funeral directors whom I knew well. I acknowledged him with a nod, at which the undertaker wound down his window. 'Hello Mr Gordon. You look as if you need a lift. We can lay you out in the back if you like. We'll have you home in no time.' The lights changed, and he was off.

'Lift?' I thought. He could have waited till I got in ... But I realised he'd already given me the lift I needed, as I chuckled and smiled all the way home.

Give someone a lift today.
Offer them a smile when they least expect it.

June 28 – Greatness

'Greatness, with private men esteemed a blessing.'
Philip Massinger, The Great Duke of Florence

William Whittingham was a Puritan Fellow of All Souls College, Oxford, in the mid-16th century. He fled to Frankfurt to escape the Marian Persecutions. Like many other Protestant reformers, it was necessary to flee from England when Queen Mary I ascended the throne and initiated her policies of hostility and persecution against Reformed churchmen.

In Germany, Whittingham met John Knox and married the sister of John Calvin. He took over Knox's role as established, ordained and recognised minister to the English congregation of exiles in Geneva.

A scholar as well as a churchman, Whittingham was one of the main translators of 'The Breeches Bible', another name for the Geneva Bible. (It gets its name from the translation of Genesis 3:7: *They sewed fig leaves together and made themselves breeches.*) Whittingham became Dean of Durham in 1563 and preached before Queen Elizabeth I. Fifteen years later he was charged with the invalidity of his ordination, but died before the accusation could be proved.

Calvin and Knox were the great Reformation figures. But without the commitment of lesser-known people, like Whittingham, who knows how reformed theology would have spread? The well-known people get the accolades. But greatness also lies with the people who are dressed in ordinary breeches, the less well-known folk, who just get on with the work.

Greatness lies not in fame or accolades,
but in the satisfaction of being the best that we can be.

June 29 – My only support

''Tis not enough to help the feeble up
But to support him after.'
William Shakespeare, Timon of Athens

William Whittingham also issued metrical versions of some of the
Psalms. One of these is this rhymed version of Psalm 23.

The Lord is my only support,
and he that doth me feed:
How can I then lack any thing
whereof I stand in need.
In pastures green he feedeth me
where I do safely lie:
And after leads me to the streams
which run most pleasantly.
And when I find myself near lost
then doth he me home take,
Conducting me in his right paths
even for his own name's sake.
And though I were e'en at death's door
yet would I fear no ill,
For both that rod and shepherd's crook
afford me comfort still.
Thou hast my table richly deckt
in presence of my foe:
Thou hast my head with balm refreshed,
my cup doth overflow.
And finally while breath doth last
thy grace shall me defend:
And in the house of God will I
my life forever spend.

June 30 – A long season

'Love me little, love me long,
Is the burden of my song.'

Anonymous, 16th-century song

I mentioned earlier 'The Breeches Bible' which the Protestant Reformer William Whittingham had a hand in translating. Here, in the language of the 16th century, is the Breeches Bible version of the 23rd Psalm.

The Lord is my shepherd; I shall not want.

He maketh me to rest in greene pasture,
and leadeth me by the still waters.

He restoreth my soule,
and leadeth me in the paths of righteousness
for his Names sake.

Yea, though I should walke through the valley
of the shadowe of death,
I will feare no euill:
for thou art with me:
thy rod and staffe, they comfort me.

Thou doest prepare a table before me
in the sight of mine aduerseries:
thou doest anoint mine head with oile, and my cup runneth over.

Doubtlesse kindnesse, and mercie shall followe me
all the days of my life,
and I shall remaine a long season in the house of the Lord.

July 1 – Complicated

'Human life is a sad show, undoubtedly:
ugly, heavy and complex.'
Gustave Flaubert, Letter to Amelie Bosquet (1864)

I shared thoughts with you earlier about my love of cricket. But did you know that in a rain-affected match the result can be calculated using the Duckworth Lewis Formula? It's a complicated method to work out how many runs a team needs in a shorter time to make the match fair. Following me? No, I didn't expect so. And that's *before* I try to explain how the Duckworth Lewis Formula actually works!

So, should I try to explain the current interpretation of the offside rule in Association Football? I don't think I'll bother with that either. There are times I think it's so convoluted that even the players don't understand it.

When the Roman Catholic Mass was in Latin – before the days of the Reformation – people had little idea what was going on. There was movement and drama, words and actions, but the ordinary folk didn't really know what was happening. Perhaps it was deliberately kept that way. If the people understand these things, they might begin to ask questions, and where would we be then?

That's where the term 'hocus pocus' comes from – people commenting on the 'magic' words used in the Mass. It's where the rhyme of the 'Hokey Cokey' originates too, a parody of the movement and drama of the Mass.

Keep it simple! Life is complicated enough without the basics being made more baffling than they need to be.

*Now, where can I get a priest who plays cricket
to explain the offside rule to me?*

July 2 – Accessible

'It is a thing plainly repugnant to the Word of God ...
to have publick Prayer in the Church,
or to minister the Sacraments,
in a tongue not understanded by the people.'

The Book of Common Prayer, Articles of Religion

I was moved when I visited Iona Abbey recently to find at the main entrance copies of the Bible in two or three dozen different languages. The Word accessible to everyone ...

In the early 16th century, the English scholar William Tyndale passionately believed that the Bible should determine the practice and doctrine of the Church, and that people should be able to read the Bible in their own language, associating himself with Martin Luther and other controversial Protestant religious reformers.

In 1524, Tyndale left England for Germany to continue his translation work in greater safety. A year after his English New Testament was completed and printed in Cologne in 1525, copies were being smuggled into England – the first-ever Bibles written in the English vernacular. Tyndale's work was denounced by the Roman Catholic Church. He was accused of heresy and went into hiding. He moved to Antwerp but was betrayed by a friend, arrested and imprisoned for over five hundred days in Vilvoorde Castle. In 1536, he was tried and convicted of heresy and treason and put to death by being strangled and burned at the stake.

By this time several thousand copies of his New Testament had been printed.

A sacrifice of the highest order, but one which, through the work of Bible Societies worldwide, has not been in vain.

July 3 – Teacher

'Experientia docet'
'Experience teaches'
Cornelius Tacitus, The Histories, Book 5

From the complications of hocus pocus, through an accessible Bible, to William. When I was a parish minister, I offered a 'communicants' class' – a confirmation class. The only one who turned up was William. He was a lad in his mid-twenties who had learning difficulties. The oldest of a big family, he was regularly about the church. He helped out with repairs, tidied away the hymnbooks, moved chairs and came to Sunday worship. I was surprised to see him at the class, as he had shown no interest in such things before. I also knew he had the reading age of someone around 5 or 6 years old, and had no grasp of complicated or abstract ideas.

I looked at my notes for the six-week programme, along with the Bibles, commentaries and study-guides on my desk. And I looked at William. I didn't know where to start. I could see six painful weeks stretching out before me.

So I began the only way I knew how. 'Tell me why you're here.' That was the beginning of a six-week journey of discovery – mostly for me. William talked about feeling at home in the church; how funny I was (nice man!); how people accepted him; how he liked Jesus' stories; what Love meant.

William was my teacher, because he took me beyond 'hocus pocus'. He dodged around complications. He helped me make faith accessible.

Teaching comes from unexpected places and unlikely people.
Thankfully, moments of learning can take us by surprise.

July 4 – Vows

'The first vows sworn by two creatures
of flesh and blood were made
at the foot of a rock that was crumbling to dust.'
Denis Diderot, Oeuvres Romanesques

William knew more about what faith meant than I could ever teach him. However, I realised I still had much to learn when we came to the first two vows for the confirmation service:

Do you believe in one God, Father, Son and Holy Spirit,
and do you confess Jesus Christ as your Saviour and Lord?

'Confess?' he said. 'Ah'm confessin' nothin'. You only confess to the polis, when you've done somethin' bad.'

Do you promise to be faithful in reading the Bible ...?

And, devout though I knew William to be, reading the Bible – reading *anything* – was beyond him.

So in the service, we used none of the prescribed questions. Instead I asked him if he knew God loved him – to which he replied with a hearty 'Aye!'

'Do you want to learn more about Jesus, William?'

'Aye!'

'Do you feel at home with the church family?'

'An' aye to that too!'

William took his vows. He kept it simple and he helped me do the same.

Was it simple? Aye!
And it was more profound than we'll ever know.

July 5 – Outward and inward

'He is the First and the Last,
the Outward and the Inward.'
The Koran, sura 57

I spent three months in the Church of the Saviour in Washington DC in 1989. I have neither the time nor the space here to unfold all the remarkable effects the Church of the Saviour had on me. But I shall choose one.

The founder of and major influence on the Church of the Saviour was Gordon Cosby. A visionary and prophet, Gordon's elucidation of his belief in the 'inward and outward journey' radically changed my thinking. The 'mission groups', the building blocks of the church, were all committed to the journey inward and the journey outward. The outward part was the service element, the project, the doing. The inward part was the growing together, the reflection and prayer. The outward journey without the inward was futile. The inward journey without the outward was self-serving.

The creation of an AIDS hospice – an outward journey with an inward journey to sustain it; the building of low-rent, accessible apartments – an inward journey with its outworking in a community enterprise; the Potter's House Community Church, coffee-shop by day and worship-base in the evenings – an outward purpose and an inward journey going hand in hand.

In a small mission group or a larger church community – outward to serve, inward to learn; outward to work, inward to grow; outward to give, inward to receive; outward to do, inward to be.

Are your journeys inward and outward in balance?

July 6 – Inward and outward

'What kind of deal is it to get everything you want
but lose yourself?'

Bible, Matthew 16:26 (The Message)

Elizabeth O'Connor in *Journey Inward, Journey Outward* wrote: 'We cannot begin to cope with what it means to build a world community unless we understand how difficult it is to be in community even with a small group of people, presumably called by their Lord to the same mission. Nor will we know the full power of the spirit while we cling to our upper rooms.'

The 'journey inward and the journey outward' concept in the Church of the Saviour has been around for centuries. Here's what Bahya ibn Paquda, an 11th-century Spanish-born Jewish philosopher, had to say, from his introduction to *The Duties of the Heart*:

We are obliged to serve God
both outwardly and inwardly.
Outward service is expressed in the duty of the members,
such as prayer, fasting, almsgiving, learning
and teaching the Torah ...
all of which can be wholly performed by man's physical body.
Inward service, however,
is expressed in the duties of the heart,
in the heart's assertion of the unity of God,
in belief in him and in his Book,
in constant obedience to him and fear of him,
in humility before him, love for him,
and complete reliance upon him, submission to him
and abstinence from the things hateful to him.

July 7 – Sitting

'For God's sake, let us sit upon the ground.'
William Shakespeare, Richard II

'Sometimes I sits and thinks, and sometimes I just sits.' It's a statement that's been around for a while, and I love the sentiment it conveys.

When I was on sabbatical leave in Washington DC in 1989, I had the privilege of going to hear people I greatly admired at public speaking engagements. The first was Archbishop Desmond Tutu in Washington Cathedral. He was *fantastic* – passionate, impish, engaging, challenging, funny, stimulating. I sat under him, and I did a lot of thinking – then and later. I think of his sermon even now.

The second was the founder of the L'Arche communities, a French priest called Jean Vanier. His book, *Community and Growth,* had had a powerful influence on me. I admired his spiritual approach to the integration of able bodied and disabled people and folk with a range of mental abilities and illnesses, as they lived, worked and worshipped together in community. I was in the front row when he arrived. I had a notebook with me. But after a few minutes of listening to Vanier's mellifluous and engaging tones, I stopped sitting and thinking and writing. I put my notebook down, and I just sat. I soaked it all in. I was washed by the beauty of his words, his ideas, his thoughts. I was blessed by Jean Vanier's presence.

I remember little of what Jean Vanier said. But I remember how he said it, and how I felt. I just sat, and was the better for being in his wise and humble presence.

Sometimes I sits and thinks, and sometimes I just sits.
I think I should do more of that …

July 8 – Try

'If at first you don't succeed, try, try, try again.'
Mid-19th-century proverb

It's said that cycling is like riding a horse. If you fall off, you must get back on right away to get your confidence back.

When I was nine years old, I had an accident with my bike. I lived in a village outside Fort William in the Highlands of Scotland where I had an uninterrupted view of Ben Nevis from my front garden. At the edge of the village, stretching as far as the eye could see, there was a huge expanse of moorland, peat-bog and small copses of trees. That was our playground! 'Cowboys and Indians', gang-huts, adventures, and, best of all, 'cyclo-cross' tracks for racing each other over the rough terrain. We'd seen the races on TV. We set up our own circuit. It was a magnet for anyone with a bike.

Cyclo-cross can be dangerous. But when it's confined to your 'track' area, you should know what you're about. However, it's *not* a good idea to try it out on busy village streets, without a helmet, going too fast, on the wrong side of the road, and not being aware of an ice-cream van parked where it isn't usually parked. I crashed into the van, went over the handlebars, hit the road, scraped my face and elbow, cried a lot and buckled the front wheel of my bike.

The following day I was to attend a Scout Jamboree in Fort William, scraped face and all. I didn't cycle there. No bike! I went on the bus. But a couple of weeks later, I was back on our cyclo-cross track, making sure there was no ice-cream van parked where it wasn't usually parked.

Try again? Yes, I'll do that.
But I'll try to learn the lessons from past mistakes too.

July 9 – Mistakes

'As she frequently remarked
when she made any such mistake,
it would be all the same a hundred years hence.'
Charles Dickens, Mrs Squeers in 'Nicholas Nickleby'

As a minister, I've made many mistakes over the years. I'm glad other folk in churches do the same.

On behalf of Mary O'Farrel, our thanks to all those sending cards and contributing to the death of her husband.

The senior choir invites any member of the congregation who enjoys sinning to join them at their rehearsal this Sunday.

Rev Wilson, our minister, is on holiday for two weeks. In his absence, massages can be given to church secretary.

Please join us as we show our support for Brian and Sophie in preparing for the girth of their first child.

There is a sign-up sheet for anyone wishing to be baptised on the table in the foyer.

The congregation should remain seated until the end of the recession.

Today's Sermon: 'How much can a man drink?' with hymns from a full choir.

It will, indeed, be all the same in a hundred years' time! So I hope we can all keep laughing at innocent mistakes till then.

July 10 – Marked

'Progress, man's distinctive mark alone.'
Robert Browning, A Death in the Desert

I have a small copy of the New Testament in my study which has always intrigued me. It has a red cardboard sleeve and inside is a New Testament marked in gold lettering, 'South Africa 1901', a year which falls in the middle of The Second Boer War. Perhaps it was given to a soldier going to war, but there is no name inside to identify either the giver or the recipient.

There is, however, this inscription, in best Victorian script, inside the front flyleaf.

The 200 verses marked in this Testament will, under the Holy Spirit's teaching, help to make plain God's way of Salvation through Christ.

There are, indeed, verses marked – some underlined in blue, some highlighted in red, and some in both. And there are 200 of them – I've counted.

I'm intrigued by two questions: 'From whom?' and 'To whom?' Did the donor buy copies in bulk, mark every one of them in similar fashion and give them away to battalions of soldiers? Was this gift to be kept anonymous, unsigned, for fear that the giver would be identified? Was a card or letter given with it so that there was no need for a signature in the book itself? I'll never know. But as I handle this book now, it's clear that the verses were marked for a reason. I hope these distinctive marks made a difference to someone.

'Read, mark and inwardly digest,' we're told.
So, I've read what's marked, for it feeds my very soul.

July 11 – Worth

'Because I'm worth it.'
1980s Advertisement for L'Oreal

In 1793 William Godwin, the 18th/19th-century English philosopher and novelist, in *An Enquiry Concerning the Principles of Political Justice,* wrote:

> *The illustrious bishop of Cambrai was of more worth than his chambermaid. There are few of us who would hesitate to pronounce, if his palace were in flames, and the life of only one of them could be preserved, which of the two ought to be preferred.*

True? Which one is of the greater value, the bishop or his chambermaid? If you've played the party game of imagining a variety of people in a lifeboat and debating which one should be sacrificed for the sake of the others, you'll know how hard it is to decide. It's about worth and value.

I once tutored a university class of engineers in Social and Moral Ethics. One of the case-studies was about which of a dozen people on dialysis deserved the kidney transplant. We had to decide which ones could be eliminated and what our criteria might be – age, family circumstances, health issues, lifestyle, and the like. We whittled the dozen down to seven. Then we agreed that the only way was to draw lots, because each was as equally deserving as the rest.

Every life is of value. The criteria we might use to decide will always be arbitrary and based on our prejudices.

If we begin by valuing every individual,
that's as good a place to be as any.

July 12 – Perfection

'He shall bring together every joint and member,
and shall mould them into an immortal feature
of loveliness and perfection.'
John Milton, Areopagitica

I mentioned William Godwin yesterday. In another of his comments
on the human condition, from his 1793 *Enquiry Concerning the Principles of Political Justice,* we find this:

> *Perfectibility is one of the most unequivocal characteristics of the
> human species.*

We would all like to be perfect. Striving for Godwin's 'perfectibility'
is fundamental to our living.

The Bible talks about 'the Fall', and wraps it up in the Genesis story
of the sinfulness of Adam and Eve in eating the forbidden fruit. Paul
reminds his friends in his letter to the Galatians (5:4) that they are
'fallen from Grace'. But we don't need the Bible to tell us that we are
less than perfect. We are well enough aware of our own imperfections.

It's right, therefore, that deep in our psyche there is this commitment to improve ourselves. Whether we do this through religious
practices, meditation, counselling, self-analysis or the like, there is still
the need to aim for 'perfectibility'.

What are we to do? Give in to our 'fallen' nature or continue to
try to improve? The latter, surely. For perfectibility *is* one of the most
unequivocal characteristics of the human species. Thank God for that!

Perfect? Not me! A good attempt at perfection? That'll do!

July 13 – Remember

'Nor will it ever upset me
to remember Elissa
so long as I can remember who I am,
so long as the breath of life
controls these limbs.'

Virgil, Aeneid, Book 4

Christina Georgina Rossetti was a 19th-century English poet who wrote a variety of romantic, devotional and children's poems. She is famous for writing *Goblin Market* and the words of the Christmas carol *In the Bleak Midwinter*.

The poem which is loved by many clergy – and by me – is Rossetti's poem *Remember*. It's requested and used at many funerals. It has offered comfort and solace to many people in times of loss. You can see why.

Remember me when I am gone away,
Gone far away into the silent land;
When you can no more hold me by the hand,
Nor I half turn to go yet turning stay.
Remember me when no more day by day
You tell me of our future that you planned:
Only remember me; you understand
It will be late to counsel then or pray.
Yet if you should forget me for a while
And afterwards remember, do not grieve:
For if the darkness and corruption leave
A vestige of the thoughts that once I had,
Better by far you should forget and smile
Than that you should remember and be sad.

July 14 – Parlour and closet

'Life is real! Life is earnest!'
Henry Wadsworth Longfellow, A Psalm of Life

I've always been a great lover of the psalms. In the hospice I was constantly pointing people to the psalms for spiritual guidance. From 'My God, my God, why have you forsaken me?' to 'Though I walk through the valley of the shadow of death I will fear no evil', all of life was there.

The writer Isaac Watts felt the same. Watts was a nonconformist minister and a popular preacher in the earlier part of the 18th century. For most of his life he was domestic chaplain to Sir Thomas Abney at Theobalds – one of the promoters of the Bank of England, a benefactor of St Thomas' Hospital and Lord Mayor of London in 1700.

Watts was a prolific hymn writer, working particularly with the psalms, which he considered a depository of all that was required to enhance everyone's spiritual growth. In the advertisement for his 'Psalms of David' in 1718, containing the complete Psalter, Isaac Watts wrote this:

The chief design of this work was to improve psalmody, or religious singing, and to encourage the frequent practice of it in public assemblies and private families with more honour and delight … the Author hopes that the reading of it may also entertain the parlour and the closet with devout pleasure and meditations … he would request his readers at proper seasons to pursue it through; and among three hundred and forty sacred hymns they may find out several that suit … the circumstances of their families and friends; they may teach their children such as are proper for their age … they may be furnished for pious retirement, or may entertain their friends with holy melody.

July 15 – Bones

'Can these bones live?'

Bible, Ezekiel 37:3

You'll be familiar with the story of Ezekiel and the 'valley of the dry bones'. The prophet Ezekiel is struggling with the state of his nation, his religion and his own downcast spirit. He's with his people in exile in Babylon and warns them about God's judgement and the coming destruction of Jerusalem. He tells them about the disasters that will befall the various nations that have oppressed his people. He offers comfort that there will be a brighter future. And he promises that the Temple and nation will be restored.

In the middle is the vision of the valley of dry bones. Ezekiel is taken in a dream to a valley covered in a jumble of bones, which are 'very dry'. 'Tell the bones to fit together,' God commands, 'and when they do, I will hold them in place with sinews and muscles and cover them with skin.' Real bodies appear where there had once been random bones. But the bodies can't move. 'Tell the wind to come and breathe life into these bodies,' God commands him. When he does, the bodies have breath and a mighty army appears.

Some vision, eh? Some encouragement for a depressed man! 'Things may appear dry and lifeless now,' God is saying, 'but just you wait.'

Dry bones, bodies; a mighty army of deliverance? I'm not sure. But did it help Ezekiel remain hopeful? It sure did. Was it the dryness of Ezekiel that had life breathed back into it? You know, that might well be true.

Can these bones live? Indeed, they can –
but only when life and purpose fill their very being.

July 16 – Starting small

'It is so small a thing ...'
Matthew Arnold, Empedocles on Etna

'*Dem bones, dem bones, dem dry bones, now hear da word of da Lord.*' The words of that Spiritual have encapsulated the vision of the prophet Ezekiel when he saw a mighty army arise from a pile of dead bones. And, indeed, it has placed the 'valley of the dry bones' firmly in the human psyche.

However, that wasn't Ezekiel's only vision. On another occasion, he was led to the Temple, and there saw a little trickle of water coming from under the side door. A voice commanded, 'Walk in the water.' He did as he was bid, and the water was over his feet. A thousand cubits were measured and he was commanded, 'Walk in the water.' And he did, and the water was up to his knees. Another thousand cubits ... 'Walk in the water.' And it was up to his waist. Another thousand and it was too deep to touch the bottom.

Ezekiel was then led to the bank of the stream where he saw an amazing sight. For where there had once been a barren desert, there was now a garden of beauty and life. Trees, flowers and animals abounded. People fished from the bank. Ezekiel was enraptured. And the voice spoke to him for a final time. 'Look!' it said. 'See where the water came from.' And when Ezekiel looked back, he saw that 'The water came from the Sanctuary.'

The stream which had changed the world had begun as a little trickle of water from under the side door.

Don't worry if you have to start small.
Step into the stream and get your feet wet.
You'll be amazed at the transformation that might result.

July 17 – Miracles

'Conscious of a continued miracle in his own person.'
David Hume, An Enquiry Concerning Human Understanding

I believe in miracles, because I've seen them with my own eyes. There are plenty of 'miracle' stories: the Red Sea splits apart and the Israelites cross in safety; Moses sees a staff turn into a serpent; Jesus turns water into wine; Paul brings a dead boy back to life. But I don't understand miracles like that. I believe what people say, if what they say is true. But I don't really understand, because I wasn't there. Perhaps I need to apply the hermeneutic I talked of earlier and find a deeper meaning. Yet I *still* believe in miracles ...

I believe in the miracle of a dying miner, troubled by failures in his life, but who finds peace before he dies.

I believe in the miracle of a boy who leaves school with no qualifications, but after a diagnosis of dyslexia goes to night-school, then college, then university, and ends up as financial controller of a multi-national company.

I believe in the miracle of an abused woman, who, despite her fears and the damage to her self-esteem, brings up three children, takes on charity work, then paid employment, and ends up as a clinical psychologist supporting other abused women.

I believe in the miracle of an alcoholic who turns his life around with the help of AA, and trains for the ministry of the Church.

Yes, I believe in miracles, the ones I understand. I believe in miracles. And I know, because I was there.

A 'continued miracle in his own person'?
What's the miracle that's in you, I wonder?

July 18 – Quirky

'And now for something completely different.'

Monty Python's Flying Circus

My first car in the early 1970s was a Ford Anglia in two-tone grey. It was old when I got it from my sister. Some might have described it as 'a heap'. To me it was simply quirky!

You might remember the Ford Anglia – the one with the inwards-sloping rear window. Well, that wasn't the *only* thing that was quirky about mine. The driver's door didn't open, so everyone, including the driver, had to climb in through the passenger side. The starter-motor wasn't bolted on tightly enough, so there was a terrible scraping noise from inside the engine every time I tried to start the car. It had a scary wheel-wobble when it reached 55 mph. The nearside front wing had been full of rust, so the whole thing was held together with chicken-wire filled in with plaster-filler. The floor leaked ... And I just *loved* the old thing.

It was a big thing to part with my Ford Anglia when I went for an 'up-market' replacement. I sold it for a fiver, as I recall. But my memories of that car are lasting and vivid. I've had better cars since – flashier, newer, faster – but none of them as quirky or as loved as my Ford Anglia.

Sometimes it's quirkiness that makes things more loveable. In an age and generation of 'sameness' and 'blandness', something that's different and unique – and quirky – just stands out.

If you have a quirk,
it might be the something memorable and unique in you
that really matters.
And if you know someone who is quirky,
try celebrating that too.

July 19 – The pattern of patience

'I will be the pattern of all patience.'
William Shakespeare, King Lear

Most of us will have learned in school the story of Bruce and the spider – a dispirited Robert Bruce, struggling with defeat, spends time in a cave on Rathlan Island off the coast of Ireland and watches a spider try, try and try again to spin its web. If a spider can try again, thinks Bruce, then so can I.

A romantic tale, perhaps, but one which contains an important truth. For a spider is not only patient and persistent in its task, but it is also delicate in its work, producing webs of amazing form and beauty.

An insight into this appreciation of a spider comes from the observation of the American poet Walt Whitman.

A noiseless, patient spider,
I mark'd, where, on a little promontory, it stood, isolated;
Mark'd how, to explore the vacant, vast surrounding,
It launch'd forth filament, filament, filament, out of itself;
Ever unreeling them – ever tirelessly speeding them.
And you, O my Soul, where you stand,
Surrounded, detached, in measureless oceans of space,
Ceaselessly musing, venturing, throwing – seeking, seeking the spheres,
to connect them;
Till the bridge you will need, be form'd –
till the ductile anchor hold;
Till the gossamer thread you fling, catch somewhere,
O my Soul.

We are also creatures of 'the gossamer thread'. It takes perseverance to build lives of form and beauty with that.

July 20 – Seeing

'O wad some Pow'r the giftie gie us
To see oursels as others see us!'
Robert Burns, To a Louse

There was a Masonic Hall beside my school when I was in P7. Occasionally the school used the Masonic Hall for events, and I was fascinated by the 'All-Seeing Eye'. I don't know to this day whether this is a feature of all Masonic Halls. But the effect of this huge eye painted on the wall has never left me. It was massive, and no matter where I went in the hall, it always followed me. The 'all-seeing eye', indeed.

When my mother told me that 'God can see everything you do', all I could think of was 'the Eye'.

It's hard to accept you're always under scrutiny from a 'divine being' or 'all-seeing eye'. But for me, at least, the problem is more at a human level. I was once asked to meet with a member of my congregation whose marriage was floundering. We met in a café, and, as she tearfully poured out her woes, I took her hand to offer comfort and support. It was only for a moment till she found her composure again. Some weeks later I was taken aside by a colleague at a church gathering, He conspiratorially told me that I'd been seen holding hands with a lady who wasn't my wife – and gave me the place, the date and the time!

Give me the divine 'all-seeing eye' any time, if I can escape the gaze of nosy, speculative and ill-informed people. They have all-seeing eyes I can well do without ...

Am I seen as I would like to be seen?
Am I known as I'd like to be known?

July 21 – Protest

'The lady doth protest too much, methinks.'
William Shakespeare, Hamlet

When I worked in the East End of Glasgow, I met some remarkable people. One of the more eccentric ones was a lady who organised a one-woman protest – and won!

For most of the folk in the West of Scotland, deciding where your allegiances lie is usually about what football team you support, Rangers or Celtic, with undercurrents of religious affiliation. And, of course, there are the colours – Blue for Rangers, Green for Celtic. Granny Betty was a true-blue Proddy. There was no doubting her allegiance.

The Council decided to repaint the common stair where Granny Betty lived – and they chose green! It was like a red rag – or a green one – to a Proddy bull. Cursing the unsuspecting painters made no difference. Complaining to the local councillor, the minister or the MP didn't change things. So Granny Betty went on a one-woman rent strike.

The following weekend it was all over the local paper. There were rumours the BBC would pick up the story. News of the protest reached the Council Chambers. And the result? The painting of Granny Betty's stair was suspended, and the relieved painters redeployed elsewhere. A few weeks later they were back – and the stair was painted blue.

Let's hear it for protesters! Sometimes they win. But protesters should beware too. Choose an issue that's worth protesting about. I'm sure you'll find much greater social ills than the colour of your stair – eh, Granny Betty?

Now, here's a thing …
If there were no protesters, where would change come from?

July 22 – Community

'Individuals pass like shadows;
but the commonwealth is fixed and stable.'
Edmund Burke, Speech in the House of Commons, 1780

Space doesn't permit a long piece about Edmund Burke, nor a lengthy paragraph about politics in the UK in 1780. But I *do* know that Burke was right when he implied that individuals will come and go, but the commonwealth, the stable community around us, remains crucially important.

George MacLeod was born in 1895. He became disturbed by an increasing awareness of the gulf between the haves and the have-nots while working as a young minister in Edinburgh in the 1920s, and he shocked many admirers by taking a post in 1930 as a minister in Govan, a depressed area of Glasgow. Before his drive and vision took him to Iona to begin the rebuilding of the Abbey precincts, to look again at the building up of 'the common life' and to found the Iona Community, George MacLeod showed he believed in the innate goodness and worth of the individual, and the contribution that everyone, regardless of class, status, education or wealth, could make to a stable society.

In Jerusalem in early 1933, while worshipping in an Eastern Orthodox Church on Easter Day, MacLeod felt a sense of recovery of the Church as the corporate Body of Christ which would strongly influence the rest of his life. This was the beginning of an outworking of a passion for the community of God's people, a community built on the worth of the individual, for the good of all.

Community ... com-unity ... Being together in harmony.
Now, that's not a bad place to be!

July 23 – Calling

'The responsibility is yours. You know the way out.'
George MacLeod, Govan Calling

Before publishing his two better-known books, *Only One Way Left* and *We Shall Rebuild*, George MacLeod published in 1934 a book of his sermons and broadcasts entitled *Govan Calling*. This is a remarkable collection, in the format of powerful address and oratorical preaching.

At first reading, *Govan Calling* portrays George MacLeod to be a very different man from the one I knew when I joined the Iona Community in 1973. By that time George was seventy-eight. Perhaps the years had mellowed him – though those who knew him well would give the lie to that. Perhaps his views on pacifism and left-leaning politics obscured the depth of his Christian understanding from the wider public. Certainly, the overt evangelical theology that informed his preaching in his earlier years had become broader and more inclusive. But in re-reading *Govan Calling* it's been good to hear the power of MacLeod's voice establishing what he stood for.

In a sermon in St Columba's Church of Scotland in London to a congregation of young people, he unfolds the story of Peter's call to discipleship, and unashamedly offers an 'altar call', bidding those present to give their allegiance to Christ. And why? Because he believed in them as much as he believed in his Lord. So he called them to believe in themselves, and what they could offer in their own discipleship.

'You have choices,' he is saying.
'Make sure you make the right one.'

July 24 – Follow

'And one clear call for me.'

Alfred, Lord Tennyson, Crossing the Bar

In the sermon by George MacLeod that I mentioned yesterday, 'The only Christ and the average man', a challenging call is thrown to those present to give themselves, like Peter of old, to the service of the Kingdom. His text is from John 21:21, in the King James Bible:

> *Peter, therefore, seeing him [John] saith unto Jesus, 'Lord, what shall this man do?' Jesus saith unto him, 'If I will that he tarry till I come, what is that to thee? Follow thou me.'*

MacLeod had an unshakeable belief in the worth of the individual – to create community, change society and turn the Church upside down. He ends his sermon thus:

> *There is a very old legend ... concerning the return of the Lord Jesus Christ after His Ascension ... The Angel Gabriel met Him at the gates of the city. 'Lord, this is a great salvation that thou hast wrought,' said the angel. But the Lord Jesus only said, 'Yes.' 'What plans hast Thou made for carrying on the work? How are all men to know what Thou hast done?' asked Gabriel. 'I left Peter and James and John, and Martha and Mary, to tell their friends, and their friends to tell their friends, till all the world should know.' 'But, Lord Jesus,' said Gabriel, 'suppose Peter is too busy with his nets, or Martha with her housework, or the friends that they tell are too occupied, and forget to tell their friends – what then?' The Lord Jesus said ... 'I have not made any other plans. I am counting on them.'*

July 25 – Reliance

'Humpty Dumpty sat on a wall
Humpty Dumpty had a great fall
All the king's horses, and all the king's men,
Couldn't put Humpty together again!'
17th-century nursery rhyme

During the English Civil War in the 17th century, the Royalist army took control of the city of Colchester, a Roundhead stronghold. They fortified the city in readiness for a counter-attack. Mounted on the tower of what became known as St Mary's Wall Church they had a massive cannon, much larger than most cannons of the time. Like the oversized people of the day, it had the nickname 'Humpty Dumpty'. As the Parliamentarians began their counter-assault, Humpty Dumpty's gunner was kept busy firing the great cannon at the advancing troops. The siege of Colchester had begun, and the town and its people were battered with cannon-fire day after day. But they still had Humpty Dumpty!

Then a stray shot hit the church tower and the huge cannon tumbled to the ground. The king's men attempted to raise Humpty Dumpty to another part of the wall, but to no avail. The cannon was too heavy and couldn't be hauled back into position – even with the help of all the king's horses.

The Royalists never recovered and eventually surrendered Colchester to the Roundhead troops. The battle had lasted for eleven weeks, and holes from musket balls can still be seen in the timbers of some old buildings.

When any enterprise is reliant on one thing, or one person,
or one approach alone, and that important element fails,
the whole undertaking can come crashing down.

July 26 – Necessity

'Teach thy necessity to reason thus;
There is no virtue like necessity.'
William Shakespeare, Richard II

In the rigours of post-World War-One Scotland, my granny, in her mid to late teens, would be sent to the 'feeing markets' in Graham Square in Glasgow with one of her sisters and wait to be chosen by a farmer. With others, she would then be one of his farmhands for the harvest season. At first it was binding sheaves into 'stooks'. But, in time, she became a dairy-maid on the big farms run by 'the Paisley Corporation', and 'milking the kye' (the cows) was her regular work.

She met and married my grandfather – a cattle-man – on these farms and soon my mother was born. Before the days of the Welfare State, and married to a hard-drinking man, my granny had to return to the milking very quickly (and after a caesarean birth too) or else she would have no money. And, of course, she took her baby daughter with her. What choice did she have? The milking was 'piece work' – the more cows you milked, the more you got paid. My mother would be laid in the straw while my granny did the milking. And from time to time my granny would suckle her baby before getting back to work. 'Milking the kye' and looking after her baby was my granny's world.

What remarkable commitment, resilience and love! My mother grew up to be what my granny called 'a fine young woman'. All because one committed mother was going to give her the best start she could.

Necessity brought out the best possible virtues in poverty and hardship.
Might we learn something from that?

July 27 – Emphasis

'It has long been an axiom of mine
that the little things are infinitely the most important.'
Arthur Conan Doyle, The Adventures of Sherlock Holmes

I get confused about emphasis. When I was younger, the way people pronounced some Glasgow street names was confusing. Why was it *Ren*frew Street when the local borough was called Ren*frew*? And when the town was called *Eld*erslie but Glaswegians talked about Elder*slie* Street, I just didn't get it.

It doesn't stop there. Change the emphasis of *Aug*ust to Aug*ust*, and you have two words with very different meanings. And what do you make of the American tourist on his way to the Highland town of *Mall*aig who asked me, 'Can you tell me where I can find Ma*leg*?' I'm not sure he would have appreciated me pointing out the obvious.

Get the emphasis right, and you can speak like the locals do. Get it wrong, and you may feel out of place.

What about an emphasis in the way we live? If we emphasise attributes that are hurtful, destructive, or nasty, then we should be made to feel out of place, not playing by the local rules of expected human behaviour. But if our emphasis is on the *right* attributes, then everyone benefits.

In his second letter to Timothy, Paul talks about the dishes and bowls in a large house. Some are used for special occasions, and some for 'ordinary'. What Timothy should aim for are the special attributes, the things that matter above everything else. 'Strive for righteousness, faith, love and peace,' Paul suggests.

Righteousness, faith, love and peace.
Any one of these is an emphasis I really like.
Now I know what's important.

July 28 – Grace

'Let your conversation be always full of grace,
seasoned with salt,
so that you may know how to answer everyone.'
Bible, Colossians 6:4 (RSV)

One day a fox came across a fine fat goose asleep by a loch. Sneaking up, the fox grabbed at the goose before she had the chance to escape and held her by her wing. With all her might, the goose struggled to free herself, cackling and hissing loudly as she did so. But the fox held tight to his prey until she was too tired to struggle any longer.

'Ah, I have you now,' the fox exclaimed. 'But before you meet your fate, I have a question for you. If you had me in your mouth as I have you, tell me, what you would do?'

'Why,' said the goose, finding her voice at last, 'that is an easy question. I would fold my hands, shut my eyes, say a grace, and then eat you.'

'Yes indeed, for that is just what I mean to do.' And, folding his hands and looking suitably humble, the fox offered a pious grace with his eyes tightly shut. But while he did so, the goose had spread her wings, and she was now flying half way over the loch.

The fox was furious with himself for having been duped out of his supper. 'I will make a rule,' he said in disgust, 'never in all my life to say a grace again till after I've eaten my fill. Grace after I'm satisfied will suffice. Grace before I eat, and I may have nothing to eat at all.'

Grace before, or grace after?
I'm never sure.
But surely it has to be somewhere …

July 29 – Autograph

'Was there ever yet anything written by mere man
that was wished longer by its readers,
excepting *Don Quixote, Robinson Crusoe,*
and *Pilgrim's Progress?*'
Samuel Johnson, Anecdotes of Samuel Johnson

When I was young I had an autograph book. I had my dad's auto-graph on the first page – *By hook or by crook I'll be first in this book. Jimmy Gordon.* My dad was the most famous person in my autograph book!

Autographs are big business. At a recent auction a letter signed by John Logie Baird, the Scottish inventor of colour TV, was estimated to be worth £600. The signature of Thomas Edison, who developed the electric light bulb, was selling for £2000. You can get a signed pen-portrait of Mark Twain for £3,000, and a full set of early auto-graphs of the Beatles for a mere £12,000.

A handwritten musical score, signed by the composer and with his or her annotations throughout, is 'An Autograph Score'. Such 'autographs' are precious and beautiful. When my wife was doing her degree in music, we went to see Handel's autograph copy of *Messiah* in the British Museum. It was deeply moving to know that the hands of the composer had rested on the pages in front of us.

Autographs are unique. Yours or mine may never sell for thousands of pounds or find themselves in the British Museum. But they are still exclusive, precious and distinctive. They distinguish us in our uniqueness.

Next time you see me, I'll sign your book for you, if you like.
Then you and I will share a moment of uniqueness together.

July 30 – Signature

'Progress, man's distinctive mark alone.'
Robert Browning, Death in the Desert

I spoke yesterday about the importance of autographs. Every auto-graph – every signature of every person – is reckoned to be as distinctive as their fingerprints. John Hancock's signature is the most prominent on the United States Declaration of Independence. As a result, 'John Hancock' has become a synonym for a signature in the USA. 'Just put your John Hancock right here, kind sir, and the deed will be done.'

Of course, there will be people who try to forge the signature of another person – on a will, a title deed, a cheque, or even on a painting. There are handwriting specialists who investigate such attempts at forgery – the slope of the writing, the joining of the letters, the loops below or above the line, the strength of the pen-strokes. A signature defines authenticity.

Signatures can mean more than handwriting too and often indicate the unique identity of something. A Coke bottle is said to be of a signature shape. Rock guitarists can create a signature sound. A wrestler may have a signature move that is distinctive to them.

We all have a signature. It's the way write our name. But we have signatures beyond that. In his letter to the Galatians, St Paul wrote about the 'fruits of the spirit', the signature of a good person: 'Love, joy, peace, patience, kindness, goodness, faithfulness, gentleness, and self-control. Against such things there is no law.'

With a signature life such as that, there can be no dispute.
That's just the kind of authentic person we'd all like to be.

July 31 – Pillars

'Wisdom hath builded her house,
she hath hewn seven pillars.'
Bible, Proverbs 9:1

St Athanasius was Bishop of Alexandria in the fourth century AD. A renowned Christian theologian and a noted Egyptian leader, he is a saint venerated in both the Catholic and Coptic traditions. A few years after his death, Gregory of Nazianzus called him the *Pillar of the Church.* In the Eastern Orthodox Church he is hailed as the *Father of Orthodoxy.*

Now, I'm delighted St Athanasius is venerated in such a positive fashion. But I have problems with the 'pillar' idea. It's a word that crops up in church circles, and it's used to describe someone who is solid and dependable, someone whose life and work can be relied on, and whose commitment is strong enough to be a support for the Church. When people in Scotland are referred to as 'Pillars of the Kirk', we know exactly what's meant.

But it's when we get to the 'Father of Orthodoxy' concept that I begin to worry. Many of the 'Pillars of the Kirk' I've known over the years have been completely *immovable* in their orthodoxy. Strong and committed they may be. But when they're stuck, unchanging, too-big-to-move, inflexible, and all that goes with 'pillars', then there's a problem.

We need pillars like St Athanasius, whose strength of wisdom and commitment can be built on. But we *don't* need pillars who are immovable and unchanging, so that we can only build a house that is never more than orthodox.

Solid and strong I can live with.
Static and unwilling to change I can't.

August 1 – Power

'To defy Power, which seems omnipotent.'
Percy Bysshe Shelley, Prometheus Unbound

I recently saw an amazing movie called *The Wave.* Directed by Rooar Uthaug and starring Kristoffer Joner, this Norwegian 'catastrophe movie' tells the story of the Norwegian village of Geiranger which is threatened with destruction when a huge mass of rock tumbles into the Geirangerfjord, setting off a tsunami three hundred feet high. The star of the movie is 'the Wave' itself, and the sheer power of such a natural phenomenon is more than adequately portrayed by remarkable cinematography and special effects.

Just after I'd seen *The Wave* there was news of a devastating earthquake in the Umbria region of Italy. At the time of writing this, reports are that 250 people have been killed, among them three British holidaymakers, and rescue workers are still searching for victims in the rubble.

The power of nature is an awesome thing. When it can be controlled – as with dam systems for hydro-electric power, or through wind-farms or wave-generators – its power can be put to good use. But when it is uncontrolled, the power of nature can wreak unbelievable destruction.

We have power too. It might be a little or a lot. It might be local or global. It might be inconsequential or crucially important. It might lie in our words or in our actions. So channel your power well, and everyone benefits. But let it loose in an uncontrolled way, then devastation and destruction will inevitably follow.

How will you use the power you have?

August 2 – Brains

'When the pulse begins to throb,
the brain to think again.'
Emily Brontë, The Prisoner

In 1998 at the age of thirty-five, Jon Sarkin, a chiropractor from Massachusetts, USA, developed a deafening tinnitus caused by a blood vessel in his head pushing against the acoustic nerve. He was operated on, but the treatment caused a massive stroke and parts of his brain had to be removed. Recovering from surgery, Jon found he was deaf in one ear, his vision splintered, and his balance permanently skewed. But, most importantly, the injury to his brain caused a personality change, and he became obsessed with drawing. Before his stroke, Jon Sarkin had done little more than doodle. But soon the urge to draw began to consume his life. It turned out that he was experiencing a condition called 'sudden artistic output', which is so rare that doctors have only recorded three cases caused by brain injury.

He took the art world by storm. In 1993, he sold eight pictures to *The New Yorker*, gave up his business and opened an art studio. In 2011 he was the subject of a book, *Shadows Bright as Glass*, by Pulitzer Prize-winning author Amy Ellis. His drawings are now worth many thousands of dollars. The explanation? The neurons in the brain had made new connections, resulting in new ways of thinking and acting, thus making Jon Sarkin the remarkable artist he is. New connections resulting in new ways of thinking and being ... the remarkable brain doing a remarkable job.

When we make new connections with each other,
might we find new ways of thinking and being together?
That would be remarkable too.

August 3 – Imaginative

'Hunting grounds for the poetic imagination.'

George Eliot, Middlemarch

My mother's favourite book was *The Robe* by Lloyd C Douglas, a popular American author of the 1940s. The book explores the aftermath of the crucifixion of Jesus through the experiences of the Roman tribune Marcellus Gallio and his Greek slave Demetrius. Marcellus is banished to command the garrison at Minoa in Palestine. In Jerusalem during Passover, Marcellus carries out the crucifixion but is troubled by his belief that Jesus is innocent. He and other soldiers throw dice to see who will take Jesus' seamless robe, and Marcellus wins. Following the crucifixion, he takes part in a banquet attended by Pontius Pilate. A drunken centurion insists Marcellus wear the robe. When he does, Marcellus suffers a breakdown and returns to Rome.

Sent to Athens to recuperate, he gives in to Demetrius' urging and touches the robe. His mind is restored. Believing the robe has some sort of innate power, he returns to Judea, follows the path Jesus took and meets many people whose lives Jesus had affected. Demetrius and Marcellus become Christians, and Marcellus returns to Rome to report his experiences to the emperor, Tiberius. Because of his uncompromising stance regarding his Christian faith, both Marcellus and his wife, Diana, are executed by the new emperor, Caligula.

An imaginative way of getting into or behind a story we think we know well; a 'robe' that embraced my mother, and many others, with new ideas and insights.

Imagination, offering a new understanding of truth and faith.

August 4 – Madness

'Though this be madness, yet there is method in't.'
William Shakespeare, Hamlet

During my time in Washington DC in 1989, our family was entertained by some very kind people at their home in the suburbs of the city. The community in which they lived had a neighbourhood swimming pool, and, as guests of the local people, we had much enjoyment using the facilities on a blisteringly hot day. Our children had a ball!

A few weekends later, we were invited back, and the children were, of course, excited about using the pool again. But that day was grey and overcast, still warm and humid, but just dull! Keen to cool themselves off, the children asked if they could go down to the pool. Our hosts looked puzzled. 'But,' they said, 'it's not pool weather.'

The wishes of the children prevailed, however, and down to the pool we all trooped. No one was swimming. The attendant had to open the changing-rooms especially for us. The Gordons were in the water with no one else to be seen. The neighbours were taking photographs. The pool attendant was highly amused. And our hosts were heard to remark, 'They're all mad, these Scots.'

'All mad'? Perhaps there *was* a touch of madness in that day. But I wonder how quick we are to label something 'madness' when we simply don't understand it; to misinterpret as a mental health issue behaviour that doesn't fit our expected patterns; worse still, not to accept a mental illness and simply label it as 'madness'?

Let's be careful of judgements.
'All mad these Scots'? Not so.

August 5 – Reassurance

'Lo, I will always be with you, even to the end of time.'
Bible, Matthew 16:20

A couple of years ago, my wife and I spent time with our friends, Michael and Susan, in Oregon in the USA. They have a timeshare in the village of Otter's Crest, on the Pacific Coast in the north of Oregon. Their house is in a complex and has one of the best views of any property. From their front room we could look down over a rocky cove, with a beautiful beach of yellow sand. Out in the bay there was an island with flocks of pelicans coming and going. There were dory boats fishing out on the Pacific. There were wonderful breakers on the shore, and, with binoculars, we could see schools of whales further out to sea. And, of course, there were glorious sunsets over the Pacific Ocean. It was idyllic, and for three nights we marvelled, photographed, talked, drank single malt and gave thanks to God. All was well.

Then one morning when we came down for breakfast, it had all gone. A mist had rolled in from the Pacific. And there was no cove, no beach, no island, no pelicans, no whales ... nothing at all. It had all disappeared. Michael came to join us. He'd seen this before. There was no panic, no sadness for him. 'Don't worry,' he said, reassuringly. 'It's still there. And even though you can't see it for now, it's not gone away. You'll see it again soon.'

Don't worry. It's still there. It's not gone away. You'll see it again soon. And we did. Later in the morning, in all its glory and wonder, the beauty returned, for us truly to enjoy.

When the mist comes down, we need patience till it clears.
When love is hidden, we need to know it has not disappeared.

August 6 – Measurements

'Give and it shall be given unto you;
good measure, pressed down,
shaken together and running over.'
Bible, Luke 6:38

I once measured something in centimetres, went to the DIY store and bought a piece of wood in inches. I had a *lot* of wood left over! It's just as well I didn't measure it in inches and buy it in centimetres. That *would* have been a disaster.

Measurements matter. When I was a smoker and my GP asked me how many I smoked a day, I always lied. The measurement he got was less than what I knew to be fact. Weight? Alcohol consumption? Age? Measurements matter. Getting them wrong doesn't do anyone any good – least of all yourself. And what about *Bake Off* or *Sewing Bee* or *Master Chef*? Wrong measurements? Disastrous cake ... Jacket doesn't fit ... Dish over-salted ...

The story in the Bible of David the shepherd boy facing Goliath the giant begins with measurements. Goliath, the Philistine champion, is massive – tall, wide, big, strong. All the measurements are in his favour. David, on the other hand, is small. The armour he tries on is *way* too big! Big defeats little? Strong defeats weak? On the measurements of power and might that's what would be expected. But you know the outcome of the story. David goes to face the giant with no armour at all and only armed with a sling and some stones. And he strikes Goliath down. David trusts a higher power. His measurements weren't what everyone else used.

Measurements matter.
Will you measure up in the right way?

August 7 – Competition

'Thou shalt not covet; but tradition
Approves all forms of competition.'

Arthur Hugh Clough, The Latest Decalogue

When I was coming to Edinburgh after two years in Glasgow, I was told by the people in the church I was working in, 'The only good thing to come out of Edinburgh is the Glasgow train.' It was a reminder of the rivalry between two of Scotland's great cities. The capital and the largest city in competition, one believing it is superior to the other.

When Glasgow became City of Culture in 1990 I heard two Edinburgh ladies on the top deck of a No. 27 bus discussing the issue. The conversation concluded with, 'And what did Glasgow ever know about culture?' Well, quite a lot, as it turns out. Which city has the Burrell Collection and the Kelvingrove Art Gallery –and lots more besides?

In 1995, a special conference of the Labour Party passed a new 'Clause Four' in its constitution.

A community in which power, wealth and opportunity are in the hands of the many not the few, where the rights we enjoy reflect the duties we owe … in which the enterprise of the market and the rigour of competition are joined with the forces of partnership and cooperation.

Competition for its own sake may only lead to bitterness and conflict. But when it's joined with the forces of partnership and cooperation, everyone benefits.

*My competition? An angel on one shoulder
and a devil on the other – and me caught between the two.*

August 8 – Emoticons

'I kept silence, yea, even from good words;
but it was pain and grief to me.'

Bible, Psalm 37:36

Working with people who are bereaved, I'm always on the lookout for new books, pamphlets and leaflets with imaginative insights into the grief process. So I was delighted to come across a little mobile-phone-sized leaflet produced by the Perth and Kinross Schools Bereavement Project, supported by Cruse Scotland. It's called *The Smart Grief Guide,* a simple, creative and accessible leaflet, produced by school students for young people who are bereaved.

The Smart Grief Guide utilises 'emoticons', frequently used by the younger generation as they communicate with each other by text and social media. Emoticons are cartoon-style depictions of the whole range of human emotions, based on the 'smiley face' idea. *The Smart Grief Guide* covers the emotions associated with bereavement, allowing young people in their grief to see that the feelings they are experiencing are quite normal. Hurt, loneliness, sadness, being strong, anger, confusion, forgetting and guilt are all there, each emoticon showing what it feels like, with a short explanation about what this means.

We know that the grief journey is full of emotion. But how do we know what's normal when we've never been on this journey before? Leaflets like *The Smart Grief Guide* can help with that. The emoticons 'tell it as it is', and help people see how normal they and their emotions are.

Show me how you feel – emoticons and all –
and I'll tell you that you're OK.

August 9 – Still Waiting

'They also serve who only stand and wait.'
John Milton, Sonnet 16

Sometimes we have to wait for a clear direction in life.

I know not where life bids me go,
Through fire and flood, through rain and snow,
To find that home of cherished rest,
Where I must stay at life's behest,
And know this as the dwelling place
Where time would have me blessed with grace.

So to my fate I'll be resigned,
To make the best of what is mine,
Surrounded by familiar things,
To wait to see what life might bring;
To be what I must be, and stay
Till life reveals a different way;

To wait, and not to know how long,
To hold my nerve, remaining strong;
To pray, and keep my hopes in check,
Not knowing what might happen next;
To be at peace – the hardest thing –
Unsure of what the day will bring.

One day I'll know where I must go –
The clearer path; the to and fro;
The ups and down; the turns and twists.
Till then, I am assured of this –
It will not change if I complain.
The waiting will not be in vain.

August 10 – Telltale signs

'In hoc signo vinces.'
'In this sign shalt thou conquer.'
Constantine the Great, traditional form of Constantine's vision

You can tell if a man is a dog-owner if he reaches into his pocket to pull out a handkerchief and a poo-bag flutters to the floor. It may be a search for car keys, or loose change, but if there's a poo-bag in there, it can fly away almost at will. It doesn't happen so much for female dog-owners, I've discovered. Perhaps they're better organised and keep their poo-bags separate from other things. But men? With all the junk we keep in our pockets it's not surprising that a forgotten poo-bag escapes our notice – and our grasp – from time to time.

It happened to me at a church reception, attended by the great and the good, with me in all my clerical finery. I took my handkerchief from my pocket and a pale-blue, delicately-scented poo-bag glided forwards to rest decorously on the uppers of my shoes. As I bent down to retrieve it, muttering an apology, the Cardinal with whom I had been in conversation made no comment. But by the twinkle in his eye, I reckoned he was a dog man himself.

Poo bags – and a twinkle in the eye – can tell us things we'd rather no one else knew. I'm not particularly adept at interpreting body language, but I know some people who are experts at it. What signs am I communicating without knowing it? Quite a lot, it seems. So I hope that they're the right ones and that other people can read me properly.

Excuse me, is that a sign from above?
No, it's just a poo bag fluttering to the floor.

August 11 – Trusting

'My sure trust is in thee.'

Bible, Psalm 71:6

A little boy walked down a beach towards the water, always in sight of his parents. As he neared the water's edge, he saw two elderly ladies engrossed in their books, sitting under a large beach umbrella.

The boy stopped beside them and looked at them very seriously. One of the women looked up from her book and asked what on earth he was doing.

'I need to ask you something,' he replied.

'Yes, and what might that be?' the lady replied, somewhat puzzled by the little lad's directness.

'Do you go to church?'

Taken aback, she replied, 'Yes, I do, actually.'

'Do you read the Bible every day?'

'Yes, I do that too,' said the lady, indignantly.

'Do you pray every day?'

Becoming rather irritated, the matronly lady replied, 'That's very personal, but, yes, I do indeed pray every day. Now, I think that's enough of your questions. Run along, and leave us in peace.'

'Can I ask you one more question, please?'

'Well, if you must,' the lady responded.

'Would you mind looking after my 50p while I go into the water?'

Where do we put our trust?
How do we know it's right?
What will you take from me
When I am out of sight?

August 12 – Attics

'Dusty, cobweb-covered, maimed and set at naught,
Beauty crieth in an attic, and no man regardeth.'
Samuel Butler, Psalm of Montreal

I was once asked by a man in the hospice if I could spend time helping him clear out his 'mental attic' before he died. It was a most appropriate image, for his 'attic' was a jumble of all kinds of things, some of which had lain untouched for years. But the task he had set himself was an important one. However long he had to live, he was determined to let go of life with his mental attic tidied. He fulfilled his promise to himself. His attic was sorted before he died.

The trouble with helping him with his tidying, though, was that I had to go into his attic with him. I could have ducked it by giving him instructions and telling him what to do. Or I could have told him he didn't need to bother, and if he wanted to see a relatively tidy attic he could have a look at mine. But neither way would have worked. I had to go into his attic with him and be there while the sorting was done. He couldn't do it on his own.

When you go into any attic, your own or someone else's, some of the dust and cobwebs will stick to you. You'll get messy. That's expected. Any carer will tell you that. So it was important for me – and it should be for you – to make sure time was spent dusting myself down. 'Attic tidiers' have to make sure they clean themselves up too. Only then can we be ready to go with someone else on another day to another attic and share another attic-tidying exercise.

*Now, is there anything in my attic
that needs sorting before I carry on with life?*

August 13 – Daytime

'O my God, I cry in the daytime,
but thou hearest not.'

Bible, Psalm 22:1

The development of daytime television in recent years elicits a variety of reactions. If you mention that you're familiar with *Bargain Hunt, Homes Under the Hammer, Flog It, Escape to the Country, Rip-off Britain, Loose Women, Judge Rinder* and an endless variety of daytime quiz shows, you run the risk of being mocked for 'having nothing to do all day but watch TV', and to be judged as a 'couch potato' or, even worse, 'lacking in intellectual discernment' – and yes, I've heard just that said in my company.

Of course, avid watchers of daytime TV might be open to such criticism. But *before* there was such a prodigious output of TV programmes in the mornings and afternoons and there was only the test card to look at till 5 o'clock, I was acutely aware of many people who were confined to their homes with no stimulation whatsoever from one day's beginning to the next. Read a book? But what if your eyesight's not good enough? Listen to the radio? But what if there's nothing there that's suitable?

Whatever you think of it, for many people daytime TV serves an important function. As my granny would say – who only ever had two channels and watched everything in black and white – it 'takes people out of themselves', allowing folk to be aware of a world outwith their own four walls, engaging them with things beyond their reach.

'This is God's day,' the Psalmist said.
Why would we mess it up instead?

August 14 – Anchors

'The ship is anchored safe and sound,
its voyage closed and done.'
Walt Whitman, O Captain! My Captain!

When I was young, I was in the Boys' Brigade. I'd been thrown out of the Cub Scouts for being rude to Akela, and my parents sought to get me back on the straight and narrow by enrolling me in the BB. They weren't wrong.

The Boys' Brigade was started in Glasgow in 1883 by Sir William Smith. With its motto of 'Sure and Steadfast' it has been an important stabilising influence on many boys – including me – for well over a hundred years.

In the 1960s the junior section of the BB was called 'The Life Boys'. We sported an old-fashioned sailor-type hat, and the emblem was a lifebelt. When I went up to the senior section – and got to wear a pillbox hat – the emblem was the anchor. Nowadays the pre-junior section of the BB which began in 1977 is called 'The Anchor Boys', showing how important the anchor remains in the organisation.

Ask any BB member – former or current – and they'll sing you the BB hymn, 'Will your anchor hold?' Living in a fishing village as I do, I know the importance of anchors. Two huge anchors overlook Port Seton harbour. Every boat, large or small, for pleasure or for work, has an anchor on board.

We need anchors in life – faith and family, stability and familiarities, purpose and fulfilment – that will hold firm in the storms, won't drag when we are battered by the winds and will keep us safe and secure in tough times.

What are our anchors now?
And will they be steadfast and sure when we need them?

August 15 – Hermits

'The bliss of solitude.'
William Wordsworth, I wandered lonely as a cloud

In the early years of the pilgrimages around Iona, there was a pattern that seldom varied. The second half, after the picnic lunch, led from the Machair, the common grazing on the west of the island, across rough terrain to the 'Hermit's Cell', thence up Dun I, the highest point on Iona, before descending again to St Oran's Chapel and home.

The Hermit's Cell has always fascinated me. It's a small oval of stones, clearly the foundation of a solid structure, set beneath Dun I. It's believed that it was a place of retreat from the medieval Abbey community, for the bliss of solitude, silence, prayer and reflection. It was a cell for the hermit life.

A more recent suggestion is that it was no more than a sheep pen, a place of shelter from the vagaries of the West Highland weather, and has nothing whatever to do with the Abbey and hermits, solitude and prayer, or time apart from others. But I like the original notion, whether it's true or not. It is necessary to escape even from a medieval abbey, a place of worship and the common life – to solitude instead of community, prayer instead of busyness, hours of silence instead of a daily routine.

I hope you find your Hermit's Cell, and if you discover that it was only a sheep pen, give yourself to the thought that at least you have a place where the bliss of solitude provides you with shelter from the vagaries of the weather on your pilgrimage that is hard to bear.

Shhhh! Quiet now!
There might be something to listen to in the silence ...

August 16 – Miracle

'Beneath the shadow of Thy Throne
Thy saints have dwelt secure.'
Isaac Watts, Our God

One of the earliest legends about the Loch Ness monster is that of St Columba's encounter with the beast. St Columba, or Columcille as he was known, had come to the west coast of Scotland from his home in Ireland, and was responsible for the spread of Christianity in Scotland and beyond. He carried with him the guilt of being partly responsible for the death of many men in the Battle of Cul-drebene, and when he landed on the island of Iona, and found that, looking back, he couldn't see the shores of Ireland, he decided to stay.

Legend has it that, on his way to visit the Pictish king in Inverness, he encountered some Picts burying what remained of one of their own people – badly savaged, he was told, by 'a creature in the loch'. The dead man's boat lay on the other side of the water, so Columba ordered one of his followers to swim over and retrieve it. While he was swimming in Loch Ness, the servant was attacked by a creature that reared out of the loch. Invoking the name of God, Columba commanded the beast to return to the depths and it vanished beneath the waters leaving the swimming man unharmed. Columba 1, Loch Ness Monster 0. Swimmer, much relieved. Picts? Well, greatly amazed, as you can imagine.

This miracle played a big part in the conversion to Christianity of the Pictish king. Are you surprised?

If I can do a miracle, can I become a saint?
Being me is miracle enough. Am I a saint now?

August 17 – Comparisons

'I will not reason and compare:
my business is to create.'
William Blake, Jerusalem

'Shall I compare thee to a summer's day?' is the opening line of Sonnet 18 by William Shakespeare. It's a rhetorical question. Shakespeare isn't asking permission to do a comparison. He launches into it, and in wonderful language the comparison of his love with the wonders of a summer's day unfolds beautifully.

Poets use metaphors and similes to make comparisons and to express emotion, beauty and love. 'My love is like a red, red rose' writes Robert Burns. And in her poem *Clouds,* Christina Rossetti says what she sees:

> *White Sheep, white sheep on a blue hill,*
> *When the wind stops you all stand still.*

But the use of comparisons isn't confined to the world of poetry. Comparisons are with us all the time and they're not always beautiful – whether as a comparison to someone else: 'She's not like the minister we *used* to have'; or a destructive metaphor: 'When he comes into a room the temperature falls by ten degrees'; or the withering simile: 'Her voice is like the jag of a needle at the dentist.'

When comparisons are used well, they are life-affirming. But when they're used destructively, they can be cruel and hurtful.

> *Beware of unhelpful comparisons;*
> *they might be as much use as a chocolate fireguard.*

August 18 – Walls again

'Let's start the rebuilding.'
Bible, Nehemiah 2:18

When the people of Israel returned from exile, under the guidance of Ezra and Nehemiah they began to rebuild Jerusalem. The ruined walls were reconstructed, a metaphor for the rebuilding of their community and their nation.

When George MacLeod began the rebuilding programme for the living quarters of the Abbey on the island of Iona, he too had a concept of community. With artisans and church ministers in training, skilled craftsmen and labourers working together, worshipping at the beginning and end of each day and sharing the common life, community was created. The physical rebuilding of the walls was a metaphor for the restoration of community.

But MacLeod took the metaphor further. Watching the stone-masons, he became aware that when a stone was taken up onto the platform where the mason was working, it might not fit into the wall immediately. But it would not be thrown down again. Instead, it would be kept to one side, ready to be used when the right place for it became apparent. Every stone, large or small, would in time find its place in the wall. The rebuilding of community wasn't possible unless every person in their place was valued.

The next time you're in an old building where the walls are exposed, look at how the big stones and the little stones fit together. In the rebuilding of community, like the rebuilding of old walls, everyone has a place. Ezra and Nehemiah knew that. So did George MacLeod.

In our churches and communities, how do we fit together?

August 19 – Conscience

'O pure and noble conscience,
how bitter a sting to thee is a little fault.'

Dante Alighieri, Divine Comedy

There are clever people in the fields of psychology and criminology who can 'read people' by tiny signs in their body language, eyes, facial expressions and the tone of their voice. As a result, they can tell whether someone is lying or not. They reckon our conscience can't be hidden and always affects the way we behave.

One day, King Akbar lost his ring. When Birbal, his trusted chief minister, arrived in the court, Akbar confided in him. 'My father gave me his ring as a gift when I was a young man,' he said. 'I fear one of my courtiers has stolen it, but I cannot accuse them all. Please help me find my ring.'

'Do not worry, Your Majesty,' Birbal replied, 'I will find your ring right now.'

Birbal cast his eye around the palace and over the assembled courtiers. Then he announced, 'Your Majesty, the ring is here in the court. It is indeed with one of the courtiers. I shall tell you now that the courtier who has a straw in his beard has your ring.'

The courtier who had the king's ring was shocked and immediately moved his hand over his beard. Birbal noticed this act of the courtier and immediately pointed to him and said, 'Please search this man. He has the king's ring.'

Akbar could not understand how Birbal had managed to find the ring. But Birbal told the king a guilty person is always scared.

A guilty conscience needs no accuser.

August 20 – Bridges

'Everyone speaks well of the bridge that carries him over.'
Late-17th-century proverb

On the B844 road, just over ten miles south of Oban on the west coast of Scotland, is the Bridge Over the Atlantic. It's a little humpbacked bridge joining the tiny Seil Island with the Scottish mainland, and its real name is the Clachan Bridge. The bridge spans the tidal waters of the Atlantic Ocean at Clachan Sound, and although it's on a single-track road, the 'hump' of the bridge is quite substantial and obscures any view of oncoming traffic. It's a delightful little place, and it is, indeed, a Bridge Over the Atlantic.

It was built between 1792 and 1793, at a cost then of £450. Nobody's quite sure who the designers and builders were. Some attribute the bridge to Thomas Telford, others to a local builder, John Stevenson. Maybe lots of people collaborated on the project. But what we do know is that the Bridge Over the Atlantic has stood the test of time. Today, forty-ton lorries cross the bridge, thanks to additional strengthening, though local legend tells of a fully laden cart of hay being used to test its safety 200 years ago.

Though I haven't been there to see for myself, I'm told that around May of each year the bridge takes on a purple appearance, as flowers of the beautiful fairy foxglove cover its surface

I like the idea of a bridge over the Atlantic, not for romantic, floral or historical reasons, but because bridges between nations matter.

Let's build bridges.
If love and friendship cross over them with big lorries or carts of hay,
we'll all be the better for it.

August 21 – Blessings

'Pour upon them the continual dew of thy blessing.'
The Book of Common Prayer, Morning Prayer for the Clergy and People

There are many blessings which have their origins in Celtic traditions in Scotland and Ireland. The most familiar is this:

May the road rise up to meet you.
May the wind be always at your back.
May the sun shine warm upon your face;
the rains fall soft upon your fields
and until we meet again,
may God hold you in the palm of His hand.

Here are two more. You can choose the one which blesses you – and others – the most.

If there is righteousness in the heart,
there will be beauty in the character.
If there is beauty in the character,
there will be harmony in the home.
If there is harmony in the home,
there will be order in the nation.
If there is order in the nation,
there will be peace in the world.
So let it be.

May you have walls for the wind,
a roof for the rain, and drinks bedside the fire,
laughter to cheer you, and those you love near you,
and all that your heart may desire.

August 22 – More blessings

'Ye fearful saints fresh courage take,
The clouds you so much dread
Are big with mercy and shall break
With blessings on your head.'
William Cowper, Olney Hymns

I mentioned Celtic blessings yesterday. Here are two more. May they bring you the blessings you seek.

May God be with you and bless you.
May you see your children's children.
May you be poor in misfortune, rich in blessings.
May you know nothing but happiness from this day forward.

The blessing of light be on you, light without and light within.
May the blessed sunlight shine on you like a great peat fire,
so that stranger and friend may come and warm himself at it.
And may light shine out of the two eyes of you,
like a candle set in the window of a house,
bidding the wanderer come in out of the storm.
And may the blessing of the rain be on you;
may it beat upon your Spirit and wash it fair and clean,
and leave there a shining pool
where the blue of Heaven shines, and sometimes a star.
And may the blessing of the earth be on you,
soft under your feet as you pass along the roads,
soft under you as you lie out on it, tired at the end of the day;
and may it rest easy over you when, at last, you lie under it.
May it rest so lightly over you that your soul may be out from under it
quickly, up and off and on its way to God.
And now may the Lord bless you, and bless you kindly.

August 23 – Condemned

'Condemn the fault and not the actor of it?'

William Shakespeare, Measure for Measure

Driving my two grandsons home, I had this conversation with them. Alexander (aged 8): 'Granny *(his other granny, not my wife)* and I worked out the gold, silver and bronze medal-winners of who are the best drivers in our family. *(This granny doesn't drive. And, of course, neither does he!)*

Me: 'Oh? And who won?'

Alexander: 'Dad, because he's best.'

Me: 'OK. And the silver medal?'

Alexander: 'That's granny. She's nearly as good as dad, but not quite.'

Me: I see. And the bronze winner?

Silence

Cameron (aged 5): Why are you not saying?'

Silence

Me: 'OK, I know it might be embarrassing. But who won the bronze? Was it me or your mum?'

Silence

Me: 'Oh, come on …'

Alexander: 'Well, actually, we decided that you and mum were equal last because you're both terrible.'

Cameron: 'That'll be because my mummy's your daughter, grampa.'

Silence

Me: 'For goodness' sake, what's that driver doing?'

Cameron: 'That's what mummy says too, grampa.'

Alexander: 'And that's why you and mum both got the bronze medal.'

Silence – for the rest of the journey home.

August 24 – Wow!

'Indeed, I am not envious, rather I am amazed.'
Virgil, Eclogues No. 1

Close to where I was brought up in the Lochaber area of the western Highlands of Scotland, there is a remarkable geological feature called 'The Parallel Roads of Glen Roy'. Along both sides of a U-shaped valley there is a series of distinctive 'parallel roads' above the valley floor.

Early travellers were told that the parallel roads were made by giants, as described in Gaelic myths. Some believed that such precisely engineered features couldn't possibly be natural and that, in some way or another, they had been made by human activity.

As the founding fathers of geological science – such as Reverend William Buckland, James Geike, Charles Lyell, Joseph Prestwich and even the great Charles Darwin – continued to expand their understanding of the natural world, it became clear that the parallel roads were caused by ice-age glaciers. The Parallel Roads of Glen Roy are neither mythical nor human-made. They are a natural product of a remarkable world. They are no more or less than the shorelines of several ice-dammed lochs over eons of time.

As our understanding of the development of our planet has progressed over the past century, there are more explanations of remarkable geological features than ever before, from the Grand Canyon through the Serengeti Plain to the Parallel Roads of Glen Roy in Scotland.

I hope we will never lose our sense of awe and wonder at such things.

Come with me to Glen Roy and say, 'Wow!'

August 25 – Preference

'Loving not, hating not, just choosing so.'
Robert Browning, Caliban upon Setebos

The Bonnie Hoose o' Airlie is a Scottish ballad recounting the burning and sacking in 1640 of the castle of the Earl of Airlie, a supporter of King Charles I, by the Duke of Argyll.

It fell on a day, a bonnie summer's day
When the sun shone bright and clearly,
That there fell oot a great dispute
Atween Argyll and Airlie.
Argyll he has mustered a thousand o' his men,
He has marched them oot right early;
He has marched them in by the back o' Dunkeld,
To plunder the bonnie hoose o' Airlie.

When I was young, 'The Bonnie Hoose o' Airlie' was presented in a different fashion.

Hey, bonnie lassie, will ye, will ye gang
Tae the bonnie, bonnie hoose o' Airlie?
Hey, bonnie lassie, will ye, will ye gang,
Tae feed my faither's ducks.
Wi' a quack, quack here, and a quack, quack there,
Here a quack, there a quack,
everywhere a quack, quack.
Hey, bonnie lassie, will ye, will ye gang
Tae the bonnie, bonnie hoose wi' me?

The song proceeds in *Old MacDonald* style. A gory story or a bit of fun for children … What's *your* preference?

August 26 – Down to earth

'Here rests his head upon the lap of Earth
A youth to fortune and to fame unknown.'
Thomas Gray, Elegy Written in a Country Churchyard

The Pueblo people are Native Americans of the South-western United States. The Pueblos built substantial dwellings made of adobe and other local materials, and lived in settled communities. They constructed their buildings in strategic positions, with many rooms and differing layouts, often in defensive positions. But despite their settled nature, the Pueblo tribes were still people of the land.

In their religious practices, they used 'prayer sticks', colourfully decorated with beads, fur and feathers (like the 'talking sticks' I'll mention later). Many of their religious stories are about relationships among people and nature, including plants and animals. They prayed to their deities and often used substances as well as words – like the white cornmeal common in their culture – seeking blessings and love. Here is a section of a prayer based on the beauty, colour and design of a traditional woven blanket.

Oh, our Mother the Earth, oh, our Father the Sky,
We bring you the gifts that you love.
Then weave for us a garment of brightness.
May the warp be the white light of morning.
May the weft be the red light of evening.
May the fringes be the falling rain.
May the border be the standing rainbow.
Thus weave for us a garment of brightness,
That we may walk fittingly where birds sing,
That we may walk fittingly where grass is green.
Oh, our Mother the Earth, oh, our Father the Sky.

August 27 – Depth

'Far beyond my depth.'
William Shakespeare, Henry VIII

Yesterday we thought about the Pueblo approach to prayer. Here's another reflection from the Native American tradition, from Tecumseh, a 19th-century Shawnee chief:

Live your life that the fear of death
can never enter your heart.
Trouble no one about his religion.
Respect others in their views
and demand that they respect yours.
Love your life, perfect your life,
beautify all things in your life.
Seek to make your life long and of service to your people.
Prepare a noble death song
for the day when you go over the great divide.
Always give a word or sign of salute
when meeting or passing a friend,
or even a stranger, if in a lonely place.
Show respect to all people, but grovel to none.
When you rise in the morning, give thanks for the light,
for your life, for your strength.
Give thanks for your food and for the joy of living.
If you see no reason to give thanks, the fault lies in yourself.
When your time comes to die,
be not like those whose hearts are filled with fear of death,
so that when their time comes
they weep and pray for a little more time
to live their lives over again in a different way.
Sing your death song, and die like a hero going home.

August 28 – Being at one

'All things and I are one.'
Zhuangzi, Chuang Tzu Chapter 2

Chief Crazy Horse, of the Native American Oglala Lakota Sioux, is quoted as speaking the words below in the 1870s when he sat smoking the Sacred Pipe with Sitting Bull for the last time. Crazy Horse was killed four days later by US Army soldiers in a hand-to-hand scuffle as they attempted to imprison him. He and his people knew about 'suffering beyond suffering'.

*Upon suffering beyond suffering
the Red Nation shall rise again
and it shall be a blessing for a sick world;
a world filled with broken promises,
selfishness and separations;
a world longing for light again.
I see a time of Seven Generations
when all the colours of mankind will gather
under the Sacred Tree of Life
and the whole Earth will become one circle again.
In that day, there will be those among the Lakota
who will carry knowledge and understanding
of unity among all living things
and the young white ones will come to those of my people
and ask for this wisdom.
I salute the light within your eyes
where the whole Universe dwells.
For when you are at that centre within you
and I am that place within me,
we shall be one.*

August 29 – Partial

'To observations which ourselves we make,
We grow more partial for th'observer's sake.'
Alexander Pope, To Lord Cobham

If you were on the game-show *Name That Tune* and they played the
theme tune from *The Archers*, could you name it? If you shout out,
'It's *The Archers*', you would be wrong. It's name that *tune*, not 'tell us
what that tune's used for'. The correct answer is 'Barwick Green', a
maypole dance from the suite *My Native Heath* from 1924 by the
Yorkshire composer Arthur Wood. Even though the tune is so familiar,
I wonder how many people would get the correct answer.

Who knows that the tune for *Mastermind* is *Approaching Menace* by
Neil Richardson, or that the opening music for the BBC's Wim-
bledon coverage is *Light and Tuneful* by Keith Mansfield, or the current
opening music for *Panorama* is a track called *Aujourd'hui C'est Toi
(Today It's You)* by French composer Francis Lai. We *think* we know
something because it's familiar, but our knowledge is flawed. What
we know is only partial.

In the beautiful hymn in praise of love which comes in the middle
of Paul's first letter to the Corinthians, there is this passage:

> *Love never ends. If there are prophecies, they will be set aside; if there
> are tongues, they will cease; if there is knowledge, it will be set aside.
> For we know in part ... but when what is perfect comes, the partial
> will be set aside.*

If we're in a 'partial' place, we don't know everything. When our love
is partial, we still have a long way to go.

August 30 – Rivers

'Still glides the Stream, and shall forever glide.'
William Wordsworth, The River Duddon

When excavations were being carried out while the Iona Community was reconstructing the living quarters around the restored medieval abbey on Iona, there were many surprise discoveries. The foundations of the Michael Chapel, to the east of the Abbey buildings, were unearthed in 1944. Two ancient pathways running west and north from the chapel ruins appeared in the excavations,

The one to the west runs beneath the medieval buildings and may be the relic of a late-Celtic pathway, for the chapel is orientated on the Celtic principle and out of alignment with the Abbey. The one to the north was formed of long granite boulders clearly covering a culvert.

Did a stream once run north to south under the Chapel itself, known about and then covered in? If so, this would almost prove the foundations were Celtic. For the Celts built their earliest chapels over running streams.

A stream under a chapel? A symbol of movement to balance the static nature of the building above? A reminder of the life and vibrancy of their religion? The river carrying the message of the Love of God beyond one group of people, in one place, at one time, out into the world? Lots to think about there ...

Or maybe it was just a chapel over a stream for Celtic worshippers to know that they could stop for water on the occasional sunny Scottish day!

Perhaps the Celts had it right.
The streams of water mattered, to the church, to the community,
to every individual who needed the Water of Life.

August 31 – Disappointment

'We may avoid much disappointment and bitterness of soul
by learning to understand how little necessary to our joy
... are the things the multitude most desire and seek.'
John Lancaster Spalding, Aphorisms and Reflections

It's very hard being a Scotland football supporter. As a proud member of the 'Tartan Army' I've followed Scotland through thick and thin – or through thin and thin, as someone has suggested. When there is Sir Chris Hoy in cycling, and Sir Andy Murray in tennis, why can't we produce stars who help us win things on the football field?

In the summer of 2016, when England, Northern Ireland, Wales and the Republic of Ireland were all at the Euros in France, and Scotland weren't there because we didn't qualify, all the disappointment came flooding back. It was hard, very hard, being a Scotland supporter when the Tartan Army were all sitting at home.

So what do we do? We get ready for the next campaign. As I'm writing this, we're in the middle of the qualifying games for the World Cup in Russia in 2018. Will Scotland be there? Who knows? Will there be more disappointments? Of course! But will we give up supporting Scotland? Will the Tartan Army fail to turn up? Certainly not. *Certainly* not.

'I pick myself up, dust myself off, and start all over again.' So sang Nat King Cole. That could be the mantra of the Tartan Army. But, more than that, it is advice to everyone who is coping with any disappointment at *any* time.

In life, disappointment is a given.
It's how we deal with it that matters.

September 1 – Still learning

'Of such deep learning little had he need.'
Edmund Spenser, Prosopopoia or Mother Hubberd's Tale

A Sunday school teacher was trying to help her class learn familiar passages from the Bible. One of these was Psalm 23. Some of the children took a long time to learn the Psalm, while a few picked it up without any problem. But for one lad, it was just too much. He tried and tried, but he just couldn't get it at all. He could barely get past the first line. The teacher reassured him that this would be fine for him and that he wasn't to worry. And she reckoned that a single not-so-good-one in her class could be lived with.

A minister was visiting the class and the teacher boasted how good the children were with scripture.

'So, let's hear one,' he suggested. 'You there ...' and be pointed to the little lad in the front row. 'What scripture have you been learning?'

The teacher was mortified. The others in the class collectively held their breath.

'Psalm 23,' chirped the little lad.

'OK, then,' said the minister. 'Stand up and let's hear how much you know.'

The little lad in the front row stood up, and in his best public-speaking voice said loudly, 'The Lord is my shepherd ... and that's all I need to know!'

'Thank you,' said the minister. 'I think your teacher has been helping you get to know scripture very well indeed.'

We don't always get all the details right.
But grasping the essence is a good place to start.

September 2 – Hospice

'For the world, I count it not an inn, but an hospital,
and a place, not to live, but to die in.'
Sir Thomas Browne, Religio Medici

Among the many things that I learned during my fifteen years as a hospice chaplain were these two important pieces of information: firstly, the concept of 'hospice' is not a modern phenomenon, and stretches much further back than the beginning of the 'hospice movement' of Dame Cicely Saunders and others in the 1960s; and, secondly, the idea of 'hospice' originally had nothing to do with death.

The word 'hospice' has the same root as hospital – as in the words of Sir Thomas Browne from the 17th century quoted above – and hospitality. A hospice was no more or less than a 'place of rest for travellers'. Hospices sprung up in Europe in the Middle Ages along the pilgrim routes. Weary pilgrims, needing rest and recuperation on their travels, would find welcome, shelter, food and care before they moved on. It wasn't about sickness (the medieval monasteries had an infirmary for people who were infirm or in need of medical care), far less about death. It was about rest at the end of a long day, in an environment of peace and care, gathering strength and resolve for the next stage of the journey.

I like that concept. It was a metaphor for my hospice chaplaincy role. Together we offered a time of rest, a period of waiting, an opportunity to gather strength – strength of the spirit if not the body – for the next stage of the journey.

Weary travellers finding a place to rest on life's journey.
Hospices matter – at any stage of life.

September 3 – Look before you leap

'And all who heard should see them there,
And all should cry, "Beware! Beware"'
Samuel Taylor Coleridge, Kubla Khan

A fox was roaming around in the dark. Not having a light to guide him and there being no moon in the sky, the unfortunate fox fell into a well. No matter how hard he tried he couldn't get himself out. Exhausted, the fox resigned himself to staying in the well till the following morning.

Just after sunrise, a goat came along. He peeped into the well and saw the fox there. 'What are you doing there, Mr Fox?' he asked.

Now, the fox was very cunning. 'I came here to drink the water,' he said. 'And, do you know, Mr Goat, this is the best water I have ever tasted. Why don't you come in and see for yourself?'

Without thinking for a moment, the goat jumped into the well, quenched his thirst and then realised that there was no way to get out. 'Oh dear, Mr Fox,' said the doleful goat, 'we are both trapped in this well.'

But the fox said, 'I have an idea, Mr Goat. You stand on your hind legs. I'll climb onto your head and get out. Then I shall help you come out too.' The goat had no knowledge of how cunning a fox could be, so he did as the fox suggested and helped him get out of the well.

The fox went on his way leaving the goat stuck in the well. 'Huh!' he said, 'if he'd been intelligent enough he would never have got in without knowing how to get out.'

'Look before you leap.'
Don't walk blindly into anything without thinking.

September 4 – Carry On

'Keep Calm and Carry On'
A 1939 government motivational poster

The *Carry On* movies – all thirty-one of them – are a British comedy institution. With a cast of familiar faces getting up to all sorts of silly things, *Up the Kyber, Camping, Columbus, Cleo, At Your Convenience* and in a host of other ridiculous situations, they have a 'carry on' of the silliest kind.

We all like a bit of a carry on sometimes, when silliness takes over and we have a right laugh. But there's a 'carry on' of another kind that matters even more.

I once had a conversation with an elderly lady in the vestibule of my church. After a few minutes, I realised that her underskirt had fallen down and was now decoratively draped around her shoes. She hadn't noticed. I didn't know what to do. Should I warn her not to move in case she tripped? In the end, I said nothing. And I was relieved when, noticing what had happened, she bent down, retrieved her underskirt, stuffed it into her handbag, and carried on with our conversation as if nothing had happened. That's the kind of 'carry on' I really like.

I've been watching the Paralympics from Rio. Time and time again there are powerful images of people who have decided to 'carry on', despite accidents and injuries, birth defects and disabilities, tragedies and life-changing events. Whatever life has thrown at them, they've decided to carry on. What an example they set!

Having a carry on can be silly.
Choosing to carry on can be profound.
I know which one has the bigger effect on me.

September 5 – Taste

'Every man to his taste.'
Late-17th-century proverb

One of the best jobs I ever had as a student was working with a Council work squad repairing the roads in the north-west of Scotland. One of our projects was to strengthen the ditches on either side of the single-track road between Glenfinnan and Mallaig. It's a much better road now, but in the 1970s it was only nine-feet wide, and, if you slipped off the edge, you were in danger of sinking up to your windscreen in peat-bog. Our task was to fill in the ditches for several miles south of Mallaig.

Whatever we were doing would be called to a halt at the *slightest* drop of rain. So we spent a lot of time in our 'hut', a cabin-type construction in a lay-by, playing cribbage, reading newspapers, and debating the future of the world.

On Friday pay-packet day, the foreman would drive to Mallaig to pick up the wages, and return at lunchtime with the pay-packets and ... several pairs of Mallaig kippers. No one asked where they came from in case 'lorry' and 'falling off' might be involved, because Friday kippers were special. They were cooked on a clean shovel in their own oil, over the gas-burner on which we made our daily 'brew'. And we partook of our feast from back copies of *The Daily Express*. It was *exquisite!* I can taste those Mallaig kippers even now.

'Every man to his taste', and I have mine – on a wet day, in a steamy hut, with my work crew, tucking into the best meal I think I have ever had.

'Every man to his taste.' Each to their own.
Isn't variety the spice of life?

September 6 – Together again

'The exercise of singing is delightful to Nature,
and good to preserve the health.'
William Byrd, Psalms, Sonnets and Songs

I've discovered the delight of 'Shapenote Singing'.

The music we sing is unaccompanied three- and four-part vocal harmony in a rustic style dating back to 18th- and 19th-century America, still a living tradition in the South and being taken up all over the English-speaking world and beyond. The songs are found in 'tune books' such as the Sacred Harp *(1844) ... and new tunes are constantly being composed. The words are usually (though not always) religious in nature, but people of all faiths and none sing this music, not as an act of worship but for sheer enjoyment. It's not a performance but a communal participative event.*

There are four shapes – Fa (triangle), Sol (circle), La (square) and Mi (diamond) – the singing sometimes being described as FASOLA. But more important is what it means: *It's not a performance but a communal participative event.* The singing takes place in a square. The singers face inwards and sing to each other. Someone picks the tune, stands in the centre, leads the singing and beats time. *The singing is communal and not for performance.* We sing for our togetherness – and that's enough.

Singing draws people together.
If it can bring them even closer physically,
it's 'delightful to Nature'
and a good preserver of our health and well-being.

September 7 – Influence

'No trivial influence ...'
William Wordsworth, Lines composed a few miles above Tintern Abbey

The Festival Centre is a beautiful multipurpose building in the heart of the Adams Morgan district, a vibrant and diverse neighbourhood in north-west Washington DC. The building was dedicated in September 1989. During that summer I spent three months in this part of DC working with the Church of the Saviour. For more than 20 years the Festival Centre has offered a 'ministry of presence' in the Adams Morgan area and to the Church of the Saviour's faith communities. It has served as a welcoming crossroads and encouraging gateway to the spiritual growth of many people.

John Levering was the driving force behind the Servant Leadership School and the Festival Centre which is its home. I spent many hours with John, and he offered a ministry of presence to me at a crossroads in my life. So today I pay tribute to the influence of this remarkable man.

I lived for a time with John and his wife, Sarah, while he was having treatment for cancer. He died while I was with them. A celebration of his life took place in the Festival Centre, the place of his vision and commitment. In his living, John Levering taught me many things. In his dying, he taught me even more. Did he know the legacy he would leave behind? Maybe he did. Did he know what his lasting influence would be on me? I suspect not. But now, as I think of him, I give thanks for his legacy in my life, as I hope you will give thanks for the influence of many people in yours.

Pay tribute now to the people that matter to you.

September 8 – Flying

'Which way shall I fly?'
John Milton, Paradise Lost

I wrote a poem for John Levering. It needs no comment.

John gave me a picture before he died.
John was an artist, and a beautiful man,
in his heart, by his faith, and with his artist's hands.
And his beauty, his love with Sarah,
his commitment to his God, changed my life.
John gave me a picture before he died.
He had listened to me
as I unfolded my search for fullness of life,
for deepening of faith, and for beauty in me.
He had listened – for that was his gift – as I offered insights –
from Iona, from family, from faith, from my journey thus far.
He had listened to me in his dying.
John gave me a picture before he died –
wild geese in flight, painted from what he had seen,
and known, and understood of faith, and life,
and the soaring of the Canada geese –
wild geese in flight, wings outstretched for their journey.
John gave me a picture before he died.
He offered me no words of explanation; none were needed.
John gave me a picture before he died.
Now I look at the picture and see the geese still flying,
untiring on their journey on,
and I see John, and Sarah,
and I give thanks for their beauty, always with me.
John gave me a picture before he died,
and I have its beauty still.

September 9 – Busy

'How doth the little busy bee improve each shining hour,
And gather honey all the day from every opening flower!'
Isaac Watts, Against Idleness and Mischief

There's a story in Luke's Gospel about Jesus visiting friends:

Martha welcomed Jesus as a guest. She had a sister named Mary, who sat at the Lord's feet and listened to what he said. But Martha was distracted with all the preparations she had to make, so she said, 'Lord, don't you care that my sister has left me to do all the work alone? Tell her to help me. But the Lord answered her, 'Martha, Martha, you are worried and troubled about many things, but one thing is needed. Mary has chosen the best part; it will not be taken away from her.'

When you're a 'little busy bee' and you don't take time to stop and reflect, you may end up with problems. At the very least, you may not give sufficient time to reflection and prayer. At the very worst, you may succumb to burnout.

I get that. I do worry, however, that Martha is given a bad press. I've criticised Marthas often enough for being too busy to stop and think. I've pleaded with Marthas to take time out. I've supported Marthas who are broken with over-work. I've been at the funerals of many Marthas. Yes, I've *also* given Martha a bad press. But remember this … if Martha isn't there doing the work, not a lot gets done.

Different people have different gifts.
Even in the one person, there are many sides.
Let's not dismiss busyness as always being a negative thing
when it may simply be the other side of a complete person.

September 10 – History

'If history records good things of good men,
the thoughtful hearer is encouraged
to imitate what's good.'
The Venerable Bede, Ecclesiastical History of the English People

Street names in any city or town offer clues to the history that surrounds a particular area. Stroll down Edinburgh's Royal Mile and even before you know it links Edinburgh Castle and Holyrood Palace (and that it's a mile long) you're aware that it's a thoroughfare associated with royalty. Turn the corner into George IV Bridge, and you have a fair idea that this street was named after a particular king. Go to the north of the city and drive along Ferry Road and it doesn't take much to work out that this road led to or from a ferry. London Road was the main road south from Edinburgh – heading to London, of course. Could The Grassmarket give you a clue to what would have happened there? Might Waterloo Bridge be named after something significant?

But what about Fishwives Causeway? What happened there, and when, and who was involved? And Moira Terrace? Who was Moira, with a street called after her *first* name, no less? And Little France Mills? Intriguing, or what?

We have pointers to history all around us, some of which require a bit of thought to get to the bottom of the real story. We have people around about us all the time too. Some of the things you know about them will be pretty obvious. But with a little attention we might learn a whole lot more.

The name or what's obvious isn't all there is.
There may be a lot more history waiting to be discovered.

September 11 – Jumping to conclusions

'This denoted a foregone conclusion.'
William Shakespeare, Othello

I once got a phone call from a man I thought I knew well. He was the father of a large family of boys who were in and out of trouble with the police and I always suspected the father was up to no good. When I answered the phone, I realised the man's speech was slurred. It was so indistinct that I had to ask him several times to repeat himself, which he did – *very* slowly. From time to time he would stumble over his words and then correct himself. I was irritated. 'Mr Johnstone,' I said, 'you've been drinking. Perhaps it would be better if you called me back when you are sober.'

There was a lengthy silence before my caller replied – *very* slowly, 'I don't drink, Mr Gordon. Perhaps you didn't know I'm recovering from a stroke I had six weeks ago.'

How quick we are to jump to conclusions. We think we know all about someone, or a situation, or a place, but our judgements are based on what's presented to us, and a lack of knowledge, and, perhaps, an unfortunate impatience. We jump to conclusions, and often get things wrong.

Jesus once met a man called Zacchaeus who, being small, had climbed a sycamore tree to see Jesus go by. Jesus stopped, called him down and invited himself to tea. The people were full of consternation. 'We know this man,' they said. 'He's a tax-collector, and up to no good.' But there was more to Zacchaeus than people were prepared to find out.

Conclusions are easy to jump to,
but if you jump too quickly,
you might be in for a nasty fall.

September 12 – Guns

'There was a little man, and he had a little gun.'
Nursery Rhyme, Tommy Thumb's Pretty Song Book (c1744)

Having brought up three children, and now spending time with two grandsons, I know how hard it is to steer youngsters away from pretending to shoot people with made-up guns. When I was young, it was no different. A shinty stick became a sub-machine gun; a walking cane was a Lee Enfield rifle; a tree branch gave you a bazooka; a twig became a revolver. And the games were Jerries and British, Cowboys and Indians, Cops and Robbers. Boys were getting shot all the time.

With the advent of computer games, and even construction toys like Lego bricks, the issue is no different. So what do we do in the face of the increase in gun crime in the USA? What stance do we take in the light of mass shootings? What do we say about the killing of innocent children in Iraq and Syria because arms companies sell guns to oppressive regimes?

I have no definitive answer – apart from emotions and gentle words. I cry – in front of my children and grandsons – when I see random killings on TV, and I tell them why. My wife will calmly tell our grandsons that people don't bounce up again in real life after they're shot, the way they do in cartoons or video games. We're not dictatorial. We don't spoil their fun. They're going to build guns out of Lego no matter what we say. But, through emotion and explanation, we plant some seeds about another way.

Blessed are the peacemakers,
for they shall be called the children of God.

September 13 – More wisdom

'Mere cleverness is not wisdom.'

Euripides, Bacchae I

King Akbar was very fond of Birbal, his chief minister, whom he trusted for his faithfulness and wisdom. The courtiers were jealous and one of them wanted to be chief minister himself. One day Akbar praised Birbal in front of this courtier. This made the courtier angry. He said that the king had praised Birbal unjustly. 'My Lord King,' he said, 'if Birbal can answer my question, I will accept that he is indeed intelligent and worthy of your praise.'

Akbar, happy to test Birbal's worth and believing in his wisdom and knowledge, readily agreed. So the courtier quickly wrote down his question and handed it to the king. The king looked worried, but, having agreed to the test, he knew he had to go through with it.

He called Birbal before him and said, 'Birbal, here is your question. If you cannot answer it, I would have to insist that you resign as chief minister.'

'Yes, master,' Birbal replied.

'Well, then,' said the king, 'this is your question. How many stars are there in the sky?'

The courtier smirked. The king waited. Birbal stood in silence, pondering the conundrum. Suddenly he rushed out of the palace and returned with a hairy sheep.

'I will answer the question in this fashion,' he said. 'There are as many stars in the sky as there are hairs on this sheep's body. My friend the courtier is welcome to count them if he likes.'

Birbal kept his job! That's wisdom for you …

September 14 – Doors

'I'd rather be a doorkeeper in the house of my God
than to dwell in the tents of ungodliness.'
Bible, Psalm 84:10

Most of the doors I pass through I simply take for granted, using them
with little or no thought. But there are some doors which are far
from ordinary for me.

One is the door into the Church of the Nativity in Bethlehem.
During a pilgrimage to Israel/Palestine, I was deeply moved by the
door through which the pilgrims enter what is believed to be the
location of Jesus' birth. It's four feet high and about two feet wide,
and to pass through it everyone has to bow low and make themselves
very small. Not surprisingly, it's known as 'The Door of Humility'.
Every pilgrim to that holy place has no choice but to be careful and
humble before they pass through the door.

The second is the entrance to St Peter's Basilica in Rome. The
Holy Door – *Porta Sancta* – which faces the Piazza San Pietro – is
only open every 25 years during a Year of Jubilee. The message by the
Holy Door is that God's mercy reaches out to mankind's frailty.
Knowing nothing of this, I strode through the entrance, assuming it
was always open, and in such a rush that I wasn't prepared for the
wonder and beauty beyond it. Stepping inside, I broke down in tears.

We might know what we will find on the other side of a door, or
we might not. We might be fearful or full of anticipation. But, whatever door it is, perhaps having to be careful, and pausing in humility
before we rush on, will better prepare us for the transition from one
side of the door to the other.

Acknowledging our frailty can give us the humility we need.

September 15 – Quarrels

'The quarrel is a very pretty quarrel as it stands –
we should only spoil it by trying to explain it.'
Richard Brinsley Sheridan, The Rivals

The street outside our local school is reasonably wide, but one day a delivery van was carelessly parked, making the street too narrow for other vehicles to pass each other. The inevitable happened ... two cars approached from opposite ends of the street, and neither was prepared to give way. They inched forward till they were bumper to bumper. There was much shouting and gesticulating, but neither driver was prepared to back off. A crowd soon gathered. Some said one driver was in the right. Some favoured the other. The stand-off escalated when the two drivers squared up to each other and almost came to blows. Each side cheered their favourite.

Just then, the school bell rang, and people went off to collect their children. The delivery driver returned. Whatever he said to the two drivers, both of them returned to their cars and backed off down the street. The delivery van made its exit, and the cars passed each other with the minimum of fuss. Two of the parents, recounting the saga to me later, concluded with this wise assessment: 'That's how war breaks out, you know.'

Written above the main entrance to Harvard Yard in Cambridge, Massachusetts there is a quotation from the Roman poet Horace. The English translation reads:

Thrice blessed (and more) are they whom an unbroken bond holds and whose love, never strained with nasty quarrels, will not slip until their dying day.

That's how peace breaks out, you know ...

September 16 – Improvement

'When we take people ...
merely as they are, we make them worse;
when we treat them as if they were what they should be,
we improve them as far as they can be improved.'
Johann Wolfgang von Goethe, Wilhelm Meisters Lehrjahre

At a recent week in the Abbey on Iona of which I was co-leader, a staff member was facilitating the welcome for the guests on the first evening. She arranged for us to chat in pairs for ten minutes to learn about someone we hadn't met before, and then for each of us to introduce that person to the rest of the group. It was informative and effective.

Before we concluded, she played a piece from Mendelssohn's *Hebrides Overture* – 'Fingal's Cave' – and invited us to reflect on what it is in an orchestra that might give us clues to building community during our week together in the Abbey. There were many suggestions – everyone playing their part; some less prominent than others; the piece can be interpreted in different ways; listening to what's going on round about you; everyone takes the credit; coping with mistakes – showing that everyone was picking up clues that mattered.

I told folk that in Edinburgh there's a group called 'The Really Bad Orchestra', giving not-so-good players a chance to play together. One of the other guests chimed in, 'We have a 'Really Bad Orchestra' in our town too. They were once asked, "But what'll happen if you get better?" to which the answer was, "We'll have to play something more difficult."'

*There should always be the challenge of 'playing something more difficult',
or otherwise how are we ever going to improve?*

September 17 – Silence

'Elected Silence, sing to me
And beat upon my whorlèd ear,
Pipe me to pastures still and be
The music that I care to hear.'
Gerard Manley Hopkins, The Habit of Perfection

I've spoken earlier of the powerful effect that my time in the Church of the Saviour in Washington DC had. As part of my reflective processes, I enrolled in a 'Spirituality' class in the Servant Leadership School, part of which was to go on a silent retreat. The Church of the Saviour runs a retreat centre, the Wellspring Community, set in woodland outside Washington in rural Maryland. I'd never been on a silent retreat before. Indeed, the only time I had ever experienced silence with other people 'in community' was during silent meals in the Abbey on Iona. I was intrigued, and nervous, about the effect and value of a much longer period of silence.

What I wasn't prepared for in the silent retreat was the *silence*. Don't get me wrong, I knew there was going to be 'silence' – as in no talking, being aware of one another, but not communicating in words. I had done *that* bit at silent meals. But I wasn't at all ready for the silence *in me*.

The time spent in silence – and the longer the retreat went on the stronger this became – began to give me space, and time, and focus for myself. It's not too much to say that my time in silent retreat in the Wellspring Community made me look at myself as I had never done before.

Silence, when the only thing that needs to be looked at,
and thought about, and prayed for, and worried about,
and listened to … is you.

September 18 – Symbols

'Here man passes, through forests of symbols,
which watch him with looks of recognition.'

Charles Baudelaire, Les Fleurs du Mal

I'm going to get myself a tattoo. Several members of my family have tattoos, but not me – not yet anyway. One day …

I'm envious of people who have tattoos. Not the ones that cover your whole body, or where there's such a lot of ink that's it's hard make out what's what. But I like tattoos that are distinctive and have a story to tell.

Some years ago I worked with a lady whose husband had died suddenly at the age of fifty-five. She struggled with that, of course, but, slowly, over time, and with a lot of good support, she began to get to grips with things. She went back to work. It gave her a frame-work for her day and something to focus on, though it was hard coming back to an empty house. Weekends were particularly difficult.

I met her about a year-and-a-half after her bereavement, and after we'd exchanged a few moments of a 'How are you?', 'Not too bad' kind of conversation, her voice dropped to a whisper and she said, 'Can I tell you something?' 'Of course,' I replied. She paused, smiled and said, 'I've got myself a tattoo.' Another pause … 'My husband was never keen. So I've waited for a while and decided I would do this for me.' I smiled in response, but before I had time to say anything she concluded, 'And don't you dare ask what it is or where it is. All you need to know is that it's a symbol that matters for me.'

I'm going to get myself a tattoo.
It's going to be a symbol for me too …

September 19 – Balm

'Balm of hurt minds.'

William Shakespeare, Macbeth

I have always been moved by the singing of the spiritual *There Is a Balm in Gilead.*

> *There is a balm in Gilead*
> *That makes my spirit whole.*
> *There is a balm in Gilead*
> *That heals my sin-sick soul.*

'The Balm of Gilead' is a fragrant medicinal resin obtained from certain trees, from Gilead in particular. It's referred to in the Bible in Genesis 37 as a balm carried from Gilead by merchants. In Jeremiah 8 the prophet picks up a familiar metaphor and asks this searching question:

> *Is there no balm in Gilead? Is there no physician there? Why is there*
> *no healing for the wounds of [God's] people?*

The sentiment of the spiritual is, of course, rooted in the subjugation of black slaves, who saw no release from their oppression, but who believed in a future freedom – in a redeemed and changed world, or in the release from this life into the blessedness – the healing balm – of God.

We all look for balm, in a better world or when we're released from this one. But the spiritual doesn't just *hope* for that balm. It tells us that there *is* such a thing.

> *Comfort, release, blessings will come. That's a belief to hold on to.*
> *Gilead could be right here and now.*

September 20 – Even more questions

'In examinations,
those who do not wish to know
ask questions of those who cannot tell.'
Walter Raleigh, Laughter from a Cloud

A father was reading Bible stories to his young daughter when he read, 'The man named Lot was warned to take his wife and flee out of the city, but his wife looked back and was turned into a pillar of salt.'

'Oh,' said the girl. 'That's very sad. But what happened to the flea?'

***

Attending a wedding for the first time, a little boy whispered to his mother, 'Why is the bride dressed in white?'

Being careful of her reply, and concerned to keep it simple, the mother responded, 'Because ... white is the colour of happiness, and today is the happiest day of her life.'

The child thought about this for a second or two then said, 'So why's the groom wearing black, then?'

***

The Sunday School teacher said to her class at the start of her lesson, 'Now, children. I need you all to listen very carefully. First of all, if anyone needs to go to the toilet, hold your hand up very high.'

A little voice from the back of the room said, 'But how will *that* help?'

September 21 – Surprises

'Respect was mingled with surprise.'
Sir Walter Scott, The Lady of the Lake

My wife and I were on holiday in Tuscany with friends. We had lunch in a *trattoria* beside a monastery, and, as the lunch wore on, the conversation became more and more convivial. We were laughing at stories about working with children. I offered my *pièce de résistance,* making a little jumping mouse from a gent's handkerchief. With the mouse jumping around and the laughter getting louder, the couple who owned the *trattoria* came to investigate. The young woman, in stumbling English, said, 'We also work with children,' and went on to explain that she and her husband supported an orphanage in Rwanda. They raised money locally and added money from their business. They went to Rwanda every year, to care for the children and to help build a school.

We were so moved by the story that spontaneously we emptied pockets and purses and handed over a wad of euros. There were tears, smiles and handshakes. Then the young woman rushed to a cupboard and returned with a poly-bag containing a dozen or so sets of wooden rosaries. 'Our children in Rwanda make these ... to sell ... You take. *Grazie! Grazie mille.* You take with thank you from children.'

A few moments of love and sharing had been filled with surprises – a jumping mouse from a handkerchief; a concern for orphaned Rwandan children; a bag of rosary beads. The surprise was complete when I returned to my hospice and offered a Presbyterian patient a set of rosary beads, and the amazing story that went with it.

A surprise is God's way of making us more aware.

September 22 – Hats

'I never saw so many shocking bad hats in my life.'
Duke of Wellington, on seeing the first Reformed Parliament in 1832

One of my eight 'Desert Island Discs' – quite different from all the rest – would be 'Leopard-Skin Pill-Box Hat' by Bob Dylan, from his 1966 album *Blonde on Blonde,* a raunchy 12-bar electric blues number, sung in typical Dylan style, harmonica and all. Not surprisingly, given the song's title, it's about a 'brand new leopard-skin pill-box hat'. It's quirky and it's fun. It's earthy and rough. It always makes me smile.

I've never worn a leopard-skin pill-box hat. I wore a *little* pill-box hat when I was in the Boys' Brigade in the 1960s. But I'd like to have a shot at Dylan's hat, just to see what it's like.

I've got lots of other hats, though, different hats for different occasions. And I've worn more 'metaphorical' hats over the years than I could usefully count – work hats and family hats; church hats and secular hats; hats with mates and hats with colleagues; off-duty and on-duty hats.

A question might be, 'What hat are you wearing today?' indicating that the questioner wants to know who you are right at this moment, what's behind your approach to things, or, as our friends in the USA might say, to find out 'where you're coming from'.

It's important to know what hat you're wearing and that other people are clear what's coming out from underneath it.

Where's that brand new leopard-skin pill-box hat
so I can see what kind of person I might choose to be today?

September 23 – Emotion

'We are sometimes stirred by emotion
and take it for zeal.'
Thomas à Kempis, De Imitatione Christi

What is it with pipe bands? Indeed, what is it with *all* pipe music for this emotional Scotsman?

I was watching a TV recording of the World Pipe Band Championships from Glasgow Green. Pipe music is in this Scotsman's heart. Some of the playing in the senior competition was simply magnificent. I was enraptured – but still in control of my emotions – until we came to a segment of the programme featuring the juvenile competition. And there, marching into the performance arena was the 'Preston Lodge High School Pipe Band'. And in an instant I was a puddle on the floor. They weren't the best band, and they didn't win the competition. But here was *my* local school pipe band; kids from *my* community; young people from *my* village on the world stage; *my* band playing *my* music – and just for *me* …

I was delighted that in Preston Lodge High School, just down the road from my home, dedicated pipe and drumming instructors were sharing their passion for pipe music with interested and receptive young people. I suspect they feel emotion too. And I hope the youngsters feel that emotion when they're playing just for me.

What is it with pipe bands? I have no idea. But I think it has to be about an emotional attachment to my country's heritage. There's emotion; there might be zeal too. I'm happy enough with that.

The music of my country stirs my very soul.

September 24 – Talking

'What is it to thee what they whisper here?
Come after me and let the people talk.'
Dante Alighieri, The Divine Comedy

Among the artefacts I have collected on my travels is a 'talking stick' which I brought home from a trip to Canada. The talking stick is a device used in many First Nations traditions when a council is called. It allows all council members to present their 'sacred point of view'. The talking stick is passed from person to person as they speak. Only the person holding the stick is allowed to talk.

The 'answering feather' is also held by the person speaking, unless the speaker addresses a question to another council member. At that time the answering feather is passed to the person to whom the query has been addressed. Each person must listen carefully to all the words that are spoken, so that, when it is their turn, they don't say what's already been said or ask irrelevant questions.

First Nations children are taught from a very early age to listen and to respect another person's point of view. There may be disagreements, but they are bound by their personal honour to allow everyone their sacred point of view. Each talking stick is unique, and, I was told, the ornamentation on a talking stick will carry its own message and meaning.

I could take my Canadian First Nations talking stick to every meeting I ever attend. What a difference it might make – in teaching me, and others, how to listen as well as speak.

Might someone else's sacred point of view
be just what I need to hear?

September 25 – Thoughts

'Test me, and discover my thoughts.'
Bible, Psalm 139:23

Here is a hymn I've written based on Psalm 139. A suitable tune is *Ich Halte Treulich Still* by Johann Sebastian Bach.

To you, my God, I come;
To you, my God, I turn.
To you I offer up my praise.
From you I seek to learn.
You know me when I rise.
You understand my ways.
You hear my words before I speak,
And bless me all my days.

I cannot hide from you
Wherever I would go.
I find you when I rise to heaven
And when I'm cast down low.
Not on the morning's wings,
Nor in the darkest night,
Will you withdraw your heavenly love
Or hide your guiding light.

You knew me ev'n before
I saw the light of day.
You shaped and formed my life as in
My mother's womb I lay.
Search me, and know my heart;
Test me, and know my thoughts,
That I might live as you would choose,
And love you as I ought.

September 26 – Foolproof

'Dear Lord and Father of mankind,
Forgive our foolish ways.'
John GreenleafWhittier, The Brewing of Soma

Mary Berry was one of the baking experts on *The Great British Bake Off* when it was aired on the BBC. From her vast experience of baking, she would offer critiques of everything the bakers did, make suggestions, and give clear guidance about how things *should* be done properly. And she was quick to criticise if anyone showed her a soggy bottom!

In the introduction to one of her many recipe books, *Foolproof Cooking,* Mary Berry makes it clear that baking should be fun, and though bakers are inevitably stressed when they're in a competition, under the glare of TV cameras or being watched by experts, cooking or baking for friends and family should be enjoyable and rewarding. So she offers recipes which are foolproof, dishes that can be depended on, with no panic or worry, so that cooking and baking is more relaxing and satisfying.

Who am I – an average cook at best – to doubt the wisdom of the legendary Mary Berry? I have to confess that, at the time of writing this, I haven't tried any of the recipes in her book. But foolproof? I'm not so sure ...

Even the most foolproof of enterprises needs care and attention. Being complacent or slapdash – and that's before you avoid incompetence – matters. If something is foolproof, you must make sure you're not the fool that proves it to be otherwise. Or you might have more foolish ways than you expect that need to be forgiven.

I wish I had a foolproof way of living. Since I don't, I guess I'll just have to go back to the recipe book from time to time.

September 27 – Teamwork

'One of the most common defects of half-instructed minds
is to think much of that in which they differ from others,
and little of that in which they agree with others.'
Walter Bagehot, On the Evils of Sectarianism

I once had a poster which said, 'Success is teamwork'. Here it is in
verse form from an unknown source:

Two donkeys, so the story goes,
were tethered each to each,
When lo, they neared two bales of hay,
that seemed within their reach.
Each sought his own: the rope grew taut,
as though each would apply
His utmost strength to take his share
or know the reason why.
They pulled and scraped and pawed and kicked,
as though indeed insane –
But not by foolish stunts could they
one single bite obtain.
Till, wearied, turning face to face,
they talked the matter o'er,
And mutually agreed that they
would thus behave no more.
At peace, they soon one bale devoured,
and ate the other, too.
How good their joint refreshment seemed,
none but those donkeys knew!
Ye humans, crude and stubborn willed,
respect the common tether;
Be wise, confer, agree, co-work,
and 'eat your hay' together!

September 28 – Hinges

'Behold, I stand at the door and knock.'
Bible, Revelation 3:20

There's a story in the Bible in Luke 10 when Jesus is asked by an expert in religious law what he must do to have 'eternal life'. 'What does the Law say you should do?' Jesus asks. The expert answers:

Love the Lord your God with all your heart, with all your soul, with all your strength, and with all your mind, and love your neighbour as yourself.

The expert asks further, 'But who is my neighbour?' In reply, Jesus tells perhaps one of the greatest ever parables, the story of the Good Samaritan. 'Which of these three do you think became a neighbour to the man who fell into the hands of the robbers?' he asks. The expert in religious law replies, 'The one who showed mercy to him.' Jesus says, 'Go and do the same.'

But I'm more interested in the beginning of the story than I am in the over-familiar ending. The heart of the Law which Jesus draws out from the expert is what Judaism calls 'the two hinges'. If one or the other doesn't work, the door doesn't open. Both hinges must work – the love of God and the love of neighbour – if the door is to do its job.

Make sure both your hinges are working well, Jesus is saying. That way you have the door to the eternal life you want, or even to a life that's more satisfying in the here and now.

'Too heavenly-minded and no earthly use.'
One hinge working well,
but a door stuck because the other hinge is broken.

September 29 – Preparations

'Be prepared.'
Motto of the Scout Association

When the Queen came to visit a factory I worked in as a student, a host of preparations were made for the big day. The hedges and shrubs around the factory were trimmed; the car-park was cleared of unnecessary clutter; the windows facing the entrance were painted; a carpet was put in the lift to the factory floor; a bare patch of grass outside the clocking-in corridor was sprayed green; and everywhere Her Majesty's entourage was to pass through was repainted.

It's been said that the Queen believes that the whole world smells of fresh paint, such are the preparations that are made for her visits. Our factory didn't buck the trend.

However ... not everyone was prepared. The official who accompanied the Queen into the lift pressed the wrong button, and the doors opened at the boiler-house and not where the welcoming party was waiting at the production floor; a scruffy lab technician wandered across the Queen's sight-line wearing the most stained lab coat you've ever seen (that's the lab technician and not HRH ...); the cord the Queen had to pull to unveil the 'Opened by ...' plaque came away in her hand, and the curtain had to be hauled away by a quick-witted official.

I'm sure the Queen didn't mind all of this. But plenty other people did! The mistakes were the talk of the canteen for weeks. And the ribbing a scruffy lab technician got can't be repeated here.

*If we're not properly prepared in spite of all our preparations,
then things can go disastrously wrong, can't they?*

September 30 – Unknown

'Thus let me live, unseen, unknown;
Thus unlamented let me die;
Steal from the world, and not a stone
Tell where I lie.'
Alexander Pope, Ode to Solitude

Alfred Arthur Rouse was sentenced to hang for murder in 1931. His case was a *cause célèbre* in its day, and his trial is one of the most notable in English legal history. Rouse was charged and convicted of the murder of an unknown man. Seeking to fabricate his own death, it's believed he picked up a hitchhiker, knocked him out and burnt his car with the man inside. The body of the man in the burnt-out Morris Minor has never been identified. Rouse believed that by setting the car alight on Guy Fawkes night, the blaze would just be thought of as another bonfire and, therefore, not out of place. But the hapless Rouse was seen leaving the location of the fire, and his arrest and conviction were inevitable.

In May 2012, a family were seeking to determine if Rouse's victim was one of their relatives who had disappeared without a trace in 1930. In January 2014, following an investigation by a forensic team from the Universities of Leicester and Northumbria, it was agreed that the missing man was not the murder victim. Scientists are still following new leads as to the victim's identity.

A person's identity matters. How sad that someone can disappear without trace, and that someone dies without there being any definitive evidence of who they are.

Tell someone today that you love them.
It might make them feel they matter more than they knew.

October 1 – Unfinished

'I have fought a good fight; I have finished my course.'
Bible, II Timothy 4:7

A poem, attributed to both A Price Hughes and Mary Lee Hall, offers us this thought:

> *If I should die and leave you here awhile,*
> *be not like others, sore undone, who keep*
> *long vigils by the silent dust, and weep.*
> *For my sake, turn again to life and smile,*
> *nerving thy heart and trembling hand to do*
> *something to comfort weaker hearts than thine.*
> *Complete those dear unfinished tasks of mine,*
> *and I perchance may therein comfort you.*

Should our tasks be left for others to complete, or might we try to finish our own unfinished tasks? In *The Walrus and the Carpenter,* Lewis Carroll has the two protagonists weeping over the quantities of sand that needed to be cleared away.

> *'If seven maids with seven mops*
> *Swept it for half a year,*
> *Do you suppose,' the Walrus said,*
> *'That they could get it clear?'*
> *'I doubt it,' said the Carpenter,*
> *And shed a bitter tear.*

What a shame it would be if we cried bitter tears because we couldn't get all our sand 'cleared away', or if we left the unfinished parts of our lives for others to shed tears over.

October 2 – What?

'I keep six honest serving men
(they taught me all I knew);
Their names are What and Why and When,
and How and Where and Who.'

Rudyard Kipling, The Elephant's Child

I was discussing with a friend recently the problem of heating the Abbey Church on Iona. 'We could use a heat-exchanger,' he said. 'What's that?' I asked. 'You take cold water from the Sound of Iona and use it to heat the Abbey,' he replied. Seeing the incredulous look on my face, he sought to clarify things. 'It's the opposite of a refrigerator. Cold goes in one end and you get heat in exchange ...' My simple mind went into meltdown. I don't understand how a fridge works in the first place, far less the other way round!

In Matthew's Gospel, Jesus gives guidance to his friends on this very issue:

Don't worry about your life, what you shall eat, or what you shall drink, or about your body and what you will wear ... Look at the birds of the air. They don't sow, or reap, or gather into barns ... Can any of you by worrying add a single hour to the length of your life? Look at the lilies! They don't toil or spin. Yet I tell you, even Solomon in all his glory was not clothed like one of these.

Note to self:
Leave the worrying about heat-exchangers and fridges to the people who know about heat-exchangers and fridges, and spend more time admiring the beauty of the birds and the lilies. You don't need to understand that. Tom

October 3 – Reminders

'Which will be remembered for a very long time.'
William McGonagall, The Tay Bridge Disaster

There's an area in the centre of Fort William known locally as 'the Parade'. Bounded by the train and bus stations, a hotel, the parish church and a row of shops, there's a green space with a putting green, several memorials and a few park benches. It's tranquil, beautiful and appealing.

So why 'the Parade'? Fort William was a town built round a fort and, simply put, this area of the town was what had been the parade-ground. 'The Parade' is a reminder of part of the town's history.

Just outside the village of Prestonpans, at 'the pans' from which the village takes its name, there is a section called 'Morrison's Haven'. There hasn't been a harbour, mooring or haven of any kind for generations. Other than the bases of the posts for the harbour's piers, there is nothing to be seen – and all of this is a *long* way from the shoreline. But in a bygone age Morrison's Haven was, indeed, a bustling harbour, taking salt and coal far and wide. The name is a reminder of the industries of past days.

Reminders of the past matter: family resemblances and characteristics; wearing dad's watch or mother's wedding ring; faded photographs of grandparents; a christening gown passed down the generations. Reminders link us to the past and show us where we came from.

What reminders will we leave behind? Will people remember the Parade where we walk or the Haven where we worked?

If reminders matter, where will ours be?

October 4 – Sleep

'The wind comes to me from the fields of sleep.
William Wordsworth, Intimations of Immortality

I don't mind if people look at their watches while I'm preaching. But I worry when they shake them to make sure they haven't stopped! And if they were to fall asleep, well ...

In the Book of Acts, there's a remarkable story of St Paul in Troas meeting with folk for worship. Paul launched into his sermon. The plan was for him and his party to leave first thing in the morning, but Paul went on and on – part sermon, part discussion, as was the custom – well past midnight. A young man named Eutychus was sitting in an open window. He fell asleep, toppled two floors to the ground and lay dead. Paul rushed down to the street, hugged the boy hard, and said, 'No more crying. Everything will be OK.' Then, he went back to his sermon and preached until dawn was breaking! And as the congregation broke up after worship, Eutychus was full of life.

An early form of CPR? A miracle? A good story, slightly embellished? A boy in a coma whom they didn't expect to survive? Who knows? But, one way or another, Eutychus falling asleep wasn't the end of him, or, indeed, the end of Paul's reputation as a preacher. Eutychus came back 'from the fields of sleep', none the worse for his experience.

If people drift off to sleep while I'm preaching, I really don't mind. They'll have to waken up of their own accord, though, and hopefully before the offering is taken. But at least I know I'll have something in common with St Paul, and that can't be a bad thing, can it?

To sleep, perchance to dream,
perchance to wake up, perchance to start again.

October 5 – More sleep

'Watch ye, therefore:
For ye know not when the master of the house cometh ...
Lest coming suddenly he finds you sleeping.'
Bible, Mark 13:35

Reflecting yesterday on Eutychus falling asleep during a sermon reminds me of a man in one of my congregations who fell asleep during every sermon I preached. Folk suggested he was closing his eyes to concentrate on the wisdom of the preacher. But his occasional snoring was a dead giveaway. He was gracious enough to wake up when the offering was being taken, though. So it wasn't all bad.

There's a story told of two elderly ladies who regularly moaned about the poor quality of their minister's preaching and the inordinate length of his sermons. During a particularly lengthy peroration, one of them fell asleep. After a time she woke up with a start and, finding the minister still in the pulpit and in full flow, whispered to her friend, 'Is he not done yet?' To which her companion replied, 'He was done a long time ago. He just doesn't know when to stop.'

I don't mind if people fall asleep during my sermons. I hope they don't. But if they *do* drop off, at least I'll know they're relaxed enough to nod off and sufficiently at peace not to be disturbed by my ramblings.

There's an old Irish proverb which runs:

*A good laugh and a long sleep
are the best cures in the doctor's book.*

If I can help you with a long and restful sleep, in whatever way, then I don't mind at all. And if you have a good laugh at my expense, I hope I can be just as gracious.

October 6 – Bereavement

'So quick, so clean an ending?
Oh, that was right lad.'
A E Houseman, A Shropshire Lad

In my work with bereaved people I use metaphors to help find ways of explaining what bereavement is like. The language of bereavement isn't extensive or even very useful. So sometimes pictures are better than words. I'll share two such metaphors today and tomorrow. I hope they help.

Picture a little burn, bubbling and bright, running down a hillside, full of life. A huge boulder has been dislodged higher up and comes crashing down the hill, lands right in the middle of the burn and sticks there. In an instant, the little stream has died – no life, no movement, no light, nothing! The water has ceased to flow. The devastation of the boulder is total.

Bereavement does that. It comes suddenly and wreaks havoc. It stops life, meaning, colour, movement and wonder. The bubbling burn is no more.

But water has an insidious way of working around a blockage. Over time, little trickles of water appear on the other side of the boulder. One trickle joins another and slowly the burn begins to flow again – taking a different path, but showing that new beginnings are possible.

Bereavement is like that too. From hopelessness and destruction new possibilities start to flow again. It will be different. New life will be possible. And the boulder will stay.

The bereavement will always be there, to be cursed and kicked.
But it's a symbol of both an ending and a beginning,
and a life that's still flowing on in a new way.

October 7 – Beaches

*'All use metaphors in conversation,
as well as proper and appropriate words.'*
Aristotle, The Art of Rhetoric

I live close to a working harbour in East Lothian, in the fishing village of Port Seton. When storms batter both sides of the Firth of Forth, it's easy to see why a good harbour is necessary. Strong walls and a good design make sure the boats are kept safe even in the worst of storms. But beyond that, there is no such protection. There are rocky beaches on both sides of the harbour, from Cockenzie to the west and towards the sands of Longniddry to the east. Jagged rocks jut out into the Forth, crevices and spaces filled with sand and seaweed, shells and pebbles.

On a calm day, when the tide is out, you get to know the geography of these pieces of coastline – where the sand lies, where the piles of pebbles are. But after a storm? The beaches can be unrecognisable. Sand has been shifted from here to there. What was once a shoreline to be walked on is now strewn with rocks and stones. Where there were piles of little pebbles there are … well … no pebbles. The outcrops of rocks are the same. It's essentially the same coastline. But the geography, the layout, the familiarity have all changed.

Bereavement does that. The devastation alters the landscape of your beach, sometimes beyond recognition. It will take a bit of time to become familiar with it again. But it will happen. And there will be calmer days when you'll get to love your new beach as much as you did the old one.

*Change and decay in all around I see.
How can I manage change when it is facing me?*

October 8 – Out of nowhere

'My heart was not in me but with you,
and now ... if it is not with you it is nowhere.'
Héloise, Letter to Peter Abelard

I don't much like cats. If I know where they are and what they're up to, I'm fine, but when they come at me out of nowhere ...

I once visited a lady who had eight cats. At least she *told* me she had eight cats, but I swear there were eleven or twelve, although they would never stand still long enough for me to do a proper count. You've heard the metaphor 'It's like herding cats'? Well, counting any more than two or three is no easier.

Tolerance stretched to the absolute limit, I would visit cat-lady. I survived being stared-out by the ginger moggy who obviously resented me sitting in his chair. I coped with a scrawny white thing being sick in the corner. I tolerated a Persian type sitting on my lap. But what disturbed me most was the cat that would disappear and then reappear – with feline stealth and scary suddenness – right beside my right ear from the back of my chair, or under my feet when I crossed my legs, or (as on one *awful* occasion) on my head following a flying leap from the arm of the sofa (that's the cat, not me!). I don't much like cats. I hate surprises. And when the two go together ...

Keep things open and honest, please. Don't let things sneak up on me unexpectedly. Just *tell* me what's likely to happen, even if it's awful. That way I might be ready for the unexpected and the scary things that come out of nowhere.

Now, where's that cat gone? It couldn't possibly be ...

October 9 – Advice

'Advice is seldom welcome
and those who want it the most always like it the least.'
Lord Chesterfield, Letter to his son, 1774

In 2012 *The Daily Telegraph* published an article under the heading 'The 101 best pieces of advice ever received'. The great and the good from the worlds of show business and commerce, art and academia, sport and television had been invited to contribute. They spoke of wise advice from parents and mentors, agents and colleagues, friends and family. It's a fascinating insight into the pieces of wisdom people have carried with them through their years.

There was a 1990s American sitcom called *Good Advice,* and a movie of the same name in 2001. So good advice matters, whether it's welcome or not. I was once preaching in a church for the first time and I left half my sermon notes at home. I had no alternative but to 'wing it', not my style at all! Confessing my mistake to someone afterwards, they offered this advice: 'Always have a contingency plan.' I'm not sure *that* advice was really welcomed!

My own 'best piece of advice' was a nugget of wisdom from a wise woman. When I decided to enter the ministry of the Church, my family were delighted, none more so than my granny, who quietly made this suggestion: 'Keep it simple, son. Just tell folk that God loves them. That'll be enough.'

It's advice I've not always heeded – to the detriment of my own faith and ministry. But it's advice I need to go back to again and again. If it's simple, it's enough.

Why over-complicate things
when keeping them simple is easier and more effective.

October 10 – Help

'A very present help in times of trouble.'
Bible, Psalm 47:1

'Is there a doctor in the house?' Tim had heard that once before. On a student pub-crawl his mate had fallen off a bar stool after their fifth round of 'after-shocks'. 'Is there a doctor in the house?' someone had shouted amid gales of laughter. No one moved. Why would you when it was just another drunk student on the floor – *and* it was your round?

This time it was for real, and no one was laughing. 'Help! Is there a doctor? We need someone over here.' Tim looked around. Over to his right the crowd had thinned out, as if they were backing away from the source of some contamination. The early evening audience for one of the small stages at *T in the Park* wasn't particularly big anyway. Someone was on the ground. A girl was shouting for help. Tim wasn't a doctor. He was only eighteen, for goodness' sake. But maybe it was the First Aid stuff he'd just finished in Ranger Scouts; or maybe he was just curious. In any event, no one else was bothering, and he felt *someone* should help.

The guy on the ground was being sick. Tim rolled him onto his side to stop him choking, made sure his airway was clear, checked him over as best he could and gave as much help as he was able to till the proper medics arrived. The guy was OK. Tim never saw the end of the rock concert. But he felt good that he'd helped a bit when help was needed.

'Doctor Ballantyne?' A voice interrupted Tim's reverie. It was a nurse in scrubs. 'You're needed in theatre.' Tim smiled to himself, and went off to be a doctor for real.

A very present help – when anyone's in trouble – for real!

October 11 – Reassurance

'Rest, rest, perturbèd spirit.'

William Shakespeare, Hamlet

When Alec moved into his new 'sheltered flat', the manager met with him to explain all the safety and security issues. The 'emergency cords' in every room were pointed out. The intercom connection with the manager's office was tried out. 'And we have a new device that's our pride and joy,' the manager explained. She pointed down the hall. 'Right there, halfway between your bedroom and bathroom, there's a pressure pad under the carpet. That way we know that everyone's up and about first thing. As soon as the pad is stood on, a light comes on in our office. If it doesn't, we'll investigate what's what.'

The following morning, the manager was at her pressure-pad console. By 9.30, all the lights were glowing red, apart from Alec's. She gave it another couple of minutes, then she buzzed him on the intercom. No reply. She headed to the flat, and, opening the front door with her passkey, shouted, 'Mr McCafferty. Are you OK?' No reply. She looked into the bedroom. No sign of Alec. The bathroom was empty. She made her way anxiously along the hall and opened the living-room door. And there he was with his feet up on his coffee table, reading a newspaper.

'Oh, Mr McCafferty, I'm so glad you're OK. The pressure-pad light didn't come on, so I thought …' Alec smiled widely. 'Oh, I knew it wouldn't come on, hen. I took a run along the hall and jumped over the pad. I just wanted reassurance that the system works. And it does!'

What might we need to jump over to put our mind at rest?

October 12 – Prisons

> "'And a bird-cage, sir," says Sam.
> "Veels within veels, a prison in a prison.'"
>
> *Charles Dickens,* The Pickwick Papers

One of the hardest things I've ever had to do as a minister was visit people in prison. Cornton Vale, Edinburgh, Polmont, Barlinnie … none of the visits were enjoyable. I liked the inmates I visited, but I never liked where they were.

The 17th-century poet Richard Lovelace wrote a poem, *To Althea, From Prison.* The final stanza is this:

> *Stone walls do not a prison make,*
> *Nor iron bars a cage;*
> *Minds innocent and quiet take*
> *That for an hermitage;*
> *If I have freedom in my love,*
> *And in my soul am free,*
> *Angels alone that soar above*
> *Enjoy such liberty.*

Lovelace was in Gatehouse Prison for encouraging the 1640 'Clergy Act' to be annulled. He suggests that obeying the King's imposed laws does not make him free. Similarly, being in a jail does not mean he is imprisoned. Freedom and imprisonment stem from the body and soul.

Richard Lovelace was a brave man. But he is also right. I don't need to visit Barlinnie and Cornton Vale to find people who are imprisoned.

> *It's a liberty of the soul that's needed.*
> *It's a freedom without walls that must be sought.*

October 13 – Image

'Bygone images and scenes of early life
have stolen into my mind.'
Samuel Taylor Coleridge, Table Talk

I once appeared at a church function in jeans and a sweatshirt. An old
elder, a stiff and traditional type, was the first to comment. Thankfully,
he wasn't critical, but he took the opportunity to tell me how things
had changed.

'When I was a small boy in the 1930s,' he told me, 'the youngest
of five children, it was always an occasion when the minister visited.
My four sisters and I would be lined up in front of the fire in 'the
good room', and the minister would shake hands with us all. Then we
would be dismissed while the minister spent time with our parents.'

He smiled as he looked me up and down. 'And another thing,' he
said, 'was the way the minister dressed. I never saw him in *anything*
other than a three-piece black suit with a gold watch-chain on the
waistcoat, brightly polished black shoes, a full dog-collar and *always* a
black Homburg.' He paused, now with a twinkle in his eye ... 'Apart
from, that is, when he took the young people on a hike over the Pentlands. It was a sunny day, and on *that* occasion he wore a three-piece
black suit with a gold watch-chain on the waistcoat, brightly polished
black shoes, a black Homburg and ... *a white shirt and dark tie* ... It was
an image thing,' he concluded, 'and one which we just got used to.'

He looked me up and down again. Perhaps he was wondering if
he would get used to *this* image too.

I'm wondering where I can get a black Homburg for my hike up
the Pentlands with the young people this weekend ...

October 14 – Blessings abound

'Yet possessing every blessing.'
James Edmeston, Lead Us, Heavenly Father, Lead Us

I was on a walk on the island of Skye. The beginning took me down to a rock-strewn shore at the end of which was a rough track up through low cliffs. The walk was pleasant, the views spectacular and the isolation peaceful. But what I wasn't expecting was the ruins of a village.

I'd worked my way up the path when I found the broken walls of a small village at the edge of the cliff. The walls of the buildings had all but disappeared, but their outlines showed the ruins of six homesteads and the walls of two paddocks. When was the small village abandoned? Were the villagers victims of the Highland Clearances? Was it isolation or economic decline? Did people simply not want to live there any more? If stones could speak …

Beside the outline of each house there was a rowan tree or mountain ash. Rowans were placed close to most Highland homes as a way of warding off evil spirits, keeping the home safe. Each home in this old village had its rowan.

The 'magic' protection of the rowans didn't do much good for *this* village, I mused. But I also pondered what blessings the rowans had overseen in the life of that village – the weddings, the births, the ceilidhs, the celebrations.

There is no magic that can protect us from 'evil', no rowan tree or rabbit's foot or anything else. So we take blessings where we can find them, and that's as good a way of warding off evil spirits as anything else I know.

Blessings abound. Blessings are free.
Blessings for you. Blessings for me.

October 15 – New

'All appeared new and strange at first.'
Thomas Traherne, Centuries of Meditations

A party of visitors, including a family with two young boys, was being shown around a stately home. The children, aged six and nine, had been well warned about behaving, concluding with, from their mother, the much emphasised 'And DON'T touch!' It was an injunction the two boys had heard often before, and they knew that being careful – and not touching – was the order of the day.

The same instruction should have been given to the boys' father. Not being as careful as his sons, he accidentally knocked a porcelain vase from its stand by carelessly swinging round and catching it with his camera bag. The vase fell to the ground with an almighty 'crash' and shattered into a myriad pieces. The father was mortified at his clumsiness. The mother was distraught. 'Good grief,' she exclaimed, 'and I told the *boys* to behave. Look what *you've* done. And that vase was two hundred and fifty years old.'

At which point the six-year-old chirped, 'Not to worry, dad. It's just as well it wasn't new.'

I've watched with horror the TV reports of the deliberate destruction of the religious and cultural heritage in Syria. Many places of worship and ancient historical artefacts have been torn down in recent years. In Iraq, ISIL has plundered and destroyed dozens of historic religious buildings. Old things matter as much as new ones. Our religious and cultural heritage remains important.

We are part of history,
and it's right that we cherish our past.

October 16 – Inspirational

'Lord, make me an instrument of your peace.'
Prayer of St Francis of Assisi

One of the most inspiring people I've ever met was the peace campaigner Helen Steven, who died in 2016 at the age of 73, after a lifetime of dedicated work for justice and peace. Helen was a passionate campaigner against weapons of mass destruction, and a believer in the value of non-violent protest. Her witness took her to Cornton Vale prison *and* to NATO headquarters where she addressed generals on the moral case against nuclear armaments.

Helen had gone to Vietnam in 1972 as part of a Quaker project working in orphanages in Saigon. Her time there was life-changing, and she became a member of the Religious Society of Friends. In 1979, she became a full-time peace and justice worker with the Iona Community, and in 1985 she and her partner, Ellen, opened Peace House in Braco in Perthshire. Over twelve years, more than 10,000 people attended the residential centre and participated in its courses about peace, justice and non-violent direct action.

In her book on prayer, *No Extraordinary Power*, Helen wrote, 'One of the hardest boundaries for me to cross was ... to engage in civil disobedience. For a well-behaved middle-class woman, whose whole upbringing had tended towards being law-abiding, respectful and conforming, it was a huge step to break the law deliberately.'

Inspirational may be an overused word, but it is an appropriate one for people like Helen Steven.

Who do you know who has lived what they believe,
put prayer into action, and inspired others to do likewise?

October 17 – Service

'Every kind of service necessary to the public good
Becomes honourable by being necessary.'
Nathan Hale, Letter to William Hull, 1776

I wrote yesterday of Helen Steven, the embodiment of all the heroes for justice and peace whose stories inspire me.

One of these is St Francis. Born in Assisi in 1182, Francis turned his back on inherited wealth, committed himself to God and lived a simple life of poverty. He established the Rule of St Francis which exists today as the Order of St Francis, or the Franciscans. He died in 1226, aged 44. This prayer is attributed to him:

> *Lord, make me an instrument of your peace.*
> *Where there is hatred, let me sow love;*
> *where there is injury, pardon;*
> *where there is doubt, faith;*
> *where there is despair, hope;*
> *where there is darkness, light;*
> *where there is sadness, joy;*
> *O Divine Master,*
> *grant that I may not so much seek to be consoled*
> *as to console;*
> *to be understood as to understand;*
> *to be loved as to love.*
> *For it is in giving that we receive;*
> *it is in pardoning that we are pardoned;*
> *and it is in dying that we are born to eternal life.*

I'm inspired by such words, for they encapsulate all that we should aspire to in service to others.

October 18 – Peace

'Peace, peace will, peace will come,
And let it begin with me.'

Tom Paxton, Peace

My thoughts for the past two days have ranged from a modern-day peace campaigner, Helen Steven, and how inspirational I find her, to the Prayer of St Francis from the 13th century, and his desire to inspire people to live a life of service to the rest of society. Today my thoughts turn to someone who also matters a great deal to me.

I could write a great deal about the great American President Abraham Lincoln. But for now, I will confess to just this – he is another of my inspirational figures from history. His second inaugural address, in March 1865, after a landslide presidential victory, was against the background of the high number of casualties on both sides of a bloody Civil War. Lincoln closed with these words:

> *With malice toward none; with charity for all; with firmness in the right, as God gives us to see the right, let us strive on to finish the work we are in; to bind up the nation's wounds; to care for him who shall have borne the battle, and for his widow, and his orphan – to do all which may achieve and cherish a just and lasting peace, among ourselves, and with all nations.*

'A just and lasting peace.' That's what we want to work towards, inspired by all who have moved and challenged us and changed us through our years.

Peace will come, and let it begin with me.

October 19 – Dread

'Or whence this secret dread, and inward horror,
Of falling into naught.'
Joseph Addison, Cato, Act 5

Of all the things that strike dread into my heart, the worst is the number 256. It doesn't instil in me Addison's 'inward horror of falling into naught,' but it does fill me with an overwhelming feeling that I'm in deep, deep trouble.

My Latin teacher in High School was the legendary 'Fossil'. Mr McGregor (Latin) had been known as Fossil by generations of pupils. He was a kindly and informative teacher who had a deeply felt passion for his subject. Because of Fossil, I can still find Latin derivations in the English language and know the plural for words ending in 'um'. (It's *referenda*, not referendums!)

I was never the best-behaved pupil. My co-conspirator was Alistair Grant. We would often be hauled out to sit in the front of Fossil's class. 'Grant and Morgan (he never got my name right) sit here so I can keep an eye on your recalcitrant behaviour.' But *much* worse was the 'punishment exercise'. Our textbook was *Paterson & McNaughton's Approach to Latin*. Fossil would get to the end of his tether and rant, 'Morgan! Write out page 256 of the Word Studies and hand it in to me first thing tomorrow.'

Aarrgghh! Not the dreaded *page 256*. It was long and complicated and had *lots* of tricky Latin words in it. Page 256! Not again! I last did that punishment exercise 50 years ago, and yet 256 is still my secret dread.

Please don't call me 'Morgan' and shout '256' in my ear,
or I will instantly feel obliged to behave!

October 20 – Guest

'Yet, if his majesty our sovereign lord
Should of his own accord,
Friendly himself invite,
And say, "I'll be your guest tomorrow night",
How should we stir ourselves,
Call and command
All hands to work!'
Anonymous, From Christ Church MS

The great cellist Yo-Yo Ma was asked what the most important thing in his life was. He answered, 'My family.' It wasn't the answer the interviewer expected. He pressed Yo-Yo Ma further on what was the most important moment in his musical career. Yo-Yo Ma replied, 'Appearing on children's TV programmes, such as *Sesame Street.*' That wasn't what the interviewer was expecting either.

'But why?' he enquired.

'Because,' Yo-Yo Ma responded, 'then I was a guest in a children's world, not expecting them to be guests in mine.'

In *Diary of a Superfluous Man,* Ivan Turgenev writes:

Superfluous … a supernumerary, that's all. Nature, obviously, hadn't counted on my showing up and consequently treated me as an unexpected and uninvited guest.

What a tragedy when someone feels like an 'uninvited guest' in his own world! What a pleasure it is to feel you are a welcomed guest in someone else's world!

*Can you help someone feel accepted
by inviting them to be an honoured guest in your world?*

October 21 – Wrong

'That all was wrong because not all was right.'
George Crabbe, The Convert

I had a stint as an invigilator for exams in a local high school. It was what was known then as 'O Grades' in Scotland, exams for pupils around the age of 16. One task was invigilating at the O Grade Woodwork Practical. It was a simple set of duties for me. All I had to do was to make available the wood, plan and exam paper. All the pupils had to do was build the item as instructed, with proper joints, fixings and measurements.

'You have three hours, ladies and gentlemen. Turn over your exam paper, and begin your work – now!'

I never took much notice of what was going on, just checking from time to time that no one was up to any mischief. After the three hours, I announced, 'That's all folks. Leave your work on the bench. Make sure your label is properly completed and your bench is tidy. Go when you're done.' When everyone had gone, my final task was to put each person's completed item in a linen bag, secure it tightly, tie the appropriate label round the neck, box everything and trot off to the Post Office. It was a case of 'Yes, that looks good' and 'Not a bad effort' and 'Excellent job' and … 'My giddy aunt! What on earth is *this*?' I can't now recall what the object was, but I do remember that one disastrous effort bore *no resemblance whatsoever* to all the rest. It was so obvious. Even a cag-handed DYI person like me could see it was all wrong.

Why can't some people see the obvious,
especially when it is so wrong?

October 22 – Evening

'When evening's come, you homeward take your way.'
Mary Collier, The Woman's Labour

Thomas Ken was an English cleric from the beginning of the 18th century who is one of the fathers of modern English hymn-singing. The hymn 'Awake, my soul, and with the sun' and the doxology 'Praise God from whom all blessings flow' will be familiar to many. But perhaps the best known of Ken's hymns takes the form of an evening prayer. Most often sung to a beautiful 16th-century tune by Thomas Tallis, it might serve as your evening prayer too.

All praise to Thee, my God, this night,
For all the blessings of the light!
Keep me, O keep me, King of kings,
Beneath Thine own almighty wings.

Forgive me, Lord, for Thy dear Son,
The ill that I this day have done,
That with the world, myself, and Thee,
I, ere I sleep, at peace may be.

When in the night I sleepless lie,
My soul with heavenly thoughts supply;
Let no ill dreams disturb my rest,
No powers of darkness me molest.

O when shall I, in endless day,
Forever chase dark sleep away,
And hymns divine with angels sing,
All praise to thee, eternal King?

October 23 – Morning

'And the evening and the morning were the first day.'
Bible, Genesis 1:5

I wrote yesterday of the hymnwriter Thomas Ken. The 'morning hymn' below was written at a time when many in the established Church considered it blasphemous to write new lyrics for church music. In that atmosphere, Ken wrote this and several other hymns for the boys at Winchester College, with strict instructions that they use them only in their rooms, for private devotions. Here is part of his hymn, the beginning of our 'prayer for the morning'.

> *Awake, my soul, and with the sun*
> *Thy daily stage of duty run;*
> *Shake off dull sloth, and joyful rise,*
> *To pay thy morning sacrifice.*
>
> *Thy precious time misspent, redeem,*
> *Each present day thy last esteem,*
> *Improve thy talent with due care;*
> *For the great day thyself prepare.*
>
> *By influence of the Light divine*
> *Let thine own light to others shine.*
> *Reflect all Heaven's propitious ways*
> *In ardent love, and cheerful praise.*
>
> *Wake, and lift up thyself, my heart,*
> *And with the angels bear thy part,*
> *Who all night long unwearied sing*
> *High praise to the eternal King.*

October 24 – Praise God

'Praise God, from Whom all blessings flow.'
Thomas Ken, Doxology

The final stanza of Thomas Ken's hymn below has come into widespread use as a doxology, perhaps the most frequently used piece of music in public worship. At Ken's request, it was sung at his funeral, fittingly held at sunrise.

*All praise to Thee, who safe has kept
And hast refreshed me while I slept;
Grant, Lord, when I from death shall wake
I may of endless light partake.*

*Heav'n is, dear Lord, where'er Thou art,
O never then from me depart;
For to my soul 'tis hell to be
But for one moment void of Thee.*

*Lord, I my vows to Thee renew;
Disperse my sins as morning dew.
Guard my first springs of thought and will,
And with Thyself my spirit fill.*

*Direct, control, suggest, this day,
All I design, or do, or say,
That all my powers, with all their might,
In Thy sole glory may unite.*

*Praise God, from Whom all blessings flow;
Praise Him, all creatures here below;
Praise Him above, ye heavenly host;
Praise Father, Son, and Holy Ghost.*

October 25 – The cross and the antlers

'The mystery of the cross shines bright.'

Venantius Fortunatus, Vexilla Regis

The Kirk of the Canongate is in Edinburgh's Old Town. The parish includes the Palace of Holyroodhouse and the Scottish Parliament. It is also the parish church of Edinburgh Castle.

Tradition has it that the Abbey of Holyrood and the Parish of Canongate were established in 1128 by King David I of Scotland when his life was spared after he had a vision of the cross of Jesus amidst the antlers of a stag while hunting nearby. Another version has King David encountering a white stag. White animals were considered magical, otherworldly creatures. The King was so overwhelmed by this sighting that he placed a 'rood' – a Holy Cross – where he had seen the white stag. So the Abbey of the Holy Rood had its beginnings.

Which carries the truth? Is either correct? Nobody is quite sure. But I do like the symbolism of the stag's horns and the cross being interlinked. Whatever the cross stands for, it surely points to the heart of the Christian Faith – love, hope and peace. Whatever the stag's antlers represent, they are surely a symbol of struggle, danger and power. The two intertwined – the cross challenging the antlers? It works for me.

I like this prayer that the people of the Canongate Kirk make available to visitors to their historic church.

Almighty God, whose servant King David founded this ancient parish as a sign of his thankfulness to you; may we too know the presence of Jesus in all the challenges and opportunities of our daily lives, and as we travel from this place, may we take with us the promise of the cross in the antlers, that He is with us always, to the close of our age. Amen.

October 26 – Pleasure

'Whatever fades, but fading pleasure brings.'
Philip Sidney, Certain Sonnets

My dad was a smoker. He'd been a heavy smoker in his younger years, particularly in the RAF during World War II. In his later years, he'd cut down considerably. He was still a smoker, though.

My mother was never keen on him smoking. Even before the smoking ban in public places, he never smoked in the house. That was my mum's 'public place'. So he smoked at the back door. In bad weather, he smoked in his greenhouse. 'Works wonders for the tomatoes,' he told me.

After my mother died, when my dad stayed with us or we stayed with him, he would slip away from the table after a meal. The children would ask, 'Where's grampa going?' 'To the back door for a breath of fresh air,' we would reply, though we knew better.

My dad was in a nursing home for some time before he died. In his final days, he had few pleasures in life. But the most important one was to be wheeled in his chair to the front door for his 'wee fag'. The last thing I did for my dad was to light a cigarette, hold it in his mouth for him to have a few draws, and repeat that till he'd had enough. It was his final pleasure, and my final memory. It mattered to us both – and no one could argue about a moment of simple pleasure.

For there's nae luck about the house,
There's nae luck at a',
There's little pleasure in the house
When our gudeman's awa.
William Julius Mickle, 'The Mariner's Wife'

October 27 – Endless questions

'... those obstinate questionings of sense
and outward things.'
William Wordsworth, Ode, 'Intimations of Immortality'

I suggested earlier that questions are always in order. How are we going to grow in our knowledge of things if we don't have a questioning mind? But what happens when questioning become nosiness or intrusiveness.

On one of the main thoroughfares in and out of Edinburgh, there's a house with a red telephone box in the front garden. Now, people have a right to put anything in their front garden as they choose – witness the tall railway signal I mentioned some time ago. But a red telephone box? Now, come on ...

I have lots of questions ... Don't they have a phone in the house and must use the phone box every time they want to make a call? Could I use it if it was an emergency? Is it a nostalgic phone box, where someone proposed or a couple had their first snog? Is it *really* a phone box, or is it used for something else – a bird house, or a garden shed, or a greenhouse? Was it bought at an auction and taken home in the back of a car? A crane? A lorry? A JCB? How long has it been there? Was it bought with the house or is it a recent addition? So many questions ... so little time ...

What will I do with all my questions? Ring the doorbell and bombard the poor owners with my whys and whats and hows and whens? Of course not. That would be too nosey, too intrusive. I'll just leave all my questions unasked.

*I'll have to live with my questions, as people do
with their red telephone box, and leave it at that.*

October 28 – Weather

'When two Englishmen meet,
their first talk is of the weather.'
Samuel Johnson, in The Idler

I'll take issue with Samuel Johnson's affirmation on this basis – such behaviour is *not* confined to Englishmen. It is also common to every Scottish person I know. Having been born in the shadow of Ben Nevis, where the average annual rainfall is over 90 inches, I'm as familiar with talk about the weather as anyone else. We say in Lochaber, 'If you can't see Ben Nevis, it's raining. If you *can* see Ben Nevis, it's just about to rain.'

When Mark Twain was giving a speech to the New England Society in December 1876, he said this:

There is a sumptuous variety about the New England weather that compels the stranger's admiration – and regret. The weather is always doing something there; always attending strictly to business; always getting up new designs and trying them on people to see how they will go.

Now, that's more like it. To see weather in all its variety; to be amazed at the changes in the seasons (or even having four seasons in one day); to admire the differences in our weather systems; to live each day as it comes *despite* the weather ... will surely give us more from life than a negative spirit of complaining about our lot.

Talk about the weather if you must, but embrace it and love it for what it is.

Get used to the weather. After all, there's a lot of it about.

October 29 – Bravery

'I have done one braver thing
Than all the Worthies did.'
John Donne, The Undertaking

Catherine Douglas is a figure from history whose story of bravery I have never forgotten. She was a member of the powerful Clan Douglas in troubled 15th-century Scotland, and lady-in-waiting to Joan Beaufort, queen to King James I. While the king was staying at a Dominican chapterhouse in Perth, a group of men led by Sir Robert Graham came to the door searching for him in order to assassinate him. The conspirators were assisted in their plot by an 'insider' who had removed the bolt from the door of the room in which James and his queen were staying.

Hearing the commotion, the king fled into a sewer tunnel, and the queen and her ladies hastily replaced the floorboards to hide his escape route. To give them time and to assist the king's escape, Catherine Douglas thrust her arm through the staples of the door to bar the assassins' entrance. Her bravery was all in vain, however, for the assassins forced the door open anyway, breaking Catherine's arm, and discovered and killed the king. Catherine's bravery did not go unheralded, however, for, according to the story, from then on she was known as Kate Barlass.

Four hundred years later, Dante Gabriel Rossetti recounted the story in verse in *The King's Tragedy*. The poem contains the line 'Catherine, keep the door!'

Bravery matters and is always worth remembering.
Will we be prepared to 'keep the door'
when someone close to us is in trouble?

October 30 – Songs

'Secret thoughts and open countenance
will go safely over the whole world.'

Scipione Alberti

For the whole of my adult life I have been devoted to the music of the American singer/songwriter Tom Paxton. Now seventy-eight, Paxton has had a musical career spanning over fifty years, being a key figure in the folk revival of the early 1960s with Woody Guthrie, Pete Seeger and others. His love songs, protest material, ballads, children's songs, funny ditties and much more have been integral to my life.

In a radio interview several years ago, Tom Paxton was asked how he got his ideas for writing songs. 'I have a notebook,' he said. 'I jot things down – ideas, phrases, odd words, even complete lines.'

'But how do you come to write the songs? What happens between jotting things down and the finished piece?'

To which Paxton replied, 'I don't write my songs. I just write them down.'

'I just write them down ...' He's being modest, of course. Being a writer I know that things don't just 'happen'. But he is telling us much more. It's about knowing what's out there and being a channel through which it can be developed. The songs are already there. If you are aware of that, you can indeed catch them and write them down. Awareness is always where it begins.

*Can I take Tom Paxton to my desert island with me,
singing any song he likes?*

October 31 – Faces

'Faces are but a gallery of pictures.'
Francis Bacon, Essays – Of Friendship

The older I become, the more memories I have of people I've loved. I have 'a gallery of pictures' I'm happy to walk through again and again to see Charles Lamb's *Old Familiar Faces.*

I have had playmates, I have had companions,
In my days of childhood, in my joyful school-days –
All, all are gone, the old familiar faces.

I have been laughing, I have been carousing,
Drinking late, sitting late, with my bosom cronies –
All, all are gone, the old familiar faces.

I loved a Love once, fairest among women:
Closed are her doors on me, I must not see her –
All, all are gone, the old familiar faces.

Ghost-like I paced round the haunts of my childhood,
Earth seem'd a desert I was bound to traverse,
Seeking to find the old familiar faces.

Friend of my bosom, thou more than a brother,
Why wert not thou born in my father's dwelling?
So might we talk of the old familiar faces –

How some they have died, and some they have left me,
And some are taken from me; all are departed –
All, all are gone, the old familiar faces.

November 1 – Saints

'I love thee with a love I seemed to lose
With my lost saints.'
Elizabeth Barrett Browning, How Do I Love Thee? (Sonnet 43)

One of my favourite poems, and one which I've used often at funerals,
is by Elizabeth Barrett Browning.

How do I love thee? Let me count the ways.
I love thee to the depth and breadth and height
My soul can reach, when feeling out of sight
For the ends of being and ideal grace.
I love thee to the level of every day's
Most quiet need, by sun and candle-light.
I love thee freely, as men strive for right.
I love thee purely, as they turn from praise.
I love thee with the passion put to use
In my old griefs, and with my childhood's faith.
I love thee with a love I seemed to lose
With my lost saints. I love thee with the breath,
Smiles, tears, of all my life; and, if God choose,
I shall but love thee better after death.

My mother and father are buried together in a cemetery overlooking
Loch Linnhe near Fort William. I'd like to say that when I sit by their
graves I feel them close to me. But I never do. At the start I felt I had
lost them for ever. But, remarkably, I now have a deeper love for them
than I've ever had, finding that love in different places and in new
forms as time goes by. I've lost count of the ways, and I expect there
will be even more yet to come.

Has love died when the people I love have died?
No, it has not, and, I know now, it never, ever will.

November 2 – Lamentation

'She bid me take life easy,
as the grass grows on the weirs;
But I was young and foolish then,
and now am full of tears.'
W B Yeats, Down by the Salley Gardens

The late Bob Davidson, Professor of Old Testament at Glasgow University, spoke at my hospice on the meaning of suffering. 'In the Bible,' he said, 'there are more verses of lamentation than there are verses of praise.' We cannot avoid sorrow and tears. Lamentation is part of the human condition.

The Book of Lamentations in the Old Testament is a collection of poems lamenting the destruction of Jerusalem in 586 BC and its aftermath of ruin and exile. These poems are still used in Judaism on the annual days of fasting and mourning. Lamentation doesn't go away.

Medical research tell us that there's a hormone in tears (adrenocorticotropic hormone, ACTH) which signals the adrenals to produce more cortisol, responsible for supporting the fight or flight response. During times of stress, an excess of cortisol increases blood sugar levels and blood pressure, getting the body ready for some serious physical activity. As the stress builds internally but has no external vent (running, fighting, etc) we feel overwhelmed and may even experience heart palpitations or panic attacks. Getting rid of ACTH through tears can alleviate the situation.

Don't we know the feeling of being completely spent and calm after a good cry?

Sorrow is part of our living. Tears are normal.
Lamentation matters – in more ways than one.

November 3 – More and more questions

'Puzzling questions are not beyond all conjecture.'
Sir Thomas Browne, Hydriotaphia

Three boys are in the school playground bragging about their fathers. 'What's your dad do?' the first one is asked.

'My dad's a poet,' he says with pride. 'He scribbles a few words on a piece of paper, calls it a poem and they give him £50.'

'What's your dad do?' the second is asked.

'My dad's a songwriter,' he says, also with pride. '£50 for a poem? That's nothing. My dad scribbles a few words on a piece of paper, calls it a song and they give him £200.'

'What's your dad do,' the third one is asked.

'My dad's a vicar,' he announces, 'and I've got you both beat. My dad scribbles a few words on a piece of paper, calls it a sermon and it takes eight people to collect all the money!'

★★★

The children were lined up in the cafeteria of a convent school for their lunch. At the head of the table was a large tray of apples. Beside the apples was a very stern nun.

'How many apples are we allowed?' one of the girls asked. Without saying a word, the nun pointed firmly to a large notice on the wall which announced, 'Take only ONE apple. God is watching.'

As they moved along the lunch-line, there was a large plate of chocolate-chip biscuits. Quickly the girl scribbled a note and left it beside the plate for the others to find. It read: 'Take all you want. God is busy watching the apples.'

November 4 – Marches

'March, March, Ettrick and Teviotdale,
Why the deil dinna ye march forward in order?'
Sir Walter Scott, The Monastery

The Pilgrimage of Grace was an uprising among the people of Yorkshire in 1536. They had many grievances, including King Henry VIII's break with the Roman Catholic Church, the 'Dissolution of the Monasteries' and the unpopular policies of the king's chief minister, Thomas Cromwell. Upwards of 40,000 people participated in the marches organised by Robert Aske, an able lawyer from an important Yorkshire family. It was Aske who coined the phrase 'pilgrimage of grace', for he saw the protest marches as a pilgrimage of the people towards truth and justice for all.

There have been many marches of protest in our history. In the Salt March, from March to April 1930 in India, thousands followed Gandhi to protest against British rule. Nearly 60,000 people, including Gandhi himself, were arrested. The Jarrow March in 1936 was a protest march from Jarrow to London against the unemployment and poverty in the northeast during the 1930s. There were the Civil Rights marches from Selma to Montgomery, Alabama, in 1965 to highlight racial injustice in the southern states of the USA. In 2002 and 2003 there were large-scale protests against the Iraq War in many cities worldwide.

Marches matter. The right to protest, and to have mass-marches to do so, is important. Let's hope every such protest march is still 'a pilgrimage of grace' as we travel towards truth and justice for everyone.

Let grace and non-violence be arks of our pilgrimages
for justice, peace and equality.

November 5 – Futilities

'Accounting that to be futile which is unproductive.'
Francis Bacon, Novum Organum, Book I

On holiday recently, I watched a black Labrador chasing birds on a beach. Terns, oystercatchers and gulls at the sea-edge were sent packing by the marauding dog. They would settle a few yards away, only to be moved on again by the crazy hound. 'This is *my* beach,' he seemed to be saying. So, if there was any bird within marauding distance, he was off on the chase.

The birds, on the other hand, didn't much like being chased. So when they saw the black Lab hurtling towards them (again!) they just up and flew away, out to sea, high in the sky, farther along the beach, far enough away to be safe – at least for a nanosecond. 'You'll have to try harder than that,' they might have replied. It's what *I* would say, after all, and wouldn't you?

Did the dog learn from the futility of his efforts? No! Did he alter his behaviour because of his mistakes? No! Did he stop chasing birds when they flew away? No! Would he go on chasing birds all day if he had the chance? More than likely!

Much has been written about Jesus' story of the prodigal son – the wasteful son, the forgiving father, the resentful brother, and the like. But the story begins and ends for me with a young man who made mistakes and was prepared to admit it. *He* learned from futilities. He altered his behaviour when things had gone wrong. Will we continue to do our futile things, like chasing birds when they run away? Or will we learn from our mistakes and do things differently?

Recognising the futility of an action might be the beginning of change.

November 6 – One thing at a time

'The shortest way to do many things
is to do only one thing at once.'
Samuel Smiles, Self-Help

When I was involved with presenting and interviewing in religious programmes with Scottish Television in the 1980s, I leant heavily on the wisdom and experience of Rev Dr Nelson Gray, head of Religious Broadcasting with STV. Early on, after we'd finished the recording of a programme in which I had a lot of interviewing to do, Nelson took me aside in the 'green room' and said, 'A word of advice. Never ask a double-headed question or two questions at once. If you do, you'll only get an answer to the easier question, and you may get no response to the more important one.'

He took me into the editing suite. I'd just interviewed a rabbi in a series called *Come Wind, Come Weather.* Nelson arranged for a clip to be played. The rabbi had been a survivor of a concentration camp in which he'd seen the unspeakable horrors of the Holocaust at first hand. At one emotional point in the unfolding of his story I'd asked, 'Can you forgive those who inflicted the Holocaust on your people?' and, without pausing for breath, I continued, 'And how do you feel now looking back on it all?' The rabbi responded by dealing with the second question. We never got into the 'forgiveness' part in the way that we should have.

The next time you see a politician being interviewed, you'll see what I mean. If a 'double-header' is asked, they'll always duck the hard part and go for the easy one.

To get to the truth, deal with one thing at a time.
You're more likely to get to the heart of the matter that way.

November 7 – Discoveries

'The discovery of a new dish
does more for human happiness
than the discovery of a star.'

Anthelme Brillat-Savarin, Physiologie du Goût

When the singing started at family gatherings, and my grandfather was *very* drunk, someone would shout, 'C'mon, auld yin. Gie us yer sang, Tam.' Here's how I remember it …

> *Ah tried tae mak' a dumplin', it cost me mony an oor,*
> *Wi' currants an' raisins an' the very best o' floor.*
> *When Maister Tam cam' hame that nicht,*
> *'A dumplin'?' said he,*
> *'Twad mak' a better fitba' fur the Celtic Committee.'*

> *For he'll no' tak' liver, he'll no' tak' lamb;*
> *He disnae care a button for Lipton's ham;*
> *He'll no' tak' haddies, and yet he'll no' tak' veal;*
> *But he's awfae fond o' totties tae a big coo's heel.*

> *Ah thocht that ah wid buy him a wee bit mutton chop.*
> *He asked me if ah'd got it in an ironmonger's shop.*
> *'Oh weel,' said he, 'ah'll tak it, but if it's richt or wrang,*
> *Ah'll buy a ha'penny candle fur tae grease your fryin' pan.'*

I thought he was making it up, till I discovered years later that it was part of a *real song*, a 'bothy ballad' from the north-east of Scotland. In an instant I saw a strange song – and a stranger grandfather – in a completely new light.

Discoveries change things, don't they?

November 8 – Propaganda

'The best things come in small packages.'
Late-19th-century proverb

The term 'Napoleon Complex' suggests that people who are short overcompensate by being aggressive and domineering. Short people (mostly men, it should be said, which is why it's sometimes referred to as 'short-man syndrome') are claimed to be more belligerent, hostile, quarrelsome or pushy than most. In John Steinbeck's *Of Mice and Men*, the 'shorty' character, Curley, always feels obliged to prove his worth by picking fights with bigger men. In the TV comedy *Dad's Army*, Private Walker calls Captain Mainwaring Napoleon, perhaps because of Mainwaring's blustering approach to things, but more likely as a dig at his shortness and roundness of girth!

Is there such a thing as a 'Napoleon Complex'? Psychologists suggest not, believing it's more a form of derogatory social stereotyping than a definable personality trait. And it was all 'spin' in the first place. British propaganda during the Napoleonic wars promoted the idea that Napoleon was short, around five feet two. The idea lingered that the Emperor Napoleon compensated for this lack of height by seeking power through war and the expansion of his empire. But historians now suggest that Napoleon was actually five feet six or seven, taller than the average Frenchman of the age, and that, because Napoleon was often seen with his Imperial Guard, he was bound to look short beside soldiers chosen for their above-average height.

Beware of stereotyping. And beware of propaganda.
Why not look for the best in people – even the short ones.

November 9 – Help

'Since there's no help, come let us kiss and part.'
Michael Drayton, Idea (Sonnet 61)

The North wind doth blow and we shall have snow,
So what will poor robin do then, poor thing?
He'll sit in a barn and keep himself warm,
And hide his head under his wing, poor thing.

This nursery rhyme from the 16th century is designed to help children appreciate the security and warmth of home in the winter, as well as being sensitive to the plight of the robin. But another version of the nursery rhyme goes like this:

The North wind doth blow, and we shall have snow,
And what will the robin do then, poor thing?
He'll sit on a twig, and we'll feed him some bread,
And he'll sing and say 'Thank you, my friends,' poor thing.

Ah, I see! There's a difference. The second version will encourage children to appreciate their warm winter homes and be sensitive to the robin too. But now the rhyme also shows that there's something that can be done to alleviate the struggles of the poor robin.

In the first it's: 'Just let him get on with it. If he's hiding his head under his wing in some barn somewhere, what's that to me?' And in the second it's: 'Where's the bread so we can feed it to that poor robin over there on that twig. And, if we do, he might sing for us and say thank you.'

Poor robin ... better fed than ignored.
Poor me ... if I don't offer to help.

November 10 – In memoriam

'For famous men have
the whole earth as their memorial.'
Pericles, History of the Peloponnesian War

The National Arboretum in Staffordshire on the edge of the National Forest is the UK's year-round Centre of Remembrance. The woodland landscape is home to over 320 memorials. It's an evolving, maturing woodland featuring 30,000 trees and a vast collection of sites, symbols, plaques, sculptures and constructions commemorating every conceivable military and community organisation you can think of. The 150-acre site is a living, growing tribute to those who have served and continue to serve our country.

That's what had the impact on me. This place is a tribute, not to glory in war or to rejoicing in victories, but to those who served and fell. The trees and memorials call on us to remember and give thanks, to find tranquillity and thoughtfulness, and to pray for peace.

While I was there, I had this thought. In the autumn, the leaves of most of the trees in the National Arboretum are absorbed into the ground. The earth will be renewed and invigorated by what has fallen, and, in time, it will further strengthen what will grow in the spring and summer.

We remember the fallen, the people who matter to us who have gone before. They lie buried in the ground. But their falling is not in vain. We remember more than their death. We remember the life they gave to those who remain, and the opportunity for growth they give us yet.

At the going down of the sun, and in the morning,
we will remember them

November 11 – Remembering

'Lest we forget.'

Rudyard Kipling, Recessional

My wife and I were waiting in Portland airport in Oregon for a flight to Chicago on the penultimate leg of our journey home after a holiday. It was standard stuff – keeping an eye on the departure board, having another coffee, reading a book – passing the time waiting for our flight to be called.

On schedule, the announcement came: *Ladies and gentlemen, American Airlines Flight 103 is ready for boarding at Gate 7B.* Yes, it's ours. Get ready to go. *Passengers with small children and anyone requiring assistance, please come to the gate. Other passengers will be called shortly. Thank you for your patience.* Us next … But not yet. For after a few minutes we heard: *Ladies and gentlemen, thank you for your patience … Could we invite members of any branch of the military to come forward next for boarding? Thank you.*

No military personnel stepped forward. But no one seemed to mind. There was no impatient shuffling, no mutterings of discontent or complaint. Instead, everyone waited. *Ladies and gentlemen, thank you for your respect. We shall board the remaining passengers in row order. Would passengers in rows 18 through 36 please present themselves at Gate 7B? Thank you.*

Maybe they do it this way in all American airports, or maybe it's just United Airlines, or maybe only in Portland. I don't know. But for a few moments, it gave us cause to wait, to pause respectfully, to remember all who offer themselves, to recall lives lost and service still given.

Ladies and gentlemen, lest we forget …

November 12 – Still hopeful

'Hopes have precarious life.'

George Eliot, The Spanish Gypsy

I've heard it said that a generation or so ago the young women in a church which had an unmarried man as their minister were known as 'the Band of Hope'.

Well, that's as maybe, but 'the Band of Hope' has got nothing whatsoever to do with marriage or the prospects of the young women of a congregation finding a suitable liaison with their unattached minister. The Band of Hope was a temperance movement set up in the 1840s to teach children the importance and principles of sobriety and teetotalism.

In the second half of the 19th century alcohol was seen as a necessity of life, next only to food and water. The Band of Hope fought to counteract the influence of pubs and brewing companies, especially on working class people, 'the poor unfortunates'. They preached total abstinence, established alcohol-free premises and organised marches and demonstrations to oppose the evils of drink. And, of course, they encouraged young people to 'sign the pledge'. This literally meant putting your signature to a document that pledged that you would never touch alcohol. There were many homes which had a framed copy of 'the Pledge' on the living-room wall.

We may smile at 'the Band of Hope' now, mock the 'signing of the pledge' and criticise the doctrinaire approach. But, to those who need it, every glimmer of hope matters.

When you are faced with evil in any form,
a pledge to do something about it is important.

November 13 – Communication

'To do good and to communicate forget not.'

Bible, Hebrews 13:16

In 1986, when Edinburgh hosted the Commonwealth Games for the second time, my friend and I managed to secure tickets for a day in one of the hospitality boxes. It was sponsored by a drinks company, and the tickets had come to me from someone in the brewing industry. It was a great day out – morning coffee and cake, a sumptuous buffet lunch, afternoon tea with chocolate and savouries, and, of course, a free bar.

My friend was a university chaplain and, at that time, I was a parish minister. But being an 'off-duty' affair, we were both dressed in a smart suit, shirt and tie.

It's not that we were ashamed of our professional life, but as any of the clergy will tell you, when people discover at a social function what you do for a living, the conversation can turn and the atmosphere can change. So being 'in mufti' was good. It would make the day more enjoyable.

But as the day wore on conversations turned to 'who are you?' 'Are you guys in the drinks business, then?' Sorry, no ... 'Industry?' No ... 'Banking?' No ... It became a kind of a who-can-find-out-what-these-two-interlopers-do-for-a-living game. Eventually, people's patience ran out. 'OK. We give up! What *do* you do?' Quick as a flash my friend replied, 'We're in communication ...'

And the game started again. 'BT?' No ... 'The military?' No ... 'Computers?' No ... Did they ever get there? I'm not telling. But I can say we had a fantastic day off ...

Is there such a thing as too much communication?

November 14 – Rules

'Ah! When shall all men's good
Be each man's rule, and universal peace
Lie like a shaft of light across the land?'
Alfred, Lord Tennyson, The Golden Year

I have been a member of the Iona Community since 1973. Since then I have endeavoured to keep the Rule of the Community. Each year every member is invited to recommit to the Community in a 'with us' process, making a decision about whether the Rule can still be held to. At the present time, that recommitment is enshrined in a personal 'with us' letter to the leader of the Iona Community.

I'll share the contents of the Rule over the next few days, but, for now, I'll reflect on this. There are things that go along with 'rule keeping' in our daily living. If you don't keep 'the rules of the road', you'll be a danger to others and are likely to commit a road traffic offence. If you don't keep to 'the rules of the game', you'll be penalised, and maybe sent off. If you don't hold to 'the rules of behaviour' in a company or organisation, you are liable for discipline or dismissal.

Is the Rule of the Iona Community like that?' The answer is 'No!' It begins with a personal responsibility. But the keeping of the Rule is shared in small groups, 'family groups', and it is there in honesty, openness and in a non-judgemental setting that the Rule is explored. We're all in it together. It's about sharing in a trusting community.

For forty-three years, here's one member of the Iona Community who's been the better for that.

'The good old rule sufficeth them …'
William Wordsworth, 'Rob Roy's Grave'

November 15 – Nourishment

'The sire turns o'er, wi' patriarchal grace,
The big ha'-Bible, ance his faither's pride.'
Robert Burns, The Cotter's Saturday Night

The first rule for members of the Iona Community is this:

*We commit ourselves to daily prayer, worship with others
and regular engagement with the Bible
and other material which nourishes us.*

It's a hard rule to follow. It takes discipline, commitment, organisation and – for me, at any rate – facing up to failure.

There's a lot in this part of our Rule that I've touched on in one way or another as we've progressed through this year. But let me highlight this phrase today: 'which nourishes us'.

The Cotter in Burns' poem turned to 'the big ha' Bible' for daily spiritual nourishment for him and his loved ones. That's what we would expect, I suppose, for a devout Christian family. So far, so good …When I joined the Iona Community over forty years ago, this part of the Rule mentioned *only* the Bible. But in recent years there has been a debate among Community members. And I'm pleased that 'other material' is now included in this part of our Rule.

The Bible remains important – that's why there are many biblical quotes in this book. But did revelation, truth and guidance stop when the books of the Bible were agreed upon? I think not. Indeed, I *know* they didn't – thank God!

*As we engage with the writings of many good people,
there's more to nourish us than we could ever expect.*

November 16 – Justice and peace

'Yes, you have ravished justice;
Forced her to do your pleasure.'
John Webster, The White Devil

The second rule of the Iona Community is:

> *We commit ourselves to working for justice, peace,*
> *wholeness and reconciliation*
> *in our localities, society and the whole of creation.*

In the unfolding of this part of its Rule, the Iona Community enshrines key principles in its 'Justice, Peace and Integrity of Creation Commitment'. We are bound in the belief that:

> *the Gospel commands us to seek peace founded on justice; costly reconciliation is at the heart of the Gospel; work for justice, peace and an equitable society is a matter of extreme urgency; as stewards of creation, we have a responsibility to live in a right relationship with the whole of God's creation; handled with integrity, creation can provide for the needs of all, but not for the greed which leads to injustice and inequality, and endangers life on earth; everyone should have the quality and dignity of a full life that requires adequate physical, social and political opportunity, without the oppression of poverty, injustice and fear; social and political action leading to justice for all people and encouraged by prayer and discussion is a vital work of the Church; the use or threatened use of nuclear and other weapons of mass destruction is theologically and morally indefensible and [that] opposition to their existence is an imperative of the Christian faith.*

November 17 – Money

'A blessing that money cannot buy.'
Isaak Walton, The Compleat Angler

The third rule of the Iona Community is:

Supporting one another in prayer
and by meeting, communicating, and accounting with one another
for the use of our gifts, money and time,
our use of the earth's resources
and our keeping of all aspects of the Rule.

Community members meet regularly in family groups to fulfil one part of this commitment, developing openness and trust and sharing mutual support built on the base of a common understanding. The most important part of this for me has been the opportunity to talk openly about money. We have an annual 'accounting discipline', where each member must account for the disposal of 10% of what remains of income after 'base line' commitments are taken care of (including an appropriate percentage to the Community) and a breakdown of personal and family income and expenditure is shared.

The most important part of this process is honesty. Where else have I been able to talk about what I have, and what my priorities are, and how I use my income? Where else can I feel less than satisfied – even when I account for the tithe that I give – when I ask myself serious questions about how I spend the remainder?

In a world of competition,
can we find ways of looking at things differently?
In a world of secrecy,
can we find a new openness that makes a difference?

November 18 – In community

'Agreeing with others ...
to join and unite into a community.'
John Locke, Second Treatise of Government

The fourth rule of the Iona Community is:

*Sharing in the corporate life and organisation
of the Community.*

The Wounded Healer by Henri Nouwen is a book aimed at men and women who want to be of service in their church or community but who have found traditional models of service either threatening or ineffective. Many people struggle with the hierarchical model in organisations, when the 'top' people recruit others to fulfil tasks they've decided need doing. There are also problems with the 'it's aye bin' model, where everything must be done the way it's always been done, and usually by the same people.

The Wounded Healer offers hope to those who struggle with all of this. Nouwen begins with the need to accept the woundedness of human nature. This woundedness, he affirms, can serve as a source of strength and healing when being in community with others. He contends that all Christians are called to recognise the sufferings of their time in their own hearts and make that recognition the starting point of their service. The only way we can helpfully work through this is in community with other wounded healers.

*Sharing in community works when we recognise
we're all broken and can be healed together.*

November 19 – Political engagement

'For Mercy has a human heart,
Pity a human face,
And Love, the human form divine,
and Peace the human dress.'
William Blake, The Divine Image

Before I leave the Iona Community, here's how politics and peace are seen – the 'human dress' we all seek to wear.

As Members and Family Groups we will: engage in forms of political witness and action, prayerfully and thoughtfully, to promote just and peaceful social, political and economic structures; work for a policy of renunciation by our own nations of all weapons of mass destruction and for the encouragement of other nations, individually or collectively, to do the same; celebrate human diversity and actively work to combat discrimination on grounds of age, colour, disability, mental wellbeing, differing ability, gender, race, ethnic and cultural background, sexual orientation or religion; work for the establishment of the United Nations Organisation as the principal organ of international reconciliation and security, in place of military alliances; support and promote research and education into nonviolent ways of achieving justice, peace and a sustainable global society; work for reconciliation within and among nations by international sharing and exchange of experience and people, with particular concern for politically and economically oppressed nations; act in solidarity with the victims of environmental injustice throughout the world, and support political and structural change in our own countries to reduce our over-consumption of resources.

November 20 – Denials

'Ich bin der Geist der stets entbehren'
'I am the spirit that always denies.'
Johann Wolfgang von Goethe, Faust

When I was a boy and living in Fort William, we had no double-decker buses. But when we were on holiday, being upstairs in a bus or a tram was quite magical, especially in the front seat – being the driver!

A little lad was once doing the same – driving the bus, guiding it through the traffic, into bus stops, around roundabouts, across traffic lights, till, suddenly, the bus stopped! A car in front had braked unexpectedly and the bus had run into the back of it. It wasn't a bad accident but the police were on the scene quickly to direct the traffic past the bus. The little boy started to wail loudly. 'Did you bump yourself?' his mum asked. 'No,' he replied through his tears. 'Did you get a fright?' 'No,' he cried. 'So why are you so upset?' The little lad stopped crying long enough to say, 'Oh mum, it wisnae me! Please tell the police it wasn't my fault!'

We've all denied things when we know it *was* our fault. When Peter was challenged that he was a follower of Jesus, he denied it three times. 'It wisnae me.' Yet he came through in the end. He knew he couldn't live with it.

Perhaps we might realise that our denials when we're at fault ultimately do us no good. Denials, when we know we're in the wrong, just allow us to get more and more entangled in a developing web of deceit.

Will someone tell a little lad on the top deck of a bus
that his denials are OK, and that the police know that
'It wisnae him!'?

November 21 – Memory

'We have all forgot more than we remember.'
Thomas Fuller, Gnomologia

I watched a BBC prom concert recently in which the Aurora Orchestra played Mozart's final symphony, the *Jupiter*, entirely from memory. It was an amazing performance. Four movements, a thousand bars of music, a veritable myriad of notes ... and, as far as my untrained ear was concerned, not one mistake.

I'm amazed enough that a soloist can perform an entire concerto without recourse to the music. It's practice, of course, playing a piece over and over again so that it becomes second nature. 'Muscle memory,' my wife tells me. But, whatever it is, it's still singularly impressive. And when a *whole* orchestra can pull it off, well ...

Each player had their own way of remembering – a violinist on a train playing an invisible instrument; a viola player in a headstand listening to an iPod; a horn player saying he has to 'feel it, like a dance'; a violinist mapping out the piece as he goes for a run, each turn corresponding to a change in the music; the orchestra leader remembering her part like a sequence of numbers; a flautist humming to her baby. They all said it was liberating.

'For Mozart,' the conductor said, 'the music existed in his head and not on the page. Freeing ourselves from the page gets us inside Mozart's head.' The presenter said they were exploring Mozart's symphony 'from the inside out'.

If we practised our memory skills more than we do,
what's inside our heads might come out more readily and more beautifully.
Now, that would be liberating, wouldn't it?

November 22 – Meaning

'Free from all meaning, whether good or bad,
All in one word, heroically mad.'
John Dryden, Absalom and Achitophel

I have grumpy-old-man tendencies sometimes. My wife helpfully suggests that you can't *become* a grumpy old man if you've been grumpy all your life. It's a case of a grumpy man getting older. Well, that's as maybe, but my current grumpiness is focused on passenger announcements on trains. On a recent journey to Glasgow we were informed that 'This train will terminate at Glasgow Queen Street.' Eh? No! This train will *not* terminate anywhere. When did you last hear an announcement saying, 'The 12.34 to Falkirk High has died, it is no more, it has ceased to be …'?

No! This train *service* might terminate at Glasgow Queen Street, and this *journey* will certainly terminate – unless they plan to plough the train through the station and into George Square. Or the length of time to be spent on this train listening to inane and linguistically-compromised announcements will terminate at Glasgow Queen Street … But one thing is certain – the train will *not* terminate. The announcement is wrong!

Words matter. If there is a clear meaning to be conveyed, using the correct words is important. OK, we know what the announcement meant. The message got through. But it still makes me grumpy when it's not right.

'Say what you mean and mean what you say'
is a good axiom to live by.
The train announcer meant what he said,
but he didn't say what he meant.

November 23 – Poetry

'Of its own accord my song would come
in the right rhythms,
and what I was trying to say was poetry.'
Ovid, Tristia, Book IV

Those of us who write poetry know it's not as easy as Ovid suggests! If 'right rhythms' came to the poetry of William Topaz McGonagall, they are very hard to find. McGonagall, a 19th-century citizen of Dundee, has been dubbed the worst poet in the history of the English language. He wrote around two hundred poems and never seemed to realise how bad he was. Here's the opening to *The Tay Bridge Disaster.*

Beautiful Railway Bridge of the Silv'ry Tay!
Alas! I am very sorry to say
That ninety lives have been taken away
On the last Sabbath day of 1879,
Which will be remember'd for a very long time.

McGonagall performed his doggerel poetry at a local circus for fifteen shillings a night. The crowd often pelted him with flour, eggs, potatoes, herrings and stale bread. But things got out of hand, so the city magistrates were forced to ban the events.

Should we mock McGonagall? I think not. For in his day, before the advent of radio and TV, he was a source of news and entertainment for the good citizens of Dundee. Even now, his poetry makes people smile. In a serious age, that can't be a bad thing at all.

Even bad poetry can be memorable.

November 24 – Graffiti

'Kilroy was here.'
1930s graffiti

I once found some graffiti on a toilet wall. It said:

To do is to be – *Socrates*
To be is to do – *Jean-Paul Sartre*
Do Be Do Be Do – *Frank Sinatra*

Funny *and* clever ... But we can't say that about most graffiti we come across. Most of it is just wanton vandalism. Of course, some graffiti has been raised to an art form. Banksy? A graffiti artist of the highest order.

But graffiti wasn't always as we know it now. The term graffiti refers to the inscriptions and figure drawings scratched or painted on the walls of ancient sepulchres or ruins, such as the Catacombs of Rome or Pompeii. From simple written words to elaborate wall paintings, graffiti has been around since ancient times. Important aspects of our history have been gleaned from graffiti. The only known form of the Safaitic language, for example – an early form of Arabic – comes from inscriptions scratched on rocks in the deserts of Syria, Jordan and Saudi Arabia from the 1st century BC. 'Kilroy was here'? But so were lots of people through our recorded history. Their graffiti tells us that.

I wonder if we might find better ways of marking *our* territory and noting our presence – like, how much love we've left behind, and how many people's lives have been changed for the better. We don't need graffiti for that ...

What message do you want to leave for others to find?

November 25 – Refreshment

'So the Lord awakened as one out of sleep:
and like a giant refreshed with wine.'
Bible, Psalm 78:66

There's an Edinburgh expression I like a lot: 'Would you like a small refreshment?' It's a gentle, polite and dignified euphemism, not relating to tea or coffee, but something stronger.

When I was a minister in Edinburgh, I called to see two elderly sisters. They took me into the 'back room', and though I was welcomed politely there was a slight tension in the air. As I was leaving, one of them said, 'If you choose to call again, would you be kind enough to let us know when it will be?' I assured them I would. But I was puzzled.

When I was due to visit again, I phoned the day before to confirm the best time to call. I arrived at the agreed time, but now I was ushered into 'the front room'. In the middle of the floor was a circular coffee-table covered by a delicate, lace doily, on which had been laid a silver tray with a bottle of *Croft Original* sherry, three crystal sherry glasses and a plate with three fingers of shortbread. Once I had sat down, the elder sister smiled and said, 'Well, minister, would you like a small refreshment?' When I'd indicated in the affirmative, three glasses of sherry were poured with great ceremony, the shortbread was appropriately allocated and we partook of our refreshment together. It was a delightful social occasion. The ritual was repeated every time I visited.

Good old-fashioned Edinburgh hospitality. None of 'You'll have had your tea' at all.

What might you appreciate from the hospitality of others?
What 'small refreshment' might you offer someone else?

November 26 – Mystery

'We soon learn that there is nothing
mysterious or supernatural in the case.'
David Hume, Enquiry Concerning Human Understanding

In my second year in university I shared 'digs' with five other students, in a post-Victorian terraced house in the centre of Edinburgh, run by two elderly sisters. Our landladies were lovely, but they weren't worldly-wise.

The students were an eclectic bunch, and we all had our own rooms. Two of us were at the top of the house – Dave Hawcroft, an eccentric engineering student who had a passion for vintage cars, and me, a quiet-living, shinty-playing Highlander who was struggling to make sense of a degree in maths and physics. Both rooms had a 'gas-miser' fire controlled by a slot-meter. The meter took 'shillings' (old money, the equivalent of 5p and roughly the size of a 10p piece) and we were *always* running out of coins. However, the enterprising engineering student put his car-maintenance skills to good use and found a way of picking the padlocks on the meters so that we could take coins out and feed them in again as often as we liked.

The meters were always emptied on a Saturday, and, being honest chaps, we made sure the money was replaced. But what two elderly ladies made of the mystery of all the coins being piled up neatly in the four corners of each meter's box we'll never know. Perhaps they thought that D Hawcroft and T Gordon had a bit of the supernatural about them. Or perhaps they were just pleased that they had some honest students in their digs.

'*Stewards of the mysteries of God.*'
1 Corinthians 4:1

November 27 – Twinning

'Those twins of learning that he raised in you,
Ipswich and Oxford.'
William Shakespeare, Henry VIII

I'm not sure I saw Ipswich and Oxford as twins before I read this quote from Shakespeare. I'll leave the good people of both towns to work out whether it's true or not. But what is prevalent these days is the 'twinning' of villages, towns and cities with one another. How often have I driven into a place that tells me it's twinned with a village in Southern France, or a town in Louisiana, or a region of Malawi?

My own village in East Lothian is twinned with Barga, a hilltop town in Tuscany. In the late 19th century, following the demise of Barga's silk industry, many young Italians emigrated to Scotland. In time, they intermarried with the Scots and many successful businesses – fish and chip shops, delis and ice cream parlours, for example – were established. These successful enterprises created wealth which was brought back to Barga and used to construct the beautiful villas which now form the 'new' area known as *Il Giardino* (the garden) outside of the historic centre. Barga celebrates *Settimana Scozzese* – Scottish Week – every year. The artist John Bellany, connected to both locations, cemented the link with East Lothian and a 'twinning' was the result.

Twinning works. When we learn from one another, become aware of our varied cultures and histories and, above all, come to value our common humanity, concerns and standards, we grow closer together.

When we're closer to one another,
we learn respect and understanding, and everyone benefits.

November 28 – Toilets

'Pure ablution round earth's human shores.'
John Keats, Bright Star

Toilets are a necessity. Hygiene, privacy and comfort in this area of our lives are important. Where would we be without our toilets? Digging a hole in the garden, perhaps?

Here's a very old joke: There was a break-in at the local police-station. All the toilets were stolen. A police spokesman said they had nothing to go on.

We may joke, but, sadly, while *we* have hygiene, privacy and comfort in our toileting, there are many who do not. Some don't even have a garden in which to dig a hole. And that's not funny. So I was delighted when a friend introduced me to Toilet Twinning, a water and sanitation charity initiative. Its website suggests we 'Flush away the world's toilet trouble with your very own twinned toilet.'

> *2.3 billion people don't have somewhere safe and hygienic to go to the toilet … [That's] 1 in 3 people across the world … Bad sanitation is one of the world's biggest killers: it hits women, children, old and sick people hardest. Every minute, a child under the age of five dies because of dirty water and poor sanitation. Around half the people in the world have an illness caused by bad sanitation … It's out of order!*

My toilet is now twinned with a latrine in Cambodia. I'll never use *that* loo, but I know my donation has twinned me with people who need practical and life-enhancing help.

> *I'm delighted people have got something to go on.*
> *We just have to get the police sorted out now!*

November 29 – Homeland

'The more foreigners I saw,
the more I loved my homeland.'
Pierre-Laurent Buirette du Belloy, Le Siège de Calais

Xenophobic? In 18th-century France that may well have been Du
Belloy's intention. But he still hints at a passion for one's homeland
being strengthened the more one travels. The more I get to know of
the world, the more I value my roots. That's not xenophobia or nation-
alism. Like the twinning of towns or toilets, when we learn from each
other, everyone benefits. But that shouldn't diminish one's pride in
one's own national identity. We all need a place we can call home.

My Ain Folk is a traditional Scottish song which my mother sang
often. It's another of my Desert Island Discs:

Far frae my hame I wander, but still my thoughts return
To my ain folk over yonder in the sheiling by the burn.
I see the cosy ingle and the mist upon the brae,
And joy and sadness mingle as I list some auld world lay.
And it's oh, but I'm longing for my ain folk,
Though they be but lowly pure and plain folk.
I am far beyond the sea, but my heart will always be
At hame in dear old Scotland wi' my ain folk.

Remove the sentimentality and you have the universal yearning for
a homeland, where you can be surrounded by your people and culture, and find true acceptance. How sad it is for those who might
never see their homeland again.

Remember those who are displaced from their country,
who yearn for a homeland to which they might never return.

November 30 – Andrew

'The dignity of this high calling.'

Edmund Burke, On Conciliation with America

Saint Andrew was a Galilean fisherman who, along with his brother Peter, became a disciple of Jesus. As an Apostle, he took the Christian message through Greece, around the Mediterranean and into central Europe, and we are told that he was martyred by crucifixion at the Greek city of Patras. A tradition developed that his cross was *crux decussate* or X-shaped – now commonly known as the 'saltire' or St Andrew's cross. It's believed that he purposely chose this form of crucifixion because he considered himself unworthy to die on the same kind of cross as had been used for Jesus.

Andrew Carnegie was born in Dunfermline in 1835, but made his fortune in the American steel industry in the late 18th and early 20th centuries. He was, in his day, one of the richest men in America and possibly in the world. But he was also one of the most generous, and, as a philanthropist, it's believed that in the latter years of his life he gave away in excess of $350 million to further the causes of peace, education, science and research.

These two Andrews, from different backgrounds, ages and circumstances, had depth, meaning and principles that underpinned their lives. They had dignity and humility in common. The one gave himself for his faith. The other gave his wealth to create the possibility of a better future for many people.

On this St Andrew's Day, can we learn from them, and build better lives for ourselves, for others, for our nation and our world because of our principles, dignity and humility?

What of myself can I give away so that others benefit?

December 1 – Veni Emmanuel

'Christmas is coming, the goose is getting fat.
Please to put a penny in an old man's hat.'
Traditional nursery rhyme

The start of December sees the beginning of the run-up to Christmas,
what the Church traditionally calls 'The Season of Advent'. One of
the familiar hymns sung in our churches during Advent is *O Come,
O Come, Emmanuel*. It's based on a translation by John Mason Neale
of the original Latin, *Veni, Veni, Emmanuel*. What we sing now is a
metrical paraphrase of the *O Antiphons*, a series of plainchant
antiphons attached to the *Magnificat* at Vespers over the final days
before Christmas during the 18th century.

One verse which always helps me in Advent:

O come, Thou Dayspring, come and cheer,
Our spirits by thine advent here;
Disperse the gloomy clouds of night,
And death's dark shadows put to flight.

Neale's original translation was:

Draw nigh, Thou Orient, Who shalt cheer
And comfort by Thine Advent here,
And banish far the brooding gloom
Of sinful night and endless doom.

I don't need to be reminded of the 'sinful nights' and the 'endless
doom' which might await me. But I *do* need the Advent assurance
that the dark shadows of pain, sorrow and death will be dispersed
when Love is in our midst.

December 2 – Advent

'Hills of the north, rejoice:
River and mountain-spring,
Hark to the advent voice;
Valley and lowland spring.'
Charles Edward Oakley, Hills of the North, Rejoice (19th century)

Here we are again, another Advent, the beginning of the run-up to Christmas. Time for a little bit of Christmas humour.

It was coming up to Christmas and Tommy asked his mum if he could have a Playstation. She told him that he would have to write to Santa Claus. But Tommy, having just finished with his school nativity play, had a better idea. 'I'd rather write to the baby Jesus,' he said. So he went to his room and wrote, 'Dear Jesus, I have been a very good boy all year, and so I would like to have a Playstation 3 for Christmas.' When he read over what he'd written he knew it wasn't *strictly* true. He decided to try again. 'Dear Jesus, I'm a good boy *most* of the time and would like a Playstation 3 for Christmas.' But he wasn't happy with this one either. He tried a third time. 'Dear Jesus, if I try *really* hard to be good, can I *please* have a Playstation 3 for Christmas?'

But he still wasn't satisfied. So he decided to go out for a walk while he thought about a better approach. On the way home he passed a house with a small statue of the Virgin Mary in the front garden. He grabbed the statue, stuffed it inside his jacket, hurried home and hid it under the bed. Then he wrote the final version of his letter.

'Dear Jesus, if you want to see your mother again, you'd better send me a Playstation 3 for Christmas.'

Smile! It's only 23 days to Christmas!

December 3 – Jokes

'It's an odd job, making decent people laugh.'
Molière, La Critique de l'École des Femmes

Only 22 days to go now ... So before you get overwhelmed with your preparations, here are some more things to make you smile. After all, it is a season of merriment, isn't it?

It was just before Christmas and the magistrate was in a happy mood. He asked the prisoner in the dock, 'What are you charged with?' The prisoner replied, 'Doing my Christmas shopping too early.'

'That's no crime,' said the magistrate. 'In fact, it seems quite a sensible approach. Just how early were you doing this shopping?'

'Before the shop opened,' answered the prisoner.

Maria went to the post office to buy stamps for her Christmas cards. 'What denomination?' asked the assistant.

'Oh! Good heavens! Have we come to this?' said Maria. 'I'm not a regular churchgoer. Just put me down as C of E and that'll be fine ...'

Q: Why are Christmas trees like bad knitters?
A: They both drop their needles.

Q: Why does Santa like working in the garden?
A: Because he enjoys going hoe, hoe, hoe.

Q: Why is Christmas just like another day at the office?
A: You end up doing all the work and the fat guy in the suit gets all the credit.

December 4 – Testing

'It is your part and duty also ...
to walk answerably to your calling,
and as becometh the children of light.'

The Book of Common Prayer (1662) from 'Baptism of such that are of riper years'

In the book of Judges, there's the story of a young man called Gideon who is getting on with life when God's angel calls him to be the new leader of Israel. 'Go with all your strength and rescue Israel from the Midianites,' he is told. 'I, your God, am sending you.' But Gideon is not at all sure. He decides to test his calling – not once, but twice.

If you will save Israel by my hand as you have promised – look, I will place a wool fleece on the threshing floor. If there is dew only on the fleece and all the ground is dry, then I will know that you will save Israel by my hand, as you said.' And that is what happened. Gideon rose early the next day; he squeezed the fleece and wrung out the dew – a bowlful of water. Then Gideon said to God, 'Do not be angry with me. Let me make just one more request. Allow me one more test with the fleece, but this time make the fleece dry and let the ground be covered with dew.' That night God did so. Only the fleece was dry; all the ground was covered with dew. [Judges 6:36-40, *New International Version*]

I'm not sure I would try to test my calling in *that* way, when a prayerful, thoughtful assessment should be enough.

If there's a Call, isn't it right to give it your best shot –
no matter what?

December 5 – Sermons

'Perhaps it may turn out a sang;
Perhaps, turn out a sermon.'
Robert Burns, Epistle to a Young Friend

A minister whose sermon had gone down very badly asked a friend afterwards, 'How would you have delivered that sermon?' 'Under an assumed name,' was the reply!

Critics of sermons are commonplace. Samuel Pepys recorded in his diary on 17th March 1661 that he'd heard 'a good, honest and painful sermon'. We know that 17th March 1661 was a Thursday. So maybe Pepys had been to church in the middle of the week, or perhaps he'd taken time to reflect on the quality of the sermon from the previous Sunday.

In any event, we're not privy to whether the sermon caused pain for Pepys or the preacher. But we're left with an honest comment about the quality of a preacher's offering. You can't help but admire the straightforward critique of the sermon's worth.

I used to think that sermons mattered, in the sense that they were things of great, lasting impact, that would remain in people's hearts and minds for ever. But I've come to the conclusion that sermons are 'of the moment'. They are to be given away, good or bad, even written of in diaries, but to be valued for their immediate and personal impact.

St Francis de Sales wrote,
'The test of a preacher
is that his congregation goes away saying not:
'What a lovely sermon!'
but: 'I will do something.'
You don't need an assumed name – or a diary – for that!

December 6 – The people

'You are the salt of the earth.'
Bible, Matthew 5:13

The pride Glasgow people have in themselves often elicits the affirmation, 'We arra peepul ...' (We are the people.) Shouldn't everyone be able to say that with pride?

Rudyard Kipling's poem *A Pilgrim's Way* offers me the essence of the worth and value of 'the people'. I'll share the whole poem over two days with little comment, other than to say that 'the people are good enough for me' as well.

> I do not look for holy saints to guide me on my way,
> Or male and female devilkins to lead my feet astray.
> If these are added, I rejoice – if not, I shall not mind,
> So long as I have leave and choice to meet my fellow-kind.
> For as we come and as we go (and deadly-soon go we!)
> The people, Lord, Thy people, are good enough for me!
>
> Thus I will honour pious men whose virtue shines so bright
> (Though none are more amazed than I when I by chance do right),
> And I will pity foolish men for woe their sins have bred
> (Though ninety-nine per cent of mine I brought on my own head).
> And, Amorite or Eremite, or General Averagee,
> The people, Lord, Thy people, are good enough for me!
>
> And when they bore me overmuch, I will not shake mine ears,
> Recalling many thousand such whom I have bored to tears.
> And when they labour to impress, I will not doubt nor scoff;
> Since I myself have done no less and – sometimes pulled it off.
> Yea, as we are and we are not, and we pretend to be,
> The people, Lord, Thy people, are good enough for me!

December 7 – All people

'All people that on earth do dwell,
Sing to the Lord with cheerful voice.'
William Kethe, The Geneva Psalter, 1561

Might someone sing with a cheerful voice because of me?

And when they work me random wrong, as oftentimes hath been,
I will not cherish hate too long (my hands are none too clean).
And when they do me random good I will not feign surprise.
No more than those whom I have cheered with wayside charities.
But, as we give and as we take – whate'er our takings be –
The people, Lord, Thy people, are good enough for me!

But when I meet with frantic folk who sinfully declare
There is no pardon for their sin, the same I will not spare
Till I have proved that Heaven and Hell which in our hearts we have
Show nothing irredeemable on either side of the grave.
For as we live and as we die – if utter Death there be –
The people, Lord, Thy people, are good enough for me!

Deliver me from every pride – the Middle, High, and Low –
That bars me from a brother's side, whatever pride he show.
And purge me from all heresies of thought and speech and pen
That bid me judge him otherwise than I am judged. Amen!
That I may sing of Crowd or King or road-borne company,
That I may labour in my day, vocation and degree,
To prove the same in deed and name, and hold unshakenly
(Where'er I go, whate'er I know, whoe'er my neighbour be)
This single faith in Life and Death and to Eternity:
"The people, Lord, Thy people, are good enough for me!"

December 8 – Fancied

'In the spring a young man's fancy turns to love.'
Alfred, Lord Tennyson, Locksley Hall

In my younger years, I worked a fair bit in radio and TV. The radio work was with BBC Schools, and the TV work was largely with Scottish Television. The bulk of my TV work was on pre-recorded programmes, doing presenting or interviewing.

On one occasion, in STV's Edinburgh studio, I was interviewing a Roman Catholic nun about her life, work and faith. The programme was 'as live', which meant that the recording suite was 'down the line' in Glasgow. Everything was going well, until, out of the corner of my eye, I saw the floor manager starting to giggle. Within seconds both cameramen were giggling too, and soon I could hear sound engineers and other crew members joining in the laughter.

The floor manager stepped forward. 'I'm sorry,' he said. 'We'll have to stop. There's a problem. It's not you. We'll get it sorted out in no time.' Soon enough, the interview was 'counted in' once more, and the programme proceeded without a hitch to its conclusion.

At the end of the recording I asked the floor manager what the problem had been. 'Oh,' he said, his face reddening, 'the recording engineer at the Glasgow end caught a close-up of the nun and burst out, "My God, she's gorgeous. Any chance of her phone number?" I couldn't restrain myself, and that started everyone else off. But it's been put down as a technical hitch, and nobody's the wiser.'

Ah … but … you see … I had the nun's phone number,
and there was no way I was going to share it with anyone else.

December 9 – Re-enactment

'How many ages hence
Shall this our lofty scene be acted o'er
In state unborn, and accents yet unknown!'
William Shakespeare, Julius Ceasar

The 'Saturday pictures' in Fort William's Picture House were for kids. With lots of others I went to the movies every week. It was six-pence (6d in 'old money', 2.5p in today's coinage) for a seat 'downstairs' and 9d in the balcony – filled with older kids who got more pocket money than I did. Roy Rogers and a variety of Western heroes were the order of the day. I remember a series called 'The Green Archer', a kind of forerunner of a 'superhero'. There was also the 1960s' equivalent of *Byker Grove* or *Grange Hill.*

Two things mattered about the Saturday pictures ... The first is that I could go by myself – a bus trip from my village into Fort William and back – very grown up. And the second was that all the kids were well equipped for the whole of the next week with things we could re-enact.

We'd seen it on the screen, now we acted it out – repeatedly. Cowboys and Indians, kids building racing carts, Robin Hood and the like were our bread-and-butter scripts for hours of play. On bikes, in a gang-hut, in the fields, across a moor, we had all the scripts we ever needed.

We do the same in adult life ... not watching a movie or TV programme with mates, but re-enacting what we see and know in the dramas of daily living. 'Living it out' it's called.

What dramas do we display that give people good things to re-enact?
What might people be 'living out' because they've seen the pictures we show?

December 10 – Holiness

'Worship the Lord in the beauty of holiness.'
Bible, Psalm 96:8

I helped care for a patient in our hospice who was a Roman Catholic sister from a small order of nuns. She was in a single room, and the Mother Superior and two of the sisters were her constant companions. Day and night they stayed with her. They never left her side for 48 hours.

Throughout their vigil, they repeated the Rosary over, and over, and over again. It became clear to anyone entering the room – for a procedure, to check medication, or just to offer support – that the room was filled with holiness. It was the only way to describe it.

The repetition of the Rosary, and the dignity and playfulness of the nuns, had created a special atmosphere around a dying woman.

The Sikh scriptures, from Guru Arjan Var Jaitasari, offer us this insight:

Better by far than any other way
is the act of repeating the perfect Name of God.
Better by far than any other rite
is the cleansing of one's heart
in the company of the devout.
Better by far than any other skill
is endlessly to utter the wondrous Name of God.
Better by far than any sacred text
is hearing and repeating the praises of the Lord.
Better by far than any other place
is the heart wherein abides
that most precious Name of God.

December 11 – More mistakes

'Think it possible you may be mistaken.'
Oliver Cromwell, Letter to the General Assembly of the Church of Scotland

The General Assembly of the Church of Scotland is far from being the funniest gathering I've ever attended. Maybe it should be standard practice to read out some of the things below, on the basis that Oliver Cromwell may well be right ...

All singles are invited to join us Friday at 7pm for the annual Christmas Sing-alone.

The Ladies' Liturgy Society met on Monday evening. Mrs Jones sang 'Put Me In My Little Bed', accompanied by the minister.

Thursday at 5pm there will be a meeting of the Little Mothers Club. All wishing to become little mothers, please see the Rev Paterson in his office.

Next Sunday, a special collection will be taken to defray the cost of the new carpet. All those wishing to do something on the new carpet will come forward and get a piece of paper.

The pastor would appreciate it if the ladies of the congregation would lend him their electric girdles for the pancake breakfast next Sunday morning.

The Associate Minister unveiled the church's new Stewardship Campaign slogan last Sunday 'I Upped My Pledge – so, Up Yours.'

December 12 – Use your imagination

'What the imagination seizes as beauty must be truth –
whether it existed before or not.'
John Keats, Letter to Benjamin Bailey, 1817

The Archers is the world's longest-running radio soap opera. On BBC's Radio 4, it's had more than 18,000 episodes. It is described as 'a contemporary drama in a rural setting'. As such *The Archers* continues to air many important social issues, including, in September 2016, the issue of domestic abuse.

The trial of *The Archers'* Helen Titchener, with millions tuning in to hear how she fared against her emotionally abusive husband, Rob, won widespread praise for highlighting the sensitive issue of domestic emotional abuse, and was even praised by lawmakers for illustrating a subject which is often kept hidden.

So far, so good. But here's the bit I *didn't* get. The BBC commissioned a court artist to depict the trial in a series of sketches so we could *see* what was happening in the court. The artist told the media that the drawings had taken longer than usual because she kept having to refer to the script. What? This is *radio,* for goodness' sake! We don't *need* an artist to depict a radio drama. It's about imagination – the tone of a voice, the nature of the script, the use of sound effects, all help create a picture for us. It's in the *mind*!

The late Sir Terry Wogan said, 'Television contracts the imagination and radio expands it.' We can use our imagination any way we like to create our own picture of the action.

We can put our own visuals around the scenes, thank you.
We don't need any court artist to show us how we should think.

December 13 – I want

'Please, sir, I want some more.'

Charles Dickens, Oliver Twist

It's getting close to Christmas. This didn't happen in our home, but, oh my, how I wish it had!

Two boys were at their grandparents' house. It was a devout home, and so, at bedtime, the two of them knelt beside their beds to say their prayers. After the usual 'God bless mummy, God bless daddy, make me a good boy ...' the younger boy launched into a prayer his brother hadn't heard before.

'Dear God, I want a new bike for my Christmas.'

'That's not a proper prayer,' the older brother whispered. 'You shouldn't expect God to give you things just because you ask.'

The younger one, undeterred by this guidance, raised his voice and said more loudly. 'Dear God, I want a new bike for my Christmas.'

Again, a stern admonition from the older brother, 'That's not what prayers are for,' he insisted.

Once again, the devout child was unmoved by his brother's wisdom, and this time shouted at the top of his voice, 'DEAR GOD, I WANT A NEW BIKE FOR MY CHRISTMAS ... A NEW BIKE ... A NEW BIKE ...'

'Oh, for goodness' sake,' the older brother said. 'Why are you shouting in your prayers? God isn't deaf!'

'I know that,' said the youngster, 'but granny is!'

Are you listening, granny?
Are you listening, God?
Anyone ... anyone ... Hello! Hello?

December 14 – Translation

'For the same things ... translated into another tongue
have not the same force in them.'
Apocrypha, Ecclesiasticus, The Prologue

Lennoxtown is a town in East Dunbartonshire, at the foot of the
Campsie Fells. And it has an excellent fish & chip shop.

I was at a retreat centre in the town with other hospice chaplains.
Some of us felt we weren't being fed enough, so, late of an evening,
I was dispatched to the local fish & chip emporium with a colleague
from Cardiff to purchase two haggis suppers and nine portions of
chips. We had to wait while a fresh batch of chips was cooked, so we
stood to one side while the whole of Lennoxtown, it seemed, came
and went.

Suddenly, a little man, clearly drunk, rolled into the shop from the
pub next door and promptly initiated a loud and heated conversation
with the chip-shop owner – in a broad, West of Scotland accent. The
drunk wanted fifty-pence worth of chips, but the owner insisted that
the cheapest portion of chips would cost seventy pence. The essence
of the lengthy exchange was whether it was possible to buy five-sev-
enths of a portion of chips. The potential customer insisted it was.
The owner insisted it wasn't.

It was comedy gold! I turned to my Welsh friend to make a comment, only to find him open-mouthed. 'It's amazing,' he said. 'I know
they're talking English, but I have *no* idea what they're saying. I got
"chips" and "50p" and *nothing* else.' I translated it all for him on the
way back to the retreat centre. He needed, and got, a good translator.

A good translation, in all its aspects, will always matter.

December 15 – Final words

'Media vita in morte sumus.'
'In the midst of life we are in death.'
Notker I of Saint Gall, Antiphon

The antiphon above is attributed to the Benedictine monk Notker I of Saint Gall, who died in 912. He wrote it when he saw construction workers building a bridge over an abyss. They were at risk of death, and Notker recognised that he was facing his own. I shared earlier a prayer I'd written about my own death. Here's more on the same theme.

I give thanks, Lord God of nations,
For all the worldly joys I have known.
But now, gracious Maker, I have the greatest need
That you grant my spirit to God,
That my soul may set out to you,
Prince of Angels, going in peace, into your power,
I pray, that the hell-fields may not humiliate me.
Anonymous, written after the Battle of Maldon, 991AD

O God, give me of thy wisdom,
O God, give me of thy mercy,
O God, give me of thy fullness,
And of thy guidance in the face of every strait.
O God, give me of thy holiness,
O God, give me of thy shielding,
O God, give me of thy surrounding,
And of thy peace in the knot of my death.
O give me of thy surrounding,
And of thy peace in the hour of my death.
A traditional Celtic prayer

December 16 – Unfortunate

'For every ill-turn of fortune
the most unhappy sort of unfortunate man
is the one who has been happy.'
Bible, Psalm 84:10

If you're following my Desert Island Discs, there's not an eighth one. I can't make up my mind. But I know the book I'll take – along with the Bible and the works of Shakespeare.

The 19th-century poet and writer James Hogg, 'the Ettrick Shepherd', wrote a book that continues to fascinate me – *The Private Memoirs and Confessions of a Justified Sinner*. The book centres on an autobiographical confession from one Robert Wringham, and follows Robert's descent into despair. It's about the universal struggle to be righteous, and the fight in everyone with the sinfulness of our nature.

Hogg, steeped in the folklore of the Borders, also wrote a story about a water cow which, according to legend, lived in St Mary's Loch, the largest loch in the Borders.

A farmer in Bowerhope once got a breed of her, which he kept for many years until they multiplied exceedingly; and he never had any cattle thrive so well, until once, on some outrage or disrespect on the farmer's part towards them, the old dam came out of the lake one March evening and gave such a roar that all the surrounding hills shook again, upon which her progeny, nineteen in number, followed her all quietly into the loch, and were never more seen.

We are all 'unfortunates' like the Bowerhope farmer. We are all flawed people like Robert Wringham. It's how we deal with our unfortunate flaws that matters.

December 17 – Keep smiling

'We're not laughing at you. We're laughing near you.'

Robin Williams as John Keating in Dead Poets Society

I'm glad there are people in our churches who are near enough to me so that I can smile – or even laugh out loud – at their innocent mistakes ...

The ladies of the Church have cast off clothing of every kind. They may be seen in the basement on Friday afternoon.

Low Self Esteem Support Group will meet Thursday at 7pm. Please use back door.

Missing – A purple lady's bicycle from the church car park.

It's Drug Awareness Week: Get involved in drugs before your children do.

Anyone not claiming lost articles will be disposed of.

Will the person who borrowed the ladder from the caretaker's cupboard, please bring it back before further steps are taken.

The class on prophecy has been cancelled due to unforeseen circumstances.

Wanted: Part-time, a Christian nanny to take care of our three-year-old who does not smoke or drink.

Honestly, no matter how near I get, I *am* laughing at them.

December 18 – Safe

'Better safe than sorry.'
A mid-19ᵗʰ-century proverb

When we were renovating our current house, we found a safe, built into the wall of a cupboard in the kitchen. We've kept the safe – though it's never used, and I'm not even sure we know where the key is now. But we were intrigued about why the safe was put there. Was it to conceal a secret stash of something a former owner of the house didn't want anyone to know about? A place to keep precious possessions out of sight when the house was unoccupied? For documents, money, jewellery, ill-gotten gains? We'll never know. All we're sure of is that somebody, at one time or another, was concerned about keeping something safe.

There are 'personal' safes on the market designed like soup tins or small dictionaries, which can sit randomly in a kitchen or on a bookshelf among other similar items. You can even get a safe that looks like a double electrical socket, which you can fit into a wall to make it look 'normal'. But only you know what's safely stored out of sight.

John Henry Newman had a concern for a safe place too. He wrote in 'Wisdom and Innocence', an 1883 sermon:

May He support us all the day long, till the shades lengthen and the evening comes, and the busy world is hushed, and the fever of life is o'er, and our work is done! Then in His mercy may he give us safe lodging, and a holy rest, and peace at the last.

A different kind of 'safe', not just hiding precious things. An important 'personalised safe', I reckon.

December 19 – Fascinated

'There's a fascination frantic.'
W S Gilbert, The Mikado

He was a shepherd-boy with a job to do. Looking after sheep is what shepherds do, and he was trying to be a good shepherd. He took care of his flock. He did as he had been told, and the sheep were fine, and so was he.

He had a stick. Not a shepherd's crook – only proper shepherds have crooks with curly handles and he wasn't a grown-up shepherd yet. But he had his own stick, and that was good enough.

One day, after a storm, he was driving his sheep along a rutted path when he came upon a puddle. He'd seen a puddle before, of course, and this one wasn't going to cause him any problems. So he stuck his stick firmly in the middle of it and went to cross over. But then he noticed something strange. He had put a straight stick into the puddle, but now it was bent, just where it entered the water. He pulled his stick out again and it was straight. He put it in the puddle, and it was bent. He pulled it out and it was straight.

He was fascinated by the effect of the puddle on his shepherd-boy stick. Why's it doing that? What's happening? It was the beginning of a process of enquiry for a shepherd-boy, and one that never, ever left him.

That shepherd-boy was Ernest Rutherford, the greatest scientist New Zealand has ever produced, who became known as 'the father of nuclear physics'. A lifetime of enquiry began with a stick bending in a puddle.

It's amazing where fascination with
the wonders of nature can take you.

December 20 – Danger

'Oft in danger, oft in woe.'
H Kirke White, 1812 hymn of the same title

At the peak of his broadcasting prowess, the doyen of radio presenters, the late Sir Terry Wogan, had a long-running segment of his show given over to cones on motorways. It began with a listener writing in and complaining about the long coned-off sections of motorways where nothing seemed to be happening – no workers, no repairs, no machines, just endless lines of cones! Over a few days the issue descended into farce, with listeners making up countless puns on the 'cone' idea. 'It's cone-fusing,' someone suggested; 'In-cone-venient,' said another; 'Causing cone-siderable delay,' another complained. It went on and on and on, like lines of cones on a motorway – until Wogan had to call a halt to all this silliness.

No one suggested that the cones were 'cone-structive', that they *were* there for a reason. They may be confusing, and it is often inconvenient, and, indeed, the delays might be considerable. But the cones have a purpose – to warn us to take care, or that there may be disruption ahead. Cones alert us to danger, and that has to be constructive.

We need to heed danger signals. Why do we teach a child to cross the road when the 'green man' shows? Because the 'red man' is a danger signal. We need people to warn us of danger too – parents, teachers, clergy, people experienced in life – who know what problems a course of action might lead to.

People who warn us of danger are really important.
Why not 'cone-gratulate' them for their sound advice?

December 21 – Changing

'To change what we can.'

Robert Louis Stevenson, More New Arabian Nights

By the time she was 21, Sue had been in seventeen different jobs. It wasn't that she lacked commitment. It's just that something better always seemed to come along. Wouldn't life be boring if you got stuck in a rut?

Some jobs had been very short-term, like the weekend she'd been a stand-in barmaid, covering for her best friend who'd got the flu. At one stage she'd been juggling four jobs at once – which took some organising and made for a *very* long day. She'd tallied up the number of jobs. 'Sixteen,' she'd informed her parents, who were always on about 'settling down to something permanent'. Sue knew it had *actually* been seventeen, but her stint as a cloakroom attendant at a pole-dancing club was not for her parents to know about.

But now, all of that was over. Working as a PA to the Director of a city art gallery was a dream job. 'Six months!' her dad had said. 'I don't believe it!' Sue didn't really believe it either. But things were definitely changing.

She'd just got to work as the phone on her desk was ringing. It was Rosie, her best friend. 'You're on the go early, Rosie,' Sue remarked.

'Yeah. But this is urgent.'

'How so?'

'Well, Sue, I've just seen your *dream* job advertised in the morning paper. Fancy giving it a look?'

Sue sighed. 'Well', she thought, 'could I make it eighteen before I'm 22?'

Dreams? Changes? Chances?

December 22 – Escape

'What mad pursuit? What struggle to escape?
What pipes and timbrels? What wild ecstasy?'
John Keats, Ode on a Grecian Urn

High up at the east end of the Abbey on Iona there is a little window set, just below the roof, in the apex of the solid and imposing east wall. It looks small compared with the dominance of the large window above the marble Communion Table. So why is it there?

It's a 'bird window', common in most medieval church buildings, an opening to offer an escape route to any bird that might unwittingly become trapped inside. A door may have been left open from the cloisters, or the west entrance, or the south aisle, and a sparrow, dove, swallow – or even, on one occasion, a peregrine falcon – might find its way inside, and, in confusion and panic, fail to find a way out. A trapped bird will intuitively fly upwards to the highest point of light, just as it would do in a forest, to make good its escape.

When Iona Abbey was being rebuilt in the early years of the 20th century, the Edwardians, concerned more about draughts than ornithology, had the open window glazed, sealed, blocking any escape for a trapped bird. The bird might still fly up to the light, but now it has no escape.

Sometimes we get ourselves trapped in something and struggle to find a way out. So it's important to make sure that a possible escape route – flying up towards the light – hasn't been blocked off by people who don't realise their mistake when they try to shut out the draughts.

If you're drawn to the light, reach for it.
Don't let anything block your way.

December 23 – Concentration

'Must I always be a mere listener?'
Juvenal, Satires No. 1

I shared with you earlier how transformative it was for me when I got hearing aids. One advantage is the use of a 'hearing loop' or 'induction loop', especially in churches. It's a sound system that boosts the signal in hearing aids and helps me focus on particular sounds. I can cut out the distracting stuff and concentrate on the words being spoken. Sermons, speeches, funeral services, presentations are all clearer. (It's a pity the loop system doesn't improve the content or the delivery, but you can't have everything ...)

On the other hand, I struggle to hear things properly in a crowded room. There's often so much noise, it's difficult to filter out what's not needed and concentrate on what's being said. There's no sound system that cuts out extraneous noise and allows me to hear only what I need to. Concentration is hard when there's too much to take in.

That's true for most things, and not just with hearing aids. There are times when there's so much going on it's hard to concentrate on what really matters. It's too easy to be distracted so that you miss the important things.

When my grandsons have their headphones on while they're watching movies or playing games on their devices, they often don't hear what I say – time for tea; make sure you've washed your hands; put your schoolbag away. But if I say, 'Anyone fancy some chocolate?' they will instantly reply in chorus, 'Me, please.' So you *can* hear what you want to hear if you concentrate well enough. Even with hearing aids in a crowded room, I'll have to give it a try.

Can you hear what matters when you try hard enough?

December 24 – Warm

> 'Wash what is dirty, water what is dry,
> heal what is wounded.
> Bend what is stiff, warm what is cold,
> guide what goes off the road.'
>
> *Stephen Langdon,* The 'Golden Sequence', for Whit Sunday

This quotation comes from the 13ᵗʰ century. But it should be the mission statement of any church community.

My first parish in the 1970s was in West Pilton, a problematic housing estate in Edinburgh. The people of the local church – the Old Kirk – were a veritable beacon of service, light, love and welcome.

Christmas was always a big thing, especially the Christmas Eve watchnight service, packed to overflowing, mostly with people making their annual trip to church. 'I'm a regular churchgoer,' one chap told me. 'I go to church faithfully once a year ...' The church service began at 11.30pm. The pubs closed at 10, and most of the customers hit the streets at about 10.30. The chip shops stayed open till midnight. For a lot of folk, it was out of the pub, into the chip shop and down to the church for the service. The slower ones hadn't finished their late-night repast by the time they got to the church. We had a system! The half-eaten fish suppers were kept warm on the radiators in the vestibule till the service was over.

We kept things warm for the waifs and strays, drunk men and noisy teenagers, large families and partygoers because the warmth of a welcome really mattered.

People who needed to feel they belonged were warmed
with their fish suppers – at least once a year.

December 25 – Christmas

'I have often thought, says Sir Roger, it happens very well
that Christmas should fall out in the middle of winter.'
Joseph Addison, The Spectator

An Irish folk carol says it all ...Merry Christmas everyone ...

Christmas Day is come; let's all prepare for mirth,
Which fills the earth and heaven at this amazing birth.

Through both the joyous angels in strife and hurry fly,
With glories and hosannas, 'All Holy' do they cry,

In heav'n the Church triumphant adores with all her choirs,
The militant on earth with humble faith admires.

But how can we rejoice? Should we not rather mourn
To see the hope of nations thus in a stable born?

Is there no sumptuous palace, nor any inn at all
To lodge his heavenly mother but in a filthy stall?

Oh! cease, ye blessed angels, such clamorous joys to make!
Though midnight silence favours, the shepherds are awake;

If we would then rejoice, let's cancel the old score,
And, purposing amendment, resolve to sin no more –

For mirth can ne'er content us, without a conscience clear;
And thus we'll find true pleasure in all the usual cheer,

In dancing, sporting, revelling, with masquerade and drum,
So let our Christmas merry be, as Christians doth become.

December 26 – Babies

'Sweet babe, in thy face, soft desires I can trace,
Secret joys and secret smiles, little pretty infant wiles.'
William Blake, A Cradle Song

Working in the post-war housing estate that was my first parish, I came across a strange custom. When each of our three children was born and we were pushing the new baby around in its pram, people would stop to admire the baby and then slip some money under the covers. 'You can't meet a new baby and not give it some silver,' we were told. *Why* this should be so, nobody knew. But we never objected. A bit of extra cash from any source always helped! One lady got into a panic because she had no 'silver' coins to give the new baby. So she took a fiver from her purse, stuck it under the pram covers, and raked about in the pram for an appropriate amount of change. Whatever the purpose was of giving 'silver to the baby', it made even less sense now!

I shouldn't analyse it too much. Babies, because they're babies, affect us in positive ways. Babies make a difference, so why shouldn't they be appreciated in some tangible way? Lord Byron in *Cain* offers us this insight:

He smiles, and sleeps! – sleep on
And smile, thou little, young inheritor
Of a world scarce less young; sleep on and smile!
Thine are the hours and days when both are cheering
And innocent.

Maybe that's why wise men from the east brought gifts of gold, frankincense and myrrh to Jesus, because they saw him as the 'little, young inheritor' *par excellence.*

Our 'young inheritors' are worth all we can give them too.

December 27 – Fun

> 'I've taken my fun where I've found it,
> An' now I must pay for my fun.'
>
> *Rudyard Kipling*, The Ladies

When I walked the West Highland Way, the six-day hike over the 90 plus miles of the trail was well planned. B&Bs were booked; new hiking boots had been broken in; rucksacks were filled with maps, cameras, and the like; and for sustenance we had an ample supply of Kendal Mint Cake, flasks of Bovril and Mars bars for the occasional energy boost. The walk was hard work, covering around 15 miles per day. It was sore on the feet. But the scenery, companionship and sense of achievement made it all worthwhile.

On day three we met up with a couple from Glasgow. While we were kitted out like proper hikers, they didn't seem to have taken it quite so seriously. Sandshoes instead of walking boots; an old-fashioned, leather-strapped rucksack that hung at 50 degrees off the chap's back; and for sustenance, several cans of lager and exotic packets of crisps. We asked them if they did a lot of walking. 'Naw,' the man said, 'ah'm a car man masel'.'

'But he's been in trainin',' his companion chipped in, grinning widely.

'Aye,' the man responded, 'ah stopped takin' the car up the top o' the road tae get ma breakfast rolls and mornin' paper.' And off they both went, whistling a happy tune.

Did they have fun? You bet they did. Did we have fun? Absolutely – but in a very different way.

> *If beauty is in the eye of the beholder,*
> *then fun is obviously in the heart of the participant.*

December 28 – Mother

'O Mother blest, whom God bestows,
On sinners and on just,
What joy, what hope thou givest those
Who in thy mercy trust.'
St Alphonsus, O Mother Blest

It was once the custom in Scotland for the women in the farming districts to help make and bind the sheaves after the grain had been cut. On one occasion, a mother, Hannah Lamond, took her little child with her, thinking she could place it safely within reach and watch over it while she was working. But, preoccupied with their work, no one noticed a golden eagle swooping down, snatching the baby and carrying it away. Consternation took hold, and some of the men made valiant efforts to climb up to the eagle's eyrie, high in the rocks. None of them succeeded.

Among the men there was a sailor, on leave from the vast clipper ships, well used to climbing the rigging to great heights. But his efforts also met with failure.

They were all about to give up when Hannah Lamond herself began to scale the cliffs. Bit by bit, higher and higher, she reached the eagle's nest. The eagle tried to beat her off with its wings, but Hannah Lamond was not to be daunted. She grabbed the baby and safely made the tortuous descent. Hannah Lamond was a heroine, and was lauded and celebrated for her bravery. But she took no praise.

'It's ma bairn,' she said, 'ma ain wee bairn. Wid a mither no dae onythin' for her bairn? For yer ain flesh an' bluid, love will find a way.'

Love will find a way ...

December 29 – Each to their own

'All my love is towards individuals.'
Jonathan Swift, Letter to Pope, 1725

When my mother's family got together, particularly at Hogmanay and New Year time, the gathering would eventually get around to singing. Everyone had their own party-piece. My grandfather would have a go at *The Soor Milk Cairt* – if he could ever remember the words past the first verse and chorus. My granny would launch into *An Auld Maid in a Garret,* with the assembled company joining in the parts they knew. My uncle Donald would lean against the mantelpiece and offer an extraordinary yodelling song, while my cousin George, a relative newcomer to the family singing extravaganza, would offer a passable rendition of *Moon River.* The whole thing fascinated me as a small boy. And the phrase 'Wan singer, wan song' or, in more modern parlance, 'Each to their own', would be an apt description of the whole event. There was rarely anything new offered. The family fell back on what was familiar. Each person had their own – and respected – place.

'Each to their own' should be a description of all aspects of family life. Not just at parties or in a home-grown karaoke event, but in working together, respecting each other, giving each person their place. I've seen too many families break apart because someone has stolen or disrespected someone else's song.

What's your song? And what are the contributions to family life you are pleased to hear from others?

Who will be applauded when they sing their song
with pride, and uniqueness?

December 30 – Endings

'New journeys now begin.'
Tom Gordon, the title of his second book

Endings are often as hard to manage as new beginnings. So, as this year draws to its close, here are some thoughts about endings:

I'm nearly done; I'm almost there;
and soon I'll say, 'Enough for now!'
The task will end, the work conclude;
'That's all!' I'll cry, and take a bow.

And if you thank me, I'll be pleased
your gratitude's been thus expressed.
And if you praise me over-much,
I'll humbly say, 'I did my best.'

If I'm ignored, I'll slip away
to take my place amid the crowd,
and ponder what I've said or done:
'Am I ashamed, or am I proud?'

But then I'll know what's gone is passed
and cannot be now be rearranged.
And I will have to face this truth:
'My past is for the future changed.'

For as I ask myself, in fear,
'Will future days be burdensome?'
I pray that I might hear this voice:
'The best, my friend, is yet to come ...'

December 31 – Last word

'This is the last of Earth! I am content!'
John Quincy Adams, uttered on his deathbed in 1848

The last words of famous people can be both revealing and challenging. Take, for example, the final words of Captain Lawrence (Titus) Oates, during Scott's ill-fated expedition to the South Pole in 1912, when he left his companions:

I am just going outside and may be some time.

And words attributed to Oscar Wilde on his deathbed, appalled as he was by the wallpaper in the room:

One of us must go.

While he was on the brink of death in August, 1867, the wife of renowned chemical scientist Michael Faraday asked him if he had ever pondered what he thought his occupation would be in the next life. In response, Faraday calmly uttered his last words:

I shall be with Christ, and that is enough.

Faraday's approach to death fascinates me, because a scientist could express himself in the language of faith. Here was no scientific certainty or provable case. Instead, here was belief, and that, for this scientist, was enough.

The selflessness of Titus Oates, the wit of Oscar Wilde, the faith of Michael Faraday ... however we approach the future, and whatever it holds, let us hope we can be selfless, laugh a little and have faith enough that will carry us forward – no matter what ...

Whatever this moment might be the last of for you,
can you say with John Quincy Adams, 'I am content'?

Notes, acknowledgements and permissions

January 11: 'A prayer for my dying' was first published in *A Need for Living* by the author, 2001, Wild Goose Publications

January 12: The Rule of St Benedict can be accessed at http://www.osb.org/rb/text/toc.html; The Rule of St Francis can be accessed at https://ofm.org/about/rule

January 14: For further information about Stepping Stones contact Chalmers Memorial Church, Port Seton, at steppingstones.mail@gmail.com

January 24: For the full text of the United Nations Convention on the Rights of the Child, see https://downloads.unicef.org.uk/wp-content/uploads/2010/05/UNCRC_united_nations_convention_on_the_rights_of_the_child.pdf

February 24 & 25: Quotations relating to The Cyrenians are taken from http://cyrenians.scot and are used by permission of the CEO, Ewan Aitken. For access to Ewan Aitken's blog, see http://cyrenians.scot/ceo-blog

March 6: The full text of the poem, 'I'm Old', by the author can be found in *Holy Ground*, ed Neil Paynter & Helen Boothroyd, 2009, Wild Goose Publications. https://www.ionabooks.com/holy-ground.html

May 6: Adapted from 'Questions', from *A Blessing to Follow* by the author, 2009. https://www.ionabooks.com/a-blessing-to-follow.html

May 13: Based on *Jesus was a Refugee,* 2016. https://www.ionabooks.com/jesus-was-a-refugee-pdf-download.html

May 23: The poem 'For all my days', by the author, was first published in *A Need for Living*, 2001, Wild Goose Publications. https://www.ionabooks.com/a-need-for-living.html

June 4: For the full text of 'The 51st Division's Farewell to Sicily' by Hamish Henderson see http://www.scottishpoetrylibrary.org.uk/poetry/poems/ 51st-highland-divisions-farewell-sicily

July 5 & 6 and **September 7 & 17:** For more on the Church of the Saviour see http://inwardoutward.org/the-church-of-the-saviour/our-story

July 22 & 23 and **August 18:** For more on George MacLeod and the Iona Community, see Ron Ferguson's books, *George MacLeod* https://www.ionabooks.com/george-macleod.html and *Chasing the Wild Goose* https://www.ionabooks.com/chasing-the-wild-goose.html

August 8: For more information on *The Smart Grief Guide* see http://smartgriefguide.co.uk

September 6: The explanation of Shapenote singing is used with permission of Shapenote Scotland. It was written by Harry Campbell and is taken from http://shapenotescotland.weebly.com where further information about Shapenote can be found.

September 8: The poem, 'John Levering's Picture', by the author was first published in *A Need for Living*, 2001, Wild Goose Publications

September 21: First referenced in *Catena*, the magazine of the Catenian Association, by the author, and used with permission. See https://www.thecatenians.com

October 16: See *No Extraordinary Power* (Swarthmore Lectures) by Helen Steven, 2005, Quaker Books

October 25: The prayer is used with the permission of the minister and Kirk Session of the Canongate Kirk, Edinburgh.

November 14–19: For a full explanation of The Rule of the Iona Community see https://iona.org.uk/movement/the-rule. For further information on all aspects of the Iona Community see https://iona.org.uk

November 28: Information taken from the Toilet Twinning website – https://www.toilettwinning.org – and used with permission.

December 30: Developed from 'Today' by the author, from *New Journeys Now Begin*. https://www.ionabooks.com/new-journeys-now-begin.html

Index – by subject

Wild Goose Publications is part of the Iona Community:

- An ecumenical movement of men and women from different walks of life and different traditions in the Christian church
- Committed to the gospel of Jesus Christ, and to following where that leads, even into the unknown
- Engaged together, and with people of goodwill across the world, in acting, reflecting and praying for justice, peace and the integrity of creation
- Convinced that the inclusive community we seek must be embodied in the community we practise

Together with our staff, we are responsible for:

- Our islands residential centres of Iona Abbey, the MacLeod Centre on Iona, and Camas Adventure Centre on the Ross of Mull

and in Glasgow:

- The administration of the Community
- Our work with young people
- Our publishing house, Wild Goose Publications
- Our association in the revitalising of worship with the Wild Goose Resource Group

www.ionabooks.com

The Iona Community was founded in Glasgow in 1938 by George MacLeod, minister, visionary and prophetic witness for peace, in the context of the poverty and despair of the Depression. Its original task of rebuilding the monastic ruins of Iona Abbey became a sign of hopeful rebuilding of community in Scotland and beyond. Today, we are about 250 Members, mostly in Britain, and 1500 Associate Members, with 1400 Friends worldwide. Together and apart, 'we follow the light we have, and pray for more light'.

For information on the Iona Community contact:
The Iona Community, 21 Carlton Court, Glasgow G5 9JP, UK.
Phone: 0141 429 7281
e-mail: admin@iona.org.uk; web: www.iona.org.uk

For enquiries about visiting Iona, please contact:
Iona Abbey, Isle of Iona, Argyll PA76 6SN, UK. Phone: 01681 700404
e-mail: ionacomm@iona.org.uk